China's World View

China's World View

DEMYSTIFYING CHINA
TO PREVENT GLOBAL CONFLICT

David Daokui Li

W. W. NORTON & COMPANY
Independent Publishers Since 1923

For information about permission to reproduce selections from this book,
write to Permissions, W. W. Norton & Company, Inc.,
500 Fifth Avenue, New York, NY 10110

For information about special discounts for bulk purchases,
please contact W. W. Norton Special Sales at
specialsales@wwnorton.com or 800-233-4830

Manufacturing by Lake Book Manufacturing
Book design by Lovedog Studio
Production manager: Anna Oler

ISBN 978-0-393-29239-8

W. W. Norton & Company, Inc., 500 Fifth Avenue, New York, N.Y. 10110
www.wwnorton.com

W. W. Norton & Company Ltd., 15 Carlisle Street, London W1D 3BS

1 2 3 4 5 6 7 8 9 0

In memory of Neil Schwartz,
whose short life reminds us that future generations
ought to enjoy and deserve a peaceful world
with the rise of China

Contents

China's World View

The Debate Takes Center Stage

O N A PLEASANT JUNE EVENING IN 2011, NEARLY 2,500 people filled Toronto's Roy Thompson Concert Hall. I stood on stage with three of North America's most influential intellectuals: Dr. Henry Kissinger, the former US secretary of state; Professor Niall Ferguson, a leading historian and political thinker; and Fareed Zakaria, the articulate and thought-provoking CNN anchor. We had gathered to debate the topic "The 21st Century Will Belong to China." It was one of the first events of the Munk Debate series founded by Pete and Melanie Munk of Canada. The tickets had sold out within a week. When I first left China to study in the United States in 1985, debating such a topic, and having people pay to attend, would have been unthinkable.

I was assigned to the "pro" side along with Professor Ferguson. From the start, Dr. Kissinger had stated that the only way he would consent to be involved in the debate was if he could argue for the "con" side. He said that he was so concerned about Western paranoia concerning China following the financial crisis that his mission was to calm the Western world's anxieties about China's emergence.

I was easily the most uncomfortable debater that evening, although Dr. Kissinger claimed it was he, citing his training in the German education system, in which debaters take turns to make points to win the support of the audience. Truly, the event was a bigger challenge for me than for all of them. Debating is not in the skillset of Chinese scholars of my generation. We were taught in the Confucian tradition of education, with a strong emphasis on avoiding open disagreement and respecting scholars and the elderly. Of course, this would include Dr. Kissinger, who, along with President Richard Nixon, "opened up" the Sino-US relationship with Chairman Mao Zedong and Premier Zhou Enlai and is regarded as a legend in China. Even more important, I disagreed and (still do) with the position that I was supposed to defend, but I had to try to win the debate.

The debate was a challenge that I had to undertake. I believe that academics like myself who are so fortunate as to study and travel around the world must work to enhance mutual understanding between China and other countries. In the wake of the financial crisis, the Chinese economy had been leading a sharp global recovery. The prices of commodities, including gold, were shooting up. It was common for many Canadians and Westerners to wonder whether China's time was indeed coming and what implications this would have for their lives.

The debate was conducted in strict Oxford style with participants presenting opening statements and the moderator requesting both sides to recommend issues to be considered. The distinguished audience included former Canadian prime minister Brian Mulroney, former US secretary of defense William Cohen, and many leading writers and thinkers from the United States and China. Topics covered included China's economic policies, whether China would become like Japan—fading away as a major economic competitor of the US, —and whether China would be able to innovate rather than only copy Western technologies.

I was surprised by the tremendous enthusiasm of the audience; those who could not gain admittance to the hall were watching it live on TV. Before the debate, a poll of the audience had revealed that 39 percent said they agreed with the "pro" position and 40 percent with the "con" position, with 21 percent undecided. Following the debate, 62 percent voted "con" and 38 percent voted "pro." It was evident that Dr. Kissinger and Dr. Zakaria had won, and convinced the audience that the twenty-first century would not belong to China. I was pleased for the same reason as Dr. Kissinger—because I do not think people in Western countries should be concerned with China's emergence. Another reason I was happy: I had not defeated a respected elder; my Confucian principles had not been compromised.

A revealing moment came during the debate that planted the seed for me to write this book, which eventually took more than a decade and much more energy than I initially anticipated. Dr. Kissinger shocked me by rhetorically asking me and Niall Ferguson: "Look at the world map—how many friends can China truly claim? Especially look at the neighbors of China—which are the largest in number for a country, how many of them are truly comfortable and trustful with the rise of China?" Coming from China and knowing how hard China has been trying to show its goodwill and earn respect from the rest of the world, I was stunned by his statement. I knew in that moment on stage that the world needed a better understanding of China and its world view, and that I needed to write a book about it.

DURING THE TEN YEARS since the Munk Debate, China has taken center stage in world politics. For many reasons, the debate in the West has escalated from "Will the future belong to China?" to "How can we stop China from damaging the free world of liberal democracy?"

In 2020, during the COVID-19 pandemic, many politicians and elites in the West began to label China as the new and most dangerous common threat, like the former Soviet Union, and advocate for a new Cold War against China. Of course, President Trump made a significant contribution to the hostility of the West toward China by openly claiming that China's rise had been at the expense of the United States, saying that China had done too well

for too long and it was time for the United States to fight back.
His secretary of state, Mike Pompeo, in effect treated China as a
warring state by recalling the US ambassador to China, closing
a Chinese consulate in the United States, and calling upon the
Chinese people to rise up and overthrow the Chinese Communist
Party. Needless to say, the hostility from President Trump and
Secretary of State Pompeo also stoked the fire of ultranationalist
and anti-West views in China. Chinese social media was ablaze
with personal attacks on Mike Pompeo as netizens bemoaned the
United States' intent to repress the rise of China.

A dramatic event happened on Saturday, January 28, 2023, that
may one day be seen as a turning point in American perception of
foreign affairs as significant as the first orbit of the USSR's Sputnik satellite in 1957. That morning, Americans woke up to break-
ing news that an ultra-high-flying balloon had appeared in the sky
of North America. This was unprecedented. The White House
alleged that it was a Chinese spy balloon as large as a football field
and flying twice as high as a commercial jet. More shocking than
the appearance of the balloon was that a commercial pilot first
spotted it, not the US military. The Chinese government stated
that the object was a meteorological balloon blown astray by the
wind. News of the balloon riveted the nation in the ensuing week.
Local police admonished rifle owners not to shoot at it as the balloon was flying way beyond the range of any hand-held weapon.
Finally, on February 4, President Biden ordered it shot down by
a missile launched from a US Air Force fighter. Regardless of the
truth, the threat of China had suddenly been perceived to be real
and present by many people in the United States.

Whether the rise of China is a threat or an opportunity for
the West can only be answered by an honest understanding of
how China works. So far, there are many books on China that
have been published outside of China, most of them written by
Westerners with deep knowledge and profound insights about the
country. However, these authors are visitors and guests of China.

They are like observers peeking through the windows of a building, and sometimes they even are invited inside. However, they do not live in the building. I am an insider—I live and work in the building. I hope to explain how the building was designed, how it was constructed, and how it functions.

I confess that I am not the most prepared or suitable author for a book of this sort. To begin with, oftentimes it is a struggle for me to write well in English since it is not my native language. To make things worse, I was trained as an academic economist, and academic economists' writing style is too rigid and dry for a general audience. Most importantly, I am fully aware that readers in the West may not trust me, since they may perceive me as being too close to the Chinese government, with ulterior motives to promote China.

As unprepared and ill-suited as I am as a general writer, I have been increasingly compelled to finish this book. Throughout the past decade, I have witnessed the widening gulf of misunderstanding between China and the West, especially the United States. Suspicion and hostility have surged alarmingly, and many Western elites have even begun to advocate for a new Cold War against China. On the other side, in China, there are also many people pushing for an ever more aggressive stand against the West, and particularly the United States. These harsh views are an extremely dangerous escalation of mutual misunderstandings. The younger generations of all societies, in China and the West, stand to lose tremendously from a new Cold War.

WHY SHOULD YOU TRUST ME? Are my views biased for China? I have encountered these challenging questions each time I speak at a public forum or give a media interview in the West. I can see the suspicion in the eyes and body language of my audience. My answer to them, and to you, is that I try to be as honest and matter-of-fact as possible. I do not face any specific pressure or incentives from inside China to say certain things, since I am an academic economist and not a government official. I do not own or run any businesses, and I have zero chance of being promoted to a high-level government position. This detachment allows me to make my own observations and judgment calls. I think this is why I am frequently invited to international forums and investor conferences such as the World Economic Forum of Switzerland. There, top executives of a specific industry have told me that they value my assessment of what is really going on in China so that they can make important strategic decisions. They cannot afford to listen to distorted views and predictions.

Why should you trust me? I myself have asked this question time and again during the long journey of writing the book. Ultimately, I think the answer should come from understanding my motivation. I wrote this book not for the purpose of obtaining fame or monetary returns, which I have much more effective and efficient ways to achieve. Moreover, at a relatively senior stage of my career in China, I am no longer hungry for them. Reputation-wise, I am running a significant risk of being attacked in China as a "traitor trying to please Westerners." Conversely, outside China, I may also be criticized as an instrument of Chinese propaganda. My sole motivation is to promote a better understanding of China by the rest of the world in order to promote more cooperation and minimize conflict of any kind. The best way to do this is to be open and honest, guarding against any possibility of misleading the readers.

My ultimate goal in writing the book is for younger generations to benefit from the rise of China by avoiding any conflict due to misunderstandings. This goal stems from my personal experiences. Forty years ago, as a young student, I was very fortunate to be able to go to the United States for graduate studies. I then benefited from my Western education through working mostly in China. Today, while many young Chinese are following my path, many young men and women from outside China are also coming here for studies and career development. This trend will certainly stop or even reverse if misunderstandings between China and the West worsen.

My worries about conflict stemming from misunderstandings and misjudgments between China and the West were heightened by the life experience of one young American friend and former colleague. His story provided me with the final and most important push to finish this book. His name is Neil Schwartz. Neil's story taught me that the rise of China can provide new opportunities for young people around the world, and also that we must not take such opportunities for granted.

Neil Schwartz was born and raised in the state of New Jersey in the United States. He was a hardworking, ambitious, and very respectful student, but he did not feel particularly comfortable in the US education system and, after graduating from college, he decided to give life in China a try. He studied Chinese and got into the international MBA program at Tsinghua University. This was the right choice for Neil. In China, he thrived. His hardworking and respectful personality made him very popular.

Neil gave himself a Chinese name, Chen Xiaoshuai, which means "young handsome guy," imitating that of a famous movie director in China. After graduating, he stayed at Tsinghua to help the university president, who later became the mayor of Beijing, to set up the university's international programs. The president liked him so much that he even tried to set Xiaoshuai up with a Chinese girlfriend, a common practice of Chinese seniors for their beloved subordinates. Xiaoshuai later went on to found his own investment company with Chinese and US investors, and most interestingly, he also learned the skills needed to become a popular speaker at China's public conferences and on TV programs, discussing President Trump and US politics—all in Chinese! These accomplishments, he often said, would not have been possible had he stayed in the United States. Unfortunately, all of these wonderful things suddenly came to an end in the summer of

2020, when Neil was in New Jersey, where he had to stay because of travel restrictions due to the outbreak of COVID-19. He came down with a mental illness, and sadly, he passed away.

The end of Neil's young life woke me to the fact that people like me have a responsibility to make our best efforts to ensure that China and the rest of the world stay closely connected, allowing younger generations to continue to benefit from this connectivity, and preventing the outbreak of another Cold War. This book is for the hundreds of millions of Neil Schwartzes in the world.

THE KEY MESSAGE OF this book is very simple: The rise of China is not a threat to the rest of the world, and in fact, will provide many global benefits. First, China is not in a position to export its ideology or overturn the current world order. This is because China's sociopolitical system relies on two thousand years of tradition in combination with the revolutionary history of the Communist Party, creating unique national circumstances that cannot be replicated. Chinese leaders and elites know well that the Chinese sociopolitical system has worked well in China so far but cannot be exported to other countries. Furthermore, this system dictates that China focus on its own domestic affairs while seeking due respect from the rest of the world. By doing so, China creates new opportunities for people around the world and makes contributions to the global public good.

This book aims to provide an insider's view of how China works and therefore why, rather than causing fear, the rise of China should be recognized as being good for the rest of the world. To do so, I first explore China's place as "number two" in the world—mostly economically—and how China's large population, non-Western political and economic institutions, and huge potential for growth cause trepidation among many observers outside China. In the next chapter, I explain the importance of history to most educated Chinese people, including Chinese leaders, and I offer a brief overview of that history to help readers understand the mentality of Chinese decision makers.

In subsequent chapters, I delve into the Chinese political system and the structure of the Chinese government so as to build a foundation for understanding the country's economy, society, and foreign policy. I begin with an explanation of the origin and operations of the Chinese Communist Party, the ruling party of China. This is perhaps the single most neglected topic in most books about modern China, the key point being that the Chinese Communist Party is fundamentally different from the Communist Party of the former Soviet Union. The Chinese Communist Party is an alert, pragmatic, and adaptive party that fought to survive through nearly two decades of brutal war before assuming national power. Its roots stretch deep into China's political history, and it is focused on nation-building rather than rigid ideology.

Following the politics and government section, I discuss how the Chinese economy works. The key here is to understand how the government interacts with the economy in a fluid and pragmatic way. The Chinese economy of today is certainly not a centrally planned command economy. Private enterprises and entrepreneurs are driven, energetic, and dynamic, which has made many sectors of the Chinese economy as competitive as their Western counterparts. I also illustrate that China's state enterprises are special entities that behave partially like private enterprises and partially like government agencies.

To understand China's economic emergence, one must also analyze Chinese society, which is the topic of this book's next section. In this regard, population is a major issue. China's one-child population policy has made perhaps a greater impact than any other policy in any part of the world. It has resulted in as many as four hundred million fewer people being born, a rapidly aging population, and pressure on society as two pairs of aging couples now often rely on one young couple to support their postretirement life. Education is another key issue; comparing China's education system with that of the United States may hold the key to understanding the future competition and cooperation between the two countries. Next up is pollution and the environment, and I explain that as bad as they are, pollution and carbon reduction present both a challenge and an opportunity for the government. This is because managing pollution is a test of government capacity, and eliminating China's pollution may be treated as an investment and growth opportunity. Following this discussion, I cover the topics of the media and the internet. Many young people have become increasingly vocal in expressing their views online, and an outsider might be surprised to see how audacious they are. This also has broad implications for Chinese society, as explicit and implicit rules have emerged to deal with extreme online views.

Building on this illustration of various aspects of China, I move on to analyze whether the rise of China is likely to continue and whether there is a Chinese model of sociopolitical governance. I first evaluate the tremendous challenges that China faces in sustaining its ongoing momentum of development before concluding that overall, it is likely that China's rise will continue. Along with this continued rise, there will be a few outstanding features of China's sociopolitical governance and China's world outlook. Such features include all-responsible government, internal discipline in the ruling party, and respect-centered diplomacy. However, such features may not warrant their own categorization as the "China Model."

After discussing the inner workings of China, in the last part of the book I present a list of views that I call China's world view. The first key view is that it's most important to "finish homework before going to parties," that is, to focus on solving domestic issues before spending much energy on global affairs. This means that Chinese leaders are mostly exhausted by domestic affairs. The second key view is that the fundamental goal of foreign policy is to gain proper respect rather than tangible interests. In combination, these two points imply that China is not in a position to expand its ideology or undermine the current world order.

Finally, I come to the key message of the book, that is, the rise of China is good for the world. I first explain that the rise of China brings goods at lower prices, allowing the average US household to avoid a significant amount of expenditure and providing more jobs and career opportunities. I estimate that one of nine workers in agriculture or manufacturing in the world's richest countries produces for the Chinese market, and one of fifteen workers in the tourism industry serves Chinese tourists. In addition, as many as four hundred thousand Chinese students are studying in the United States, and their spending is equivalent to the United States exporting 10 percent of its automobile production to the rest of the world.

I also show that China's rise will provide more public goods for the world. Examples include a faster pace of scientific research, an additional space station, better efforts in combating climate change, and peacekeeping. Finally, the rise of China provides healthy competition for countries like the United States and prompts these countries to allocate more funding to education and research in science and technology, which have recently been falling for domestic political reasons.

All in all, the key message of this book is that the rise of China is good for people in every part of the world, and that it will be even better if only we can clear up misunderstandings and anxieties about China.

CHAPTER 1

China as
Number Two

T O LAY OUT THE BACKGROUND FOR THE DISCUS-
sions of the book, in this chapter I explain why the rise of
China has caused widespread and deep concerns for many in the
West. The first point of tension is that China does not seem to
share the same ideology as the West. Moreover, the Chinese ideology, as presented by the Chinese government and officials, is hard
for a Westerner to understand. The second factor is the huge size
of the population and therefore the potential for China to grow
even bigger, overtaking the United States as the largest economy
before long. The third and fourth factors are money and the timing of China's rise. That is, many Western countries, including the
United States, are currently not in the best political or economic
shape, which has made the rise of China all the more discomfort-
ing. These three factors make it particularly important to have a
clear, factual understanding of how China works and what the
implications of the rise of China are for the West.

SINCE THE START OF the twenty-first century, China has
found itself thrust into an awkward and uncomfortable position
as the world's number two power behind the big number one, the
United States. Indeed, China is currently the second-largest economy in the world, with an annual GDP of approximately $18.3
trillion in 2022, trailing only the United States at $25 trillion.

In many noneconomic aspects, China has also often placed second behind the United States, and sometimes has even placed first. Examples include the publication and citation of scientific papers, number of granted international patents, and expenditure on research and development (R&D). Many in the United States and the West are worried by projections that by some time between 2030 and 2035, China will catch up with the United States in the total size of its economy, and one by one, many other national indicators.[1]

In the past hundred years, there have been many other "number twos," and none of them has been successful in replacing the United States as the world superpower. The Soviet Union was growing very rapidly during the 1930s and took advantage of the Great Depression in the West to pull ahead in its domestic infrastructure construction. In the 1970s, the West German economy was also growing quite rapidly, and the deutsche mark was positioned to challenge the US dollar's international currency status. Later, in the 1980s, *Japan Is Number 1*, a best seller by Harvard professor Ezra Vogel, was seriously considered by many American readers.

Today, China's emergence has aroused debates as to whether it will replace the United States as number one. One camp argues that China should not be feared by the West since China faces numerous severe problems of its own. Perhaps the most important

1 Economists often argue that the actual size of the Chinese economy has already become larger than that of the United States. According to a 2020 report by the World Bank, the purchasing power parity exchange rate of the Chinese currency RMB is 4.18 for each US dollar. That is, 4.18 RMB can buy as much goods and services in China as one US dollar does in the United States. At this exchange rate, the Chinese economy by 2021 was already 20 percent larger than the United States'. In this book, I stick to the conventional calculations of the size of the Chinese and US economies, which are calculated by market exchange rate, since this is based on market transactions and is more widely used.

and popular view has been articulated by political scientists such as Dr. Fareed Zakaria, who argue that history shows that when an economy reaches a per capita income over $10,000—which China had attained by 2021—its population will demand democracy, usually setting off a tumultuous process that will slow down or even reverse the trend of economic growth. These arguments are seemingly credible but demand careful analysis.

Despite the arguments that China will eventually collapse or no longer present a significant threat to America's supremacy, many in the West have become increasingly concerned about China's rise. I explain in the following sections that a few unique factors make the rise of China particularly alarming to many analysts in the West.

To begin with, China has been developing very fast without the standard institutions of a Western democracy, and this fact constitutes a threat to many observers and analysts. China is clearly a market economy: Most goods and services are bought and sold freely, land and capital are actively traded, and the overwhelming majority of enterprises are owned and operated by private businesspeople. Yet China does not follow the practices or possess the institutions of a Western democracy: There are no general elections for national leaders, no permission for open entry of new political parties, and the press, for the most part, is under government control. These qualities set China apart from the former Soviet Union, where the market was replaced by direct government planning, thus making historical analysis of China based on the US-Soviet competition obsolete.

Because China does not follow the system of Western liberal democracy, many Western analysts are deeply concerned that if China becomes more powerful, it will jeopardize the way of life valued by Western democracies. For example, they worry that China will use technology and financial leverage to spy on the

American government and citizens, influence US elections, and purchase US companies, controlling their decisions to the detriment of US interests. As I illustrate later in the book, the concern that China threatens Western democracies is unfounded because, in the Chinese system, the government is overwhelmingly concerned with domestic affairs. China's diplomacy is and will be centered around earning respect rather than tangible interests. The Chinese government would never be able or aspire to impose the so-called Chinese model, if it even exists, on other countries, as this model only works in China, relying on thousands of years of culture and education.

NEVER BEFORE IN HISTORY has the world's number two been as large as China in terms of population, and a large population means great potential. Compared with the former Soviet Union, Germany, and Japan, China's population is 4.8 times, 10 times, and 28 times larger, respectively. This massive population is what allows the Chinese economy to be 73 percent the size of the US economy (as of 2022) with only about 17 percent of the per capita income at the market exchange rate. And a simple law of industrial or postindustrial market economies is that the larger the population, the greater the unified market, and therefore the greater the potential. Unified Germany after 1871 and the United States after the Civil War in 1865 both established a unified national market, leading both economies to grow very rapidly. Such a historical pattern is likely to repeat itself in the case of China, only with larger magnitude. China is positioned to host the world's largest economy before long, with a conservative forecast at 2035.

Many in the West worry that China's large size and growth potential will change their way of life. One example is Hollywood. By late 2020, China's movie market had grown bigger than that of the United States, taking its spot as the largest in the world.

As a consequence, Hollywood executives have devised ways to attract Chinese moviegoers, such as casting Chinese stars or even producing special Chinese versions with added or customized plots that cater to Chinese audiences. After graduating from a US university, my niece was once hired by a Hollywood producer to polish American screenplays and make them appeal to Chinese tastes. In the past, most Chinese characters in Hollywood films were depicted as devious criminals. The classic example is Dr. Fu Manchu, a dark and cruel character in a series of movies from the 1930s to the 1960s who embodied racist US stereotypes of Chinese people. Today, positive representation of Chinese characters in American-made movies is increasing. For example, in a movie based on the Boston Marathon terrorist attack, a Chinese student's Mercedes Benz SUV was hijacked by the terrorist. While watching the movie, I was very curious about how the screenplay would depict the student. In the end, he was portrayed as a decent and resourceful young man who helped the police track down the suspect.

Artificial Intelligence (AI) is an illustration of China's potential ability to catch up with the United States. In early 2023, the world was shocked by the release of the ChatGPT and GPT4, promising to be the most significant technological breakthrough in decades. Within a month, the Chinese company Baidu launched its own version of ChatGPT. Not surprisingly, many users laughed at Baidu for how poor its technology was in comparison to ChatGPT's. However, China is poised to rapidly catch up with the United States in AI because the progress of AI technology depends on three factors: engineers, computing power, and data. China has by far the world's largest contingent of engineers, graduating each year 4.4 million new engineers from colleges, almost the same number as make up the US engineering workforce in total. Not surprisingly, the number of academic publications in AI from China is on par with that in the United States. Meanwhile, China has the world's second largest reserves of computers and computing power following the United States. Although the US government has embargoed the sale of high-speed computer chips to China, for AI computing, connected computers can often do the same work as a few super-fast computers. As for data, China has the world's largest population of internet users, generating a huge amount of data for machine learning, which is the key to AI. All these factors suggest that the United States and China will be the leaders in AI development for years to come.

OF ALL THE COUNTRIES in the world, China owns by far the largest stock of money to purchase foreign goods and assets, even though the Chinese economy is not yet the largest. This is because Chinese households and enterprises save more proportionately to their income or profit than their counterparts in the West. This makes China's rise even more visible and controversial to outside observers. Broadly defined, *money* refers to cash plus bank deposits. It is the most liquid form of asset. At the end of 2022, China's money stock RMB (Chinese currency) was equivalent to 39 trillion US dollars (one and one-half times the GDP of the United States) at the market exchange rate. Roughly 40 percent of this amount is held by households, 50 percent by corporations, and around 10 percent by government agencies.

No wonder Chinese individuals are buying houses in California, Florida, New York, and Vancouver, while Chinese enterprises are purchasing enterprises like Smithfield—a US meatpacking company—and other manufacturing firms in the Midwest. Chinese money is also flowing into Latin America and Africa. This is perhaps only the beginning of an era of massive outward Chinese investment. The Chinese government already has $3 trillion of foreign currency reserves in hand, ready to be tapped by private investors in China. As of 2022, this is worth 12 percent of the US economy, and could hypothetically buy about 7 percent of all companies listed on US stock exchanges, more than half of the goods produced in Japan in one year, or two times all the stocks listed in London or Australia. This magnitude is worrisome to many outside China.

Controversies arise when Chinese corporations enter foreign markets and buy foreign companies. A good example is Germany, whose success rests in the large number of family-owned small and medium companies boasting years of trade knowledge in their respective sectors. Combined with the Chinese market, these companies could be even more successful, but many German policy makers are fearful that the new Chinese owners might move companies out of Germany or siphon off their technology, rendering the German economy less competitive. Sany is a nonstate company making construction equipment and one of the world's largest in its field. In 2012, Sany gained ownership of Putzmeister, a medium-sized German company in the same industry. The owner of Sany, Mr. Liang Wengen, was not permitted to visit the factory before the purchase was finalized due to German concerns over technology theft. He told me that when he first stepped into the production area after the deal was finally done, he felt that he had gotten a better deal than he originally thought. Putzmeister had even more technology than he anticipated and would be highly valuable to Sany. Of course, such a takeover could never happen today, as Chinese companies are now perceived to present a huge threat to Germany, and any such transactions elicit vehement political and media opposition.

THE INCREASINGLY VISIBLE RISE of China comes at the worst possible time for the United States and the West. They face many troubles, and as a result, their confidence has taken a hit, causing them to overstate and overreact to the rise of China. When China began to reform and open up during the 1980s, the West had charismatic and confident leaders. These ideologically

charged leaders were tough and confident, yet pragmatic in dealing with the former Soviet Union. As for China, these leaders
felt that they could change China through trade and educational
exchanges, leading China to become a larger version of Japan or
South Korea.

I recall, as a young student in the mid-1980s in the United
States, that I was imbued by the optimism, openness, and confidence of the country. In lecture halls, I heard speeches by many
iconic Western public figures, from Ted Kennedy to Ted Turner.
Regardless of their political stances, these figures were all relaxed,
humorous, and confident not only about their views but also about
the United States as a nation. Meanwhile, my American friends
would patiently and proudly explain to me things like the seemingly chaotic and brutal game of American football as well as the
local and presidential elections.

The confidence of the West peaked in the 1990s after the collapse of the former Soviet Union. However, at the beginning of
the twenty-first century, the terrorist attacks in New York City
triggered twenty years of war in Afghanistan and eight years of
war in Iraq, costing thousands of American lives and over 1 trillion US dollars. By 2008, the global financial crisis and the ensuing European debt crises greatly eroded the West's optimism and
confidence, leading many to wonder whether China would take
over, as I described at the beginning of this book.

The lost confidence of the United States greatly amplifies and
distorts the threat of the rise of China. In politics, continually
fewer people in the United States believe that the United States
and the West can change China. Instead, with the political chaos
during the Trump presidency, culminating in the stunning farce
on Capitol Hill on January 6, 2021, many worry that it is China
that will interfere with and change the United States. This worry
caused the former top US diplomat, Secretary Pompeo, to say
something incredibly undiplomatic: He called for the Chinese
people to rise up and overthrow the "evil" Chinese Communist

Party. This would be equivalent to top Chinese officials calling on US citizens to vote out the Democrats and install Donald Trump as an autocrat!

The bad timing has made many US policy makers and analysts often behave like sour coaches of a sports club, blaming the opposing team for playing dirty rather than finding ways to improve themselves. President Trump constantly blamed China for many socioeconomic problems in the United States. For example, he claimed that China "stole" US jobs and technology through trade. The US administration eventually imposed tariffs as high as 25 percent on almost all goods imported from China, kicking off the largest trade frictions since World War II, especially considering the wide scope and huge volume of Chinese exports to the United States. By early 2022, it became clear that the tariffs hurt US households so much that the Biden administration found ways to significantly roll them back.

The blame game against China is often accompanied by aggressive diplomacy and negotiations. In a CNBC interview, I called this the "barking dog" strategy. President Trump carried his real estate developer's approach into his dealings with China. In the trade war, he would ask for a long list of concessions from China and openly tweet his tariff threats. This made negotiations unnecessarily difficult, as Chinese culture often pays more attention to how a demand is made than what the demand is. A polite request is more likely to be successful than an aggressive one. The Biden administration has been less aggressive but still is unnecessarily so. For example, in March 2021, President Biden's young director of national security, Jake Sullivan, opened a face-to-face session with his Chinese counterpart by saying: "We are negotiating with you from a position of power." A position of power, whatever it means and regardless of its truthfulness, is an unusual expression in diplomacy. It is most likely that this rhetoric was for the US domestic audience, implying that the United States is still the more powerful one and will not make any concessions.

Sullivan's Chinese counterpart rose to the occasion, responding that "we Chinese never yield to any bully." The whole sequence was unnecessary and counterproductive. The confident President Reagan would not have spoken to his Soviet counterpart in the same fashion.

It is very unfortunate that the bad timing of China's rise has made it more difficult for China and the United States to work out their differences. The two sides are not very far apart on many issues concerning China's economy, since Chinese leaders know that further opening up and reform is needed for China's own good. Even with the aggressive President Trump in office, the two countries' leaders could have worked something out. In fact, I heard President Xi say in a session that he told President Trump, "Some people say that I do not like you and I wish that you were out of office. This is not true. You represent US interests and I represent Chinese interests. That's it. As individuals, we are friends." In a speech in St. Petersburg, Russia, in June 2019, President Xi also openly stated that President Trump was his friend.

Because of the events of the Trump presidency, many people in China, both educated and uneducated, have come to the conclusion that the United States as a whole cannot accept further development of China and will do everything in its power to squeeze and contain China into remaining number two forever. They point to the fact that when the Japanese economy reached three-quarters the size of the US economy in the 1980s, the United States waged a trade war against Japan so that today's Japan would never be in a position to challenge the United States. Now, the Chinese economy finds itself in the same position as Japan once did—its economy is three-quarters the size of the US economy. As such, US behavior is focused on impeding China.

For all these reasons, including China's non-Western ideology, large size, huge stock of money, and bad timing, the rise of China has been identified as one of the gravest challenges in historical terms for the United States and Western democracy as a whole. Is the rise of China truly an epic challenge to the United States and the West? To answer this question, we need to understand how China works and how China views the world. In the next chapters, I dive into these topics. I hope by the time you reach the latter part of the book, you will agree with me that the rise of China is eventually beneficial for the world and therefore should not be feared.

CHAPTER 2

History Is the Key to Understanding Today's China

A LL CHINESE ARE HISTORIANS. OF COURSE, I AM exaggerating. I say this to explain that people in China love to use historical figures or episodes to understand, comment, insinuate, or subtly criticize politics today. History shapes the world view of most Chinese in an extremely important way.

In this chapter, I first explain that Chinese leaders draw inspiration from history when making critical decisions. Moreover, Chinese leaders are disciplined by their expectations of how they will be judged by history. I also explain that most people in mainland China perceive the country's modern history as starting with the Opium War (1840–1842), which was the start of the "century of humiliation." As a direct implication, the common view in mainland China is that Hong Kong and Taiwan have to be properly united with China in order to end the humiliation. Most important, perhaps, is that most Chinese, based on history, do not expect a rising China to replace the United States as the world's hegemon, but they do believe that US-led preemptive attacks on China must be resolutely fended off.

MAO ZEDONG WAS EXTREMELY well-versed in Chinese history. Until his death, he kept stacks of history books alongside his huge wooden bed. He drew inspirations from history for his most critical decisions. One famous example is how the history behind the Peking Opera play *A Farewell to My Concubine* inspired Mao to keep fighting in the Chinese Civil War.

In 1949, the Communist Party had occupied northern China despite the overwhelming strength of the Nationalist Party forces, which had been given US military equipment. The Communist Party was at a crossroads, considering whether China should follow the Korean and the German model: divide the country into two parts, with the north controlled by the Communist Party and the south controlled by the Nationalists.

Chairman Mao was inspired by the famous story about War Lord Xiang Yu, who 2,200 years ago was the most powerful leader to rebel against the son of the first emperor, Qin Shihuang. Xiang Yu controlled almost the entire country when his most fierce competitor, Liu Bang, acknowledged his power and asked whether they could coexist peacefully. All of Xiang Yu's advisors told him to assassinate Liu Bang at a well-choreographed banquet, but Xiang lacked a killer's instinct. His hesitation proved to be fatal for him.

Liu Bang's diplomacy was a trap. A few years later, he returned in force and cornered Xiang Yu against a river, giving him nowhere to escape. The night before Xiang Yu was captured, he had his last drink with his favorite concubine. She performed her final dance for him with a sword and then killed herself as an act of loyalty.

Mao was taken with the themes of history expressed in "A Farewell to My Concubine": beauty, love, heroism, power, politics, success, and failure. Referring to this tragedy, Mao warned his Communist colleagues never to make the same mistake as Xiang Yu. "When we get our momentum," he said, "we shall carry on and eliminate our enemy. We will win the whole country." So in April 1949, Mao issued a command for the People's Liberation Army to cross the Yangtze River and take over the southern part of China. On the evening he captured the capital Nanjing, he said, "We will never become complacent." Mao, a tremendous romantic poet in his own right, wrote a poem on that night referring to the history of Xiang Yu.

IN ADDITION TO INSPIRING leaders' decisions, history can also act as a source of discipline for Chinese leaders, who are always deeply concerned with how their actions will be evaluated by future generations. As such, the weight of historical judgment acts as an informal accountability measure in the Chinese political system. This phenomenon was abundantly clear to me with my close observations of Premier Wen Jiabao in the lead-up to the 2008 stimulus package.

The eyes of three hundred of China's most influential figures were fixed on Premier Wen Jiabao as he began speaking about the economy. I looked to my left and saw the head of the *People's Daily* (the most influential and official newspaper of China). Not far away sat the head of China's nuclear industry, a former student at my school, the Tsinghua University School of Economics and Management, who was then the target of a corruption investigation (before eventually serving time). From the start, it was clear to me that this meeting with the premier was different from those I had attended on many previous occasions.

It was November 10, 2008, during the heart of the eruption of the global financial crisis following the bankruptcy of Lehman Brothers. The premier was the main speaker, and the moderator was then-executive premier and later premier Li Keqiang. I was asked to attend with virtually no notice and given no details about the meeting's substance. I assumed it would be a meeting simply to discuss certain reform policies.

When I entered the room, I was shocked to see so many key decision makers: the governors of all thirty-one provinces, directors of the provinces' development and reform commissions, the CEOs of the largest state-owned enterprises, and CEOs and chairmen of the largest commercial banks. Also in the audience were the heads of China's major media, including CCTV and the *People's Daily*. And one scholar: me. My guess was that I was invited because I often publicly comment on China's economic policies and might be considered an opinion maker regarding economics. In addition, I try to be as much of a nonbiased academic as possible, not involving myself in ideological debates or politics.

The venue of the meeting was a huge hall in the Western Beijing Hotel (Jing Xi Hotel). The meeting hall is virtually twice the size of the largest ballroom in any New York City five-star hotel. This is where all the largest central government meetings have been held, including the all-important Third Plenum of the Eleventh Party Congress in 1978, which began the era of reform and opening up. The hotel complex is massive, surrounded by military guards—and only cars with the proper passes can enter.

Not only did the prominence of the attendees make it clear this was no ordinary meeting, so did the speaking style of the premier. The premier usually spoke slowly and deliberately, but this time his pace was noticeably quicker than it was at previous meetings I had attended. He was wearing a white dress shirt and black zip-up jacket, the standard attire for informal meetings of Politburo members (the thirty-plus-member committee at the center of power of the Chinese Communist Party). He spent the first forty-five minutes of his two-hour talk explaining the huge challenges facing the economy, saying that industrial output and exports were declining, and that although the statistics did not appear too alarming at a glance, the negative trend they reflected was repeatedly emphasized by the premier. He said that this was an extreme situation facing the Chinese economy, and that action must be taken.

It was then that we discovered the reason for the meeting: The premier announced that the government would be rolling out a 4 trillion RMB (approximately 634 billion USD) stimulus for 2009 and 2010. I calculated on the spot that this was equal to 7.5 percent of GDP for each of the two years—roughly the ratio of China's trade surplus to GDP. My quick inference was that the government assumed that the surplus might disappear completely, so it wanted to use the stimulus to offset that worst-case scenario.

The premier continued that it was imperative to implement these policies immediately. He stressed the necessity of effective implementation, making an analogy to martial arts. "We will not behave like a showy martial artist (who pretends to be a master), whose moves are inaccurate, whose moves look good and are fancy but mellow in actual impact," the premier said. "Rather, we want swift, accurate, powerful, and effective strikes."

The entire room fell silent. Expressions of genuine shock could be seen on the faces of all three hundred attendees.

The premier continued in his stern tone and even waved his fist in the air as he spoke, an uncharacteristic display of emotion. He proclaimed that if the 4 trillion was not enough, the government "has more weapons available and will spend even more. We will do everything we have to in order to stop the decline of the economy."

At this point, all attendees were frantically taking notes, trying to capture every word. This was especially true of the local government officials, who knew they would have to relay all this information to their colleagues in their home provinces. In addition, they could use many of the premier's words to lobby or make requests to the central government for investment funds. A scene like this is rare, because often when top officials deliver important speeches, written notes are prepared and distributed for the attendees ahead of time. But in this case, the last-minute urgency of the meeting did not permit this.

The meeting ended at 11:30, which is the usual end time for such gatherings. Chinese government officials wake up very early in the morning and are in the habit of eating an early lunch before a noontime nap, so I could already hear many stomachs growling.

As the attendees stood and prepared to file out of the room, many of them began whispering to each other, trying to digest what they had just witnessed. Then, Executive Premier Li Keqiang announced that instead of going to lunch, the directors of the provincial reform and development commissions (the most powerful economic branch of a local government) were to go to a separate room and discuss how to implement the stimulus package.

Why was Premier Wen so anxious, intense, and seemingly paranoid as he rolled out the stimulus? History is the answer. He did not want to be recorded in history to be a slow-acting decision maker facing a brewing crisis. His predecessor Premier Zhu Rongji was at the verge of committing such a mistake at the very beginning of the Asian financial crisis in 1998. Zhu had been in charge of the economy and had been focused on controlling economic overheating. Fortunately, Zhu quickly understood the character of the Asian financial crisis and rolled out a sequence of stimulus package reform policies, including a quadrupling of college enrollment.

It is quite clear that Premier Wen did not realize that years later the stimulus package would come under attack by Chinese economists, who blamed the policy for putting the Chinese economy heavily in debt. The debt to GDP ratio increased from 100 percent to over 250 percent between 2008 and 2015. My honest view is that any sensible person in his position would make the same decision. Facing the uncertainty, loss, and damage that would have come with choosing not to implement a stimulus package would have been too much to bear. I made this simple point during an interview with Chinese media in Washington, DC, in 2015 while attending a conference of the World Bank and IMF. When I returned to China, I received a phone call from the former premier's office. Having retired for over two years at that point, he was seeking more evidence behind my argument. This is rare. China's retired officials are not supposed to contact incumbent officials or active scholars and vice versa—such dealings are perceived as interfering in the decision making of current leaders. And yet, Wen Jiabao went out of his way to contact me. That shows me how concerned he is about the people's assessment of his policy.

OVER THE PAST SEVERAL YEARS, I could not help comparing Chinese leaders and their US counterparts about their sense of history. As I explained, Premier Wen Jiabao was very concerned about the lasting public response to the policies he enacted while in office. In contrast, when I had the chance to meet former US president George W. Bush, I found him to be almost the opposite. I moderated a virtual town hall meeting between a retired George W. Bush and the inaugural cohort of the Schwarzman Scholars, and the meeting went extremely well. As a private citizen, George W. Bush was relaxed, down to earth, and personable, and had a great sense of humor. When the students asked him difficult questions, such as how to deal with the crisis in Syria, his response was, "I don't know. I need to consult the experts on this." It was clear that he was enjoying his private life.

His openness and easygoing nature were surprising to me because if he were a Chinese leader, George W. Bush would not be able to enjoy his retirement so thoroughly. Rather, he would be constantly plagued with blame for the two unfortunate episodes that occurred on his watch: the US invasion of Iraq in 2003 and the global financial crisis in 2008. In other words, Western political systems place a much stronger singular focus on present leaders, with checks and balances built into the government to try to balance their authority. In China, history itself is a very important check on power: Current leaders have to think twice when making decisions, since the weight of history's judgment constrains their behavior. In the United States, my observation is that when a president leaves office, all is gone. History will make judgments, but the president would not personally bear a heavy load of accountability. The presidential libraries are mostly for scholarly research and mostly not the center of current political debates.

MOST CHINESE PEOPLE ARE accustomed to having a long-term view and perceiving history in cycles. In ancient Chinese history, it was common to have a powerful empire ruling the country for a few hundred years, followed by a period of civil war or foreign invasion, chaos, and breakup into small kingdoms. The cycle would then repeat as the country was reunited again, sometimes with the help of external invaders, as was the case with the Yuan Dynasty (under the Mongolians) and the last Chinese dynasty, the Qing Dynasty founded by the Manchurians from northeastern China. Thus, many Chinese people observe big-picture patterns as they view the sweep of history.

From the long-term historical view, most Chinese believe that today China is in the rising part of a cycle following the "century of humiliation" from 1840 (the Opium War) to 1945 (the end of the Japanese invasion). The last emperors of the final dynasty got into deep troubles dealing with Western powers and were forced to sign a sequence of treaties, known as the unequal treaties, authorizing concessions. Then the Nationalist Party overthrew the last dynasty in 1911, establishing the Republic of China. Unfortunately, this regime proved unsuccessful at uniting the country and addressing social problems such as inequality. China remained in disarray until the Communist Party assumed national power in 1949, and from this historical perspective, the Communist Party is recognized as a hero among many people of China. The century of humiliation is fresh in their memory, and this contributes to the popularity of Xi Jinping's calls for China to revive itself and reclaim its place as a well-respected and powerful country.

A very popular belief in China is that five hundred years ago, China's economy was the biggest and most prosperous in the world. This statement grossly overstates the glory of China's economic history. Over the past decade, my coauthor, Professor Guan Hanhui of Peking University, and I have spent several years estimating the total size of the historical Chinese economy. In modern economic terms, the total size of an economy is measured by the gross domestic product (GDP). We spent years exploring the archives of the Chinese national library, recording the physical output of grain, paper, iron, coal, and artistic items such as porcelain, to reconstruct the total GDP of various Chinese dynasties. Prior to our research, scholars such as the late Angus Madison had to guess China's per capita income and multiply this figure by the size of the population, yielding grossly inaccurate results.

Our findings were shocking: The per capita income of China began to decline one thousand years ago, dating back to the Song Dynasty. From 980 until 1840, the beginning of China's modern history, the per capita income of the Chinese economy declined despite an increase in total output, which grew at a rate of 0.35 percent. The reason for this was very simple: The rapid increase in population outpaced the growth of arable land and capital, so that on the per capita level, capital and land were declining. Furthermore, the productivity of labor did not increase significantly in the ancient Chinese economy. With the chronic decline in per capita income, extreme poverty and a surplus of agricultural labor took root.

Based on our calculations, by 1775, China's per capita income was only 30 percent of that of the UK. Our conclusion has a clear implication: There was no way for China to have developed its own Industrial Revolution, since labor was so abundant that it did not allow for the invention of labor-saving technologies.

Against this backdrop of economic stagnation, the encounter between China and modern Western civilization proved to be disastrous for the Chinese, starting with the Opium War of 1840–1842. In a sequence of unequal treaties that ended lost wars, the Qing emperors gave up the island of Hong Kong to Britain, the city of Qingdao to Germany, Taiwan to Japan, and a huge area of land in the northern region as large as Germany, France, and the UK combined to tsarist Russia.

Over the past 180 years, generation after generation of social elites and politicians have debated and advocated for their own vision of how a modern China should emerge from its humiliating confrontations with Western civilization. Almost all Chinese leaders believe that unless the country makes itself stronger, it will again fall victim to more advanced nations and powers. Among all leaders, Deng Xiaoping put it most succinctly: "When we remain backward, we will be beaten again, economically, militarily, and eventually culturally, and China will lose its identity in the world." This belief, bordering on paranoia, is behind the politics practiced during the past thirty-plus years of rapid growth.

Attitudes toward China's historical humiliations inform contemporary stances on Taiwan and Hong Kong. Both Taiwan and Hong Kong are immensely important for mainland Chinese leaders, who enjoy unimaginable support from the population on these issues. Why? The answer does not stem from pure economics or geopolitics, but from history. Taiwan was first taken away from mainland China after the First Sino-Japanese War of 1895, when it was ceded to Japan as part of a huge war settlement. At the end of World War II, Japan was forced to give up Taiwan to mainland China. In 1949, Chiang Kai-shek's Nationalist government retreated from the mainland to Taiwan at the end of the Chinese Civil War. Chiang Kai-shek intended to use Taiwan as a base for a comeback to mainland China in a continuation of the Civil War, but of course he never realized his dream. Since then, both the Communists and the Nationalists have claimed to be the only legitimate government of all of China, including Taiwan. In recent years, the situation has gotten increasingly tense as popular sentiment on Taiwan has shown a growing call for independence from the mainland, with provocative support from certain foreign governments. Why is this such a sensitive issue? To the people in the mainland, Taiwan is a deep historical wound stemming from abuse by Western powers and Japan, and it has never had a chance to heal. A simple analogy would be if the United States had lost Hawaii to Japan during World War II. Until Hawaii could be reunited with the United States, this episode of the war would never end.

The issue of Hong Kong can be understood in a very similar way. The colonization of Hong Kong by the UK was the very beginning of the century of humiliation. That's why any indication of Hong Kong moving toward independence rips open yet another deep wound, bringing historical trauma to the surface. As a result, China has been extremely strict about not tolerating any foreign influence or undue comments from other countries about the issue of Hong Kong.

To a Western observer and many people in Taiwan and Hong Kong, self-determination is a natural right. However, to most of the people on the mainland, history matters. The determination to bring Taiwan and Hong Kong under the mainland's sovereignty, which is a tricky and sophisticated concept, is paramount. Anything besides sovereignty can be discussed. In fact, the mainland government has offered Taiwan authority to keep its army and keep everything unchanged so long as Taiwan comes back to the sovereignty of the mainland. As for Hong Kong, all political reforms can be worked out so long as it does not elect leaders calling for Hong Kong's independence from the mainland.

How do most Chinese view the United States from a historical perspective? At a risk of oversimplification, my observation is that most people recognize that the United States is and remains the most powerful and domineering country in the world. In contrast, most people believe that historically, China never ruled or conquered the world, even during powerful dynasties. Instead, powerful dynasties successfully fended off invasions, mostly from the north, and then made peace with the invaders by various means, including marrying off royal princesses to heads of the northern powers. Bringing this historical experience to the present day, many Chinese believe that today's rising China should fight back against any US-led efforts to contain China, especially on issues like Taiwan, Hong Kong, and China's claimed sovereignty over certain islands in the South China Sea. Once China is able to successfully counter US containment policies, China will make efforts to facilitate peace with the United States and its allies. Marrying out Chinese princesses is not an option, as times have changed. But there are far more alternatives today, including social and economic collaborations. It is important for the world to understand these popular Chinese views based on Chinse history.

What is the most visible impact of history on today's China? The answer has to do with the Chinese Communist Party. It is the world's largest and soon-to-be longest-ruling party, with a unique approach to sociopolitical governance. The party is a product of Chinese history, and it is arguably the most important key to understanding today's China. This is the topic I turn to next.

CHAPTER 3

The Chinese Communist Party

I T CAN NEVER BE OVEREMPHASIZED THAT IN ORDER to understand today's China, one must develop a deep understanding of the Chinese Communist Party. Toward this goal, in this chapter, I explain three simple but very important points. First, as the largest political party in the world, the Chinese Communist Party comprehensively governs the country from each village or city building to the very top. Second, before assuming national power, the Chinese Communist Party fought through twenty-two years of brutal military wars, suffered from many catastrophic setbacks, and learned in harsh ways that in order to win and stay in power, they have to be pragmatic and adaptive. In this regard, the Party is very different from those in Eastern Europe and the former Soviet Union. Third, the party is delicately organized and managed, drawing on thousands of years of Chinese history of political governance. Meritocracy is a principle that has been inherited from history.

IN CHINA, THERE'S A SAYING: The party leads everything. This refers to the fact that the party manages all critical social affairs of society. The institutions of the party overlap with those of the government; it has the authority to preside over government decisions at both central and local levels.

As a result, the party is huge in membership and its organization stretches all the way from the center of political power down to the grassroots level. With 96.71 million party members by mid-2022, the basic party units serve as an effective avenue for mobilizing resources and managing societal affairs. The best and most recent illustration of this has been the role of grassroots party units in combating COVID-19, when they were tasked with enforcing lockdowns, monitoring quarantines, and ensuring that residents could access the necessary groceries and supplies. This would be as if in the United States, President Biden issued a compulsory vaccine policy and the local branches of his Democratic Party were responsible for enforcing such a policy. Obviously, the Democratic Party does not have such a capacity. In reality, the Democratic Party or the Republican Party, with a size about half that of the Chinese Communist Party, are mostly focused on getting their candidates elected as opposed to everyday governance.

Because it plays such a central role in governance, and due to its unique history, the party has always had a founding mission. Under the leadership of Xi Jinping, the founding mission of the party has been further articulated. In his own words, the mission of the party is to seek well-being for the Chinese people and rejuvenation for the Chinese nation. To an outsider, the party's founding mission is not too different from that of other strong political parties around the world such as the People's Action Party of Singapore or Mexico's Institutional Revolutionary Party.

Therefore, a simple question arises: Given the well-articulated mission of the party, why put "communism" in its name? This is obviously an important question that few people ask in China. Many people in the world, including conservative politicians, have developed their hatred for the party because of the term *communism*. The most important answer is: history. In 1921, founders of the party, including Mao Zedong, drew their inspiration from the Russian October Revolution in 1917. They believed that the October Revolution was not only a victory of the poor but also that Russia would become a fair, strong, and prosperous nation after the revolution. And they believed that this is what China needed. Such a vision was extremely attractive for the young and educated elites in a poor, weak, and proud nation like China. The October Revolution was led by a communist party. Thus, China needed its own communist party.

It is an interesting and revealing fact that Jiang Zemin, the late former party leader, and his senior colleagues seriously examined the issue of dropping "communism" from the name of the party. This was not long after the collapse of the former Soviet Union in the early 1990s. However, the conclusion was a resounding no. Why? "Should we drop Communism out of our name, many who supported us and believed in communism and made tremendous sacrifices will no longer side with us," said Jiang, according to a senior party theoretician who participated in the discussion. In other words, dropping the term *communism* is a betrayal of the party's history.

But how does the Chinese Communist Party reconcile itself with the Marxist doctrine that capitalism should be buried and a communist society should be built to replace it? Since the start of reform and opening up, the Chinese Communist Party under Deng Xiaoping has developed a theory that creating a communist society is a goal that will be realized far in the future. Until then, a type of socialism should be promoted in which private ownership of capital should be allowed in order to provide incentives for the economy to develop. Meanwhile, some social inequality should be tolerated so long as most people are making progress in their economic well-being. In official language, this is called the primitive stage of socialism, and this stage will last a long time. In practice, this means that the party manages the market economy with government intervention to prevent extreme volatility and inequality.

————

THE HISTORY OF THE Communist Party, which marked its one hundredth anniversary in July 2021, has deeply shaped its character. Its history can be best understood by dividing it into three periods. The first period covers the first fifty-five years, 1921–1976, mostly under the leadership of Mao Zedong. The second period covers the next thirty-five years, mostly under the influence of Deng Xiaoping, 1977–2011, and the third period started in 2012 under the current leadership of Xi Jinping.

During Mao's reign, he was widely revered and viewed as a god within the party. Even today, many people in China retain a great deal of respect for Mao Zedong, although others do not share this view. Among the educated, a discussion of Mao often brings out strong emotions and turns a gathering of family or friends unpleasant. On the other hand, many less-educated Chinese people still regard Mao as a god and even hang a button showing his picture in their car's rearview mirror in order to receive his blessing for safe travel. Others less fond of Mao claim that had Mao's eldest and most favored son not been killed during the Korean War, today's China might be like North Korea, with the Mao family ruling the country just like the Kim family in North Korea. In any case, Mao certainly is the most important political figure in modern Chinese history.

Mao was among the fifteen young men who founded the Communist Party in 1921 in a French enclave in Shanghai, where the police were relatively less aggressive in controlling Marxist movements. Mao was not a key leader during the first ten years of the party. Rather, the leaders were professors and students who had studied Marxism at leading Chinese universities, or in France, Germany, and the Soviet Union.

Six years after its founding, the Chinese Communist Party ran into a huge crisis: Party members were being massacred by the opposing Nationalist government. Mao had argued that the party needed its own military force, but the scholarly founders of the party had disagreed. In response, Mao initiated on his own a peasant revolt in 1927 along the border of two provinces where Nationalist control was weak. After the revolt, Mao organized these peasants into a small guerrilla army and set up their base in a mountainous region called Jing Gang Shan. Within a few years, these troops had grown into the Red Army, with a membership of one hundred thousand.

In the following years, the Communist Party established military bases in southern China with Mao Zedong as one of their leaders. Initially, the bases were extremely politically successful, mobilizing poor farmers to support the Communist Party and its army. Meanwhile, the Red Army was using guerilla war tactics to fight against the all-powerful Nationalist Party's army under Chiang Kai-shek. However, the situation turned drastically worse around 1933, when the Communist League based in Russia began sending senior officials to "guide" the Chinese Communist Revolution. Since the Soviet Communist Party was regarded as the father of all communist parties, their advice was carefully heeded. Mao Zedong was ousted and severely criticized by the party members who had studied in the Soviet Union. The Communist League sent foreign experts to command the Red Army under the leadership of an Austrian named Otto Braun, who wrested military control from Mao. Before coming to China, Braun had been a rising officer in the Austrian-Hungarian army until he was captured by the Soviets and converted into a Communist. He was treated like a god by the Chinese Communists, but unfortunately, Braun's military performance in China was anything but godlike. He used German tactics to engage in positional warfare, which played right into the hands of the much better equipped Nationalist Army.

As a consequence of the military disaster of Mr. Braun, the Red Army was forced to embark on the famous Long March, a brutal eight-thousand-mile journey from southern to northern China. By the end of the Long March, the main force of the Red Army had shrunk from eighty-five thousand to thirty thousand soldiers. It was during this retreat that Mao was able to demonstrate his military prowess, masterfully executing elaborate maneuvers to escape his opponent's attacks in a "hit and run" approach. Mao's success won him a great deal of his supporters, and thus the Long March was the beginning of his ascent to power. Mao would remain the leader of the party until his death in the fall of 1976.

Despite the fierce conflict with the Nationalists, by 1937, Mao realized that he needed to form an alliance with them in order to have any hope of driving out invading Japanese forces, which posed a grave threat to China. Thus, Mao made tremendous efforts to restrain the Communist Party's rage against the Nationalists and form a military alliance. This helped the Communist Party survive, because without the alliance, they would have been fighting two wars at the same time. This reversal of strategy from fighting against the Nationalists to forming an alliance with them is a prime example of the Communist Party's willingness to adapt and be pragmatic in order to survive and succeed. To this day, the Communist Party fully realizes that despite its all-powerful rule over the country, it faces many dangers and must implement constant changes.

Eventually, after the Communists and Nationalists prevailed over the Japanese forces, the civil war resumed from 1945 to 1949, when the Communists emerged victorious and founded the People's Republic of China in October of 1949. So ended the first phase of Mao's leadership. Overall, most people in China agree that during this first period, Mao was largely wise in his major decisions, ultimately leading the Communists to victory over the Nationalist Party. However, after the Communist Party came into power, Mao made a series of mistakes that are openly acknowledged by the Communist Party, despite Mao's historical importance. Why does the party openly criticize Mao's mistakes? It is because many people, including senior party members, were severely affected by his poor policies. To criticize Mao is to protect the party's authority. The two most severe and openly criticized mistakes were the Great Leap Forward, which occurred during 1957 and 1958, and the Cultural Revolution, between 1966 and 1976.

The Great Leap Forward began when Mao returned from a visit to the Soviet Union celebrating the fortieth anniversary of the Russian Revolution. During his three-week stay in Moscow, he was not impressed by the situation of the Soviet Union, telling his colleagues: "Look at the Russians on the street. They appear to be depressed. China's socialism should do a better job." A few weeks after returning from Moscow, in a poetic style, Mao launched a series of campaigns to boost morale and spur mass mobilization. In one campaign, Mao hoped to triple China's steel output, while in another, he collectivized farmers into production teams. Both moves proved to be disastrous. People melted all kinds of quality hardware, including cooking tools and other necessary devices, and recycled them, artificially increasing steel production. Meanwhile, collectivizing the farmers took away their incentive to work. In many cases, grain farmers actually ate their seeds, expecting to benefit from the crops cultivated by others.

By 1959, Mao readily recognized that he had made a major mistake with the Great Leap Forward. Though his vision had been to stimulate investment and collectivize farmers, the result was a catastrophic famine. The actual number of deaths during the Great Leap Forward is still under dispute, but many historians agree the number was at least 10 million. In the aftermath of this calamity, in April 1959, Mao stepped down from the presidency of the country, while remaining as the chairman of the party. In effect, he meant to retire from the daily operations of the government and let pragmatic colleagues like Liu Shaoqi and Zhou Enlai take over. By 1962, the economy began to recover.

An important event in the former Soviet Union sowed the seed for Mao's second major mistake. Following Joseph Stalin's death in 1953, Nikita Khrushchev took his place as the new leader of the

Soviet Union. Barely three years after that, when the Twentieth Party Congress of the Soviet Communist Party had officially concluded, Khrushchev suddenly called an extra session for the next day. He delivered a long report to the stunned delegates in which he harshly criticized Stalin for all his mistakes, kicking off a massive campaign designed to tarnish Stalin's legacy. Once hailed as a god and hero, Stalin was now publicly crucified as a devil. Back in China, the fact that Mao made a bad decision in the Great Leap Forward, and that his colleague Liu Shaoqi had facilitated the recovery, made Mao extremely uncomfortable and insecure. Mao cared enormously about his legacy and worried that he would suffer a fate similar to Stalin's. He began to regard other rising party leaders such as Liu with suspicion and embarked on a mission to reclaim and protect his power.

Mao waged the Cultural Revolution to squash his political opponents—such as his once favored successor, Liu Shaoqi—who he suspected would follow Khrushchev's example. He fought this battle using a kind of grassroots, guerilla tactic. Mao traveled around the country in his specially detailed train, meeting with local officials and attacking the municipal government of Beijing as well as the central government. He asked people: "If China had a revisionist like Khrushchev, what would you do? Would you take my side or the side of the revisionists?" Because Mao was hailed as a god, the people replied, "We'll follow you."

Knowing that some senior officials were disillusioned with the catastrophe of the Great Leap Forward, Mao focused his appeal on young people, including high school and college students. He knew that many young people still worshipped him, as the concept of Mao as a god had been ingrained in them throughout their school years. Mao leveraged his power to call upon these young people to rise up against their leaders, such as their high school principals and university presidents.

The most famous incident took place at Tsinghua University Affiliated High School, where students answered Mao's call by drawing large character posters criticizing their teachers and the school principal. These students signed the posters using the pen name *Red Guards*, the personal and loyal guards of Mao. The Red Guards exploded into a massive movement that terrorized local party officials, school personnel, intellectuals, and anyone else labeled as revisionist, bourgeois, or antirevolutionary. Arguably, the phrase *Red Guard* is the most ingenious and successful stroke of political marketing in modern Chinese history. It was coined by a few junior high schoolers at the Tsinghua High School.

By 1968, all high schools, universities, and most primary schools had ceased operations. All major government agencies had been paralyzed, with their Communist Party branches replaced by revolutionary committees. The court, the procuratorate, and the police had all but stopped functioning. Massive amounts of historical and cultural heritage had been destroyed. China was in chaos. Even the Red Guards themselves had split into factions and begun to attack one another.

By July 1968, Mao had reached the goal of eradicating his political enemies, with Liu Shaoqi being snatched by the Red Guards without any legal or administrative procedures and dying in prison a year later. Worried about losing control, Mao finally called for an end to the Red Guards' terror. He then called the Red Guards to go to the countryside, calling it poetically the biggest classroom for students, where they would fly high and realize their dreams. This marked the beginning of the second stage of the Cultural Revolution. The years of the Cultural Revolution eventually created so much social chaos and discontent that it abruptly ended, less than one month after Mao's death, when his wife, Jiang Quing, was imprisoned.

WHEN MAO DIED IN 1976, the era of Deng Xiaoping began. Although Deng Xiaoping was never officially named general secretary of the Communist Party or president of China, his power was pervasive, and he was considered the country's paramount leader from 1978 until his resignation in 1989. However, the Deng Xiaoping era stretched beyond Deng's own rule and into the terms of his predecessors Jiang Zemin and Hu Jintao, as Deng's policies and philosophies continued to have a deep effect on the country.

As an extremely pragmatic person, when he first came into power, Deng Xiaoping knew that Mao was still widely beloved. Thus, to denounce Mao would have been unwise and politically divisive. At the same time, the Cultural Revolution and Great Leap Forward still evoked unpleasant memories among many people. To walk the fine line of public opinion, as soon as he assumed power in 1981, Deng Xiaoping enacted an official report of the Communist Party titled *The Official Verdict on Major Historical Events of the Communist Party*. In it, he stated that the Cultural Revolution had been a complete mistake by Mao, although Mao had been a great leader prior to that. Deng Xiaoping quickly sought acceptance of this verdict, which contained general principles but was not detailed. This was Deng Xiaoping's style. He left the details to be figured out by future generations so that the current generation could focus on more pressing issues.

As early as 1980, reflecting on the painful experience of the Cultural Revolution, Deng Xiaoping implemented a system of retirement policies in the Communist Party and the government, requiring officials to step down at a certain age. He also implemented sweeping economic reforms known as "reform and opening up," during which he opened the Chinese economy to the outside world and began to privatize state-owned industries. Deng's strategy was to transition China's economy slowly and methodically, "crossing the river by feeling the stones" and testing new policies gradually in special economic zones. Unlike Mao, Deng was extremely pragmatic, once proclaiming, "I don't care if the color of the cat is black or white, as long as it catches mice." Deng's guiding concept was extremely simple: The founding mission of the Communist Party is to let people live better and to make the country more powerful. Thus, all of Deng's policies aimed toward this end. He hated and avoided ideological debates. I often joke that Deng is the best advertiser of Nike shoes: Just Do It (don't debate)! In practice, this translated into his call for watching and learning from the success of other countries and for a philosophy in China's foreign policy called Tao Guang Yang Hui (hide your shine and bide your time)—in other words, keep a low profile in international relations.

While Deng Xiaoping was a pragmatic Just-Do-It leader, under his guidance the party had a major ideological shift. This happened in the early 2000s when Jiang Zemin was general secretary of the party. Until then, according to classical Marxism, the Communist Party was to be the vanguard to overthrow the capitalist system. Instead, Jiang stated that the Communist Party should represent three elements—this is known as the Three Represents Theory. First, the party represents the progressive direction of economic development. Second, the party represents the progressive culture. Third, the party represents the progressive direction of social change. Under the Three Represents Theory, the Communist Party aims to become a party of elites and is not too far removed from the ideology of a social democratic party in Western Europe.

THE PARTY HAS OFFICIALLY claimed it is now in a new era, which began in November 2012 when Xi Jinping formally became president and general secretary of the Communist Party. Xi's guiding principle is not to forget the founding mission of the Communist Party, which, as laid out in Xi's documents and speeches, espouses his goal of leading China's revival. The single most important tenet of Xi Jinping's leadership philosophy is that the party has to be on top of everything, and in order for the party to perform this role well, the discipline within the party should be strengthened, including a strict anticorruption protocol. In the previous Deng era, there were many discussions and cases of reforming Chinese politics by separating the party from the government, that is, for the party to reduce its control of the government and for the government to become more democratic and independent of party operations. For example, in the Deng era, there were many cases of having open elections of mayors of cities with multiple candidates for each position. On several occasions, the party's most favored candidates failed to be elected.

Mao, Deng, and Xi represent three very different styles of leadership. Mao was complex as a person and a leader. In a letter to his wife in 1966, just when he was waging the Cultural Revolution, he described himself as a monkey and a tiger in one body. That is, he was rebellious, self-doubting, and restless like a monkey and yet very pragmatic and confident like a tiger when fighting his enemies. He wanted to be worshipped and yet he was sarcastic about his personal cult, telling Edgar Snow, a trusted American journalist, that being saluted as a king was like being baked on a grill. He could be ruthless as a world-class strategist and yet, very different from other dictators, he never believed in political assassination. His ultimate goal was to make his enemy get down on their knees and say: I was wrong and you are right. He was held to be an ingenious leader for plotting and implementing strategies that helped the Communist Party assume national power. However, his vision for a modern China based on a state-controlled economy and egalitarian principles fared poorly with not only his colleagues but also ordinary citizens. Most interestingly, he sensed his failure a few years before his death and tried to reverse it by various means. He fared miserably in this. He was like an aging superstar in basketball, refusing to sit on the bench after missing many shots and stubbornly shooting another long-distance air ball while the fans were politely cheering. Truly a tragedy.

Deng was almost the opposite of Mao. He was short in stature and equally short in his speeches. He was often surprisingly brief and honest when speaking. Deng said: "Being poor is not socialism. Let us get rich first before worrying about other things because otherwise we will be wiped off the earth by the powerful." He was also credited for saying: "To get rich, make friends with the US." It is fun to read Deng's *Selected Works*, which contains many articles only as long as a few hundred words. Deng knew the problems of the latter-day Mao all too well and chose to phase out of politics while he was still active, like a sports star just after a year of peak performance.

Xi is very different from Mao and Deng. When Xi walks into a room, you can see he is a serious, calm, respectful man. He is down to earth, hardworking, and mindful of details. In a small meeting I attended, Xi said, "I want to taste the steamed bun myself, I don't want other people to chew it for me." He meant that he wanted to have firsthand knowledge as much as possible. I have also heard him talking about keeping tabs on popular topics on social media to have a greater connection to the people and the issues that matter to them.

Xi's rise to China's top political position came by perseverance. When Xi was nine years old, his father, a deputy premier (Zhou Enlai was the premier), was put in jail under suspicion of having sponsored a novel hinting that Mao and the party were saved by his faction at the end of the Long March. During the Cultural Revolution, when Xi Jinping was sixteen, he was sent to the countryside. He spent years enduring extreme hardships in a poor village. Xi recalled during a TV interview that he was constantly hungry during this time. He later emerged as a leader of the village, helping villagers to harness new technologies such as using biogas for fuel instead of burning corn husks. In the era of Deng, his father was rehabilitated, and Xi joined the government, working up from low-level positions all the way to being the top leader of a few provinces. His first wife sought to divorce him, wanting to emigrate to the UK. For one year, every week, he would make phone calls to the UK to persuade her to come back. Despite his family background, on several occasions, he ran into dead ends in his political career, since his immediate supervising official had prejudice against him. He had to uphold himself and looked for help from other sources.

As a loyal son of his revolutionary parents and the party, Xi faces a few fundamental challenges that his predecessors never encountered. The obvious one is that China is now perceived as a big threat to the West, as is discussed in many parts of this book. Xi is a believer in direct communications with top foreign leaders and has tried to make friends with Joe Biden, Vladimir Putin, Angela Merkel, and Donald Trump. Donald Trump, despite his aggressive stance against China, has always referred to Xi as his friend. Perhaps more significant than the challenge from the West is the domestic one. Xi has a vision for a modern China with orderly governance by an ethical and effective Community Party. He personally hates corrupt and dishonest government officials, calling them the trash of society. As an upright leader and tough fighter against corruption, he is regarded as a savior of the party and Chinese military, which suffered badly from the problem of venality. But he faces a challenge from changes in the Chinese population. The population is becoming increasingly prosperous and well educated, with over 50 percent of young people attending college. Also, as of 2022, the middle-income group is now four hundred million, about one-quarter of the population. The increasingly well-educated and economically well-off segment of the population tends to be more argumentative and expressive than their poor and uneducated parents. It is a challenge for Xi to communicate and respond effectively to the increasingly segmented society. Obviously, no Chinese leaders confronted such an issue until now.

THE CHINESE COMMUNIST PARTY is easily the world's largest and most powerful political party, having ruled the world's largest country for over seventy years and boasting almost one hundred million members.

People usually join the party when they are young. In order to join the party, a person must submit an application, including a personal statement and recommendations from party members. A branch committee consisting of three to twenty members then vote on the application, and if they decide to approve it, the applicant enters a one-year probation period before becoming a full member.

When seeking to expand its membership, the party focuses on two main groups. The first category is college students, young professionals, and other well-educated people who will likely grow up to work for the government in some capacity. The second category is composed of grassroots-level party members, who are usually manual workers or peasants. There is a general plan as to how many new party members to recruit. In recent years, a larger quota has been assigned to the recruitment of grassroots party members because they are regarded as vital to maintaining the party's governing stability. For example, every village has a party committee that often overlaps with the village committee of governance. Thus, many local governance issues, ranging from poverty reduction to garbage collection, go through the party committee at the grassroots level. The party committee of the village is even more important than the city council of a small township in the United States, since top-down policies are implemented by the party committee.

Why do young people choose to join the party? The answer is actually quite simple: because the party manages personnel decisions. To become a government official, it is almost essential to join the party. To make a simple comparison, college graduates in the United States wishing to enter public service often attend law school first. The list of notable figures who have taken this path includes Presidents Clinton and Obama.

In China, young people aspiring to careers in public service will join the party instead.

The party has an organizational presence at virtually every level in every aspect of society. Every village has a party committee, every department of a university has a party branch, and even factories have a party branch. The more important an organization is, the higher its party branch is ranked. These party branches typically make two types of decisions. The first takes place mostly in party committees of provinces or cities and is by far the most important: personnel decisions. For example, the party committee of a province is headed by the province's party secretary, who is the province's top official, followed by the governor. The provincial party committee makes the nomination decisions for all municipal-level mayoral candidates (who will later be officially elected by the corresponding people's congress) and party secretaries in the province. By the time the party committee votes on each personnel decision, the organization department (essentially the human resources department of the party) will have already done a significant amount of background research on the various candidates.

Party branches can also be involved in personnel decisions outside of the government. For example, the party branch of a university is heavily involved in the process of choosing a new dean of a school of the university. The party branch will first conduct surveys among professors and students to select candidates, and then gather opinions on the candidates from key staff members and professors. Eventually, the party branch will meet to make a selection, and will then post the decision on its website for seven days to allow for public comments. If seven days pass without any major valid complaints, the decision will be finalized.

The second type of decision made by party committees concerns major operations of local governments, universities, or ministries. For example, the target of economic growth for a city in the coming year will first be discussed in the municipal party committee before becoming a more detailed policy plan in the city government. Party committees and branches are also tasked with ensuring that government policies are successfully implemented on the local level. This was the case during COVID-19, when local party committees played a significant role in disseminating public health information and ensuring that quarantines and mask requirements were respected. In another example, when the Chinese government was working to eliminate absolute poverty between 2018 and 2020, each village's party committee was in charge of making sure that government subsidies and policies for the poor were being implemented in their area. The work of party committees was one of the key mechanisms in poverty reduction.

In the era of Xi Jinping, there have been reforms to beef up party operations. For example, the party has publicized a series of regulations regarding how party committees should be organized, how decisions should be made, and how members should be recruited. These elements are called "party construction." For example, one of these regulations requires party committee members to hold regular meetings called democratic life meetings, during which they analyze their actions and areas for improvement through self-inspection and self-criticism.

It is interesting to compare the Chinese Communist Party's practice of promotion with analogous practices in the United States or the West in general. The Chinese approach places emphasis on long-term evaluation and accumulation of experience through step-by-step hierarchical promotions in addition to qualifications and meritocracy. What is good about this practice is that by the time individuals are finally promoted to senior official positions, they possess extensive work experience. For example, before he was named the national leader of China, Xi Jinping was the leader of a provincial-level city, Shanghai, and before that he was the leader of one of the most economically important provinces in China, Zhejiang. Even earlier, he was the head of Xiamen

and Fuzhou, cities at the forefront of China's "opening up."
Before Xiamen and Fuzhou, he was a county mayor in an agricultural county near Beijing. Thus, Xi Jinping carries with him to the
presidential office substantial experience as a government official
at multiple levels. This is striking in comparison to, for example, President Trump, who had never served a day in public office
in his life prior to his inauguration. One may argue that a leader
like President Trump carries great momentum for implementing
change since he is not versed in the existing practices. However,
for an extraordinarily large country like China, the cost of sudden
changes can be very high.

The drawback to the Chinese step-by-step approach to selecting party and government officials is that candidates often lose
their "genius" or impetus to conceive new ideas once they move
up within the hierarchy. As such, China's foreign policy community has never seen and will never see the emergence of a
figure like Henry Kissinger, who totally changed the strategic
thinking regarding American foreign policy. In China, it would
also be unimaginable to have a forty-something-year-old leader
such as David Cameron and Tony Blair of the UK, or US presidents John F. Kennedy, Bill Clinton, and Barack Obama. This
is why drastic policy changes in China are difficult to achieve.
From this perspective, one appreciates even more the monumental events of Mao's death and Deng's ascendance after the
Cultural Revolution. Deng was a truly new leader and completely different from his predecessor, yet he was vastly experienced in Chinese domestic affairs and uniquely positioned to
make drastic changes.

When the party faces a true crisis such as the military failures
of the Long March or the widespread discontent following the
Cultural Revolution, the party will usually elect a new leader. In
the case of the Long March, Mao Zedong fought hard to win
the leadership role, and in the aftermath of the Cultural Revolution, Deng Xiaoping did the same. A top leadership change

is the primary mechanism historically used by the Communist Party to implement drastic policy shifts in response to massive crises. In other situations, the party gravitates toward gradual policy changes according to feedback regarding the policies already in place.

The topic of the Chinese Communist Party is too important to be explained in just one chapter. Thus, in the next chapters, I explain how the party governs the country through the operations of the central government and local governments, and how the party strives to fight corruption. All together, these chapters provide a full picture of how the huge country of China is governed.

CHAPTER 4

The Central Government

THERE IS ONLY ONE SIMPLE POINT THAT I TRY TO explain in this chapter, which is that in China, various government and semigovernment agencies are all coordinated by the Communist Party, forming a sophisticated system of social-political governance. I use the central government to illustrate this. Also, I explain that there are clear rules and logic to the operations of the governance machine, such as specific rules of promotion and discipline. Checks and balances do exist among the agencies, although they are not out in the open.

For example, one feature of China's integrated system of governance is the concept of rank. Rank is a key part of the identity of an official when rotating through or moving up in the complex of the party or government agencies. The highest-ranking officials are the seven members of the Communist Party's Politburo Standing Committee, who are ranked as state leaders. These seven members have the role of president, premier, head of the National People's Congress, and so on. Below them are those ranked as deputy state leaders. They include the chief staff of the party, vice premiers, and party secretaries of the four most important provinces and municipalities. Third in rank are the ministers and provincial governors. Fourth in rank are the deputy ministers and deputy provincial governors. Fifth in rank are ministry director generals and mayors of subprovincial municipalities. Sixth are the ministry deputy director generals and mayors of third-tier cities. In addition, there are five lower ranks reaching to the base of the party and government hierarchy.

Why is rank so important? The simple reason is that rank reflects the status of an official, including salary and welfare benefits. Also, unless an individual is disciplined for wrongdoing, every few years until retirement that individual will move to a different position of the same rank or one rank up. For example, the minister of commerce could be appointed the party secretary of a province, which is a move to the same rank. That person could also be appointed as the party secretary of Beijing or Shanghai, one rank up.

What is surprising is that in Chinese society, all white collar professionals and their employing agency are implicitly associated with a government rank. For example, a dean of a school or college at my university, Tsinghua University, would be identified with the rank of a division chief (seventh in the hierarchy) since Tsinghua is ranked the same as a department of the Ministry of Education (sixth).

Why may nongovernment officials care about their implicitly associated rank? First, it is a vanity issue. At official events, the seating arrangement and the order in which participants are introduced are often determined by rank. Second and more important, rank matters hugely if a person ever decides to join the government. For example, a dean of a school at my university can be appointed as a deputy department general of a ministry of the central government, which is a promotion by one rank. That same dean cannot be promoted to a department general, two steps up, since individuals can be promoted only one rank at a time. Of course, many scholars, including myself, do not care about rank. However, many do care deeply and print their rank on their business cards.

THE CENTRAL COMMITTEE OF
THE COMMUNIST PARTY

Let us now go through various branches of the government, broadly defined. The first branch is the Central Committee of the Communist Party, which houses three key departments: the Organization Department, which is the human resources department of the party; the Publicity Department, which is in charge of news and media; and the United Front Work Department, which is responsible for outreach to non-Communist Party elites, including entrepreneurs. The Central Committee also has a secretariat that arranges the meeting schedules of top leaders and manages document flows, among other routine tasks. At the very top of the Central Committee is Secretary General Xi Jinping, who meets every week with his six colleagues on the Politburo Standing Committee (PSC). With the secretary general at the helm, these seven (sometimes five or nine in the past) Standing Committee members make up the center of power in China.

Below the Standing Committee is a twenty-plus-member Politburo (usually twenty-five). Some of the Politburo members are party secretaries of key provinces or municipalities such as Beijing and Shanghai. The Politburo usually meets once a month, either to make decisions on key issues or to hold study seminars and so forth. For example, one seminar topic might be the value chain of the modern economy. On such occasions a scholar would be invited to speak, and then Secretary General Xi Jinping would deliver a prepared speech.

Below the Politburo is the Central Committee at large, composed of about two hundred people. Most of these individuals serve as provincial governors and ministers of government ministries. The entire Central Committee meets once a year for a plenary session. Once every five years, a Party Congress is held and a new Central Committee is elected, which will vote for a new Politburo, Standing Committee, and secretary general.

In each province or municipality, the structure of the Central Committee is more or less duplicated on a local level, with the secretary of the party committee as the top official.

THE STATE COUNCIL

The second arm of the central government is called the State Council, which is often compared to the cabinet of a Western government. The State Council is headed by the premier, who is also a member of the Politburo Standing Committee. The premier leads the other twenty-plus ministers of various government departments, and they all meet once a week to review documents and decisions that require their attention. Such meetings often include heated discussions. As a hypothetical illustration, the minister of education may propose a reform to change the nine-year compulsory education requirement to twelve years, to be sent to the National People's Congress for legislation. During the deliberation, the minister of finance might point out that there are not enough funds to carry out the proposed initiative. Discussions can be intense, so ministers need to do their homework carefully. Also, the premier may not get what he wants, since a minister may come up with good counterarguments.

From time to time, the premier invites scholars to speak to the ministers about the economy or certain aspects of technology. I have participated in such events multiple times under premiers Wen Jiabao and Li Keqiang. During and following my seven-minute presentations, the premier would ask questions and make comments, creating a lively discussion, with some of the vice premiers and ministers occasionally jumping in to answer questions.

On one occasion, I stated that the policy of toll-free highway travel on holidays was not economically sensible. The premier quickly pointed at the minister of transportation, asking: "What is going on? What is the rationale for the no-toll policy on holidays?" As you can see, the cabinet meetings are always very interactive and less hierarchical than people might think. I even noticed that some key officials, such as the governor of the Central Bank or the minister of finance, would discuss among themselves even as the premier was speaking. The atmosphere was rather academic or democratic.

It might be very surprising to an outsider that the Chinese central government is actually very small compared to most Western counterparts, meaning that China is actually more decentralized than most people think. For example, the Chinese Ministry of Agriculture only has about one thousand employees, mostly based in Beijing, while each province has its own bureau of agriculture that reports to the provincial governor. In contrast, the US Department of Agriculture has more than one hundred thousand employees, many of whom are situated in individual states. Of course, each US state also has its own agriculture department.

THE NATIONAL PEOPLE'S CONGRESS

Next is the legislative branch of the Chinese government, the National People's Congress (NPC). Here, please keep in mind that the NPC is very different from the concept of a congress or parliament in a Western democracy. First, the NPC is composed of a large membership of almost three thousand delegates, representing different provinces or municipalities and elected for a term of five years by the People's Congress in their home province. Therefore, this is a system of indirect election. This is like the old practice in Massachusetts, in which the state legislature elected the state's senators. These three thousand members meet only once a year for about twelve days in March, when they gather to hear, review, and vote on reports by the premier, chief justice, and chief prosecutor. They also evaluate proposed legislation and vote on revisions to the constitution.

Every five years, the NPC members also vote on the appointments of the country's next president, premier, ministers, and so on. This process is not the same as a standard election normally seen in a Western country. Instead, there is one candidate proposed per position, and the votes demonstrate the approval rating for each appointment. In the 1990s, at the city or provincial level, sometimes candidates for city mayors or provincial governors would receive less than 50 percent of the vote from the city or provincial people's congress and lose the election. Nowadays, before the election, there are meetings with each group of the delegates to urge them to vote positively for the candidates. Even so, for most positions, there are still a few negative votes or abstentions; not all officials get 100 percent positive votes.

The NPC has a Standing Committee consisting of about 150 members, who are voted on by the NPC every five years from among approximately 180 candidates. This group is akin to a combination of the US Senate and House of Representatives. It functions as the chief legislative body of the country and meets once every other month, although major and new laws must be voted on by the whole NPC. Candidates for the Standing Committee are proposed by the Communist Party and elected by the entire NPC. Most of the Standing Committee members are not full-time members. For example, the president of my university has been a member of the Standing Committee since 2018. He must attend every session, which creates major hurdles in his schedule that we must work around.

Are there cases of legislation being voted down by the NPC or its Standing Committee? The answer is no. This is because a proposed piece of legislation must face rounds of consultative discussions before making it to a vote. During the consultative process, objections are voiced and debate occurs. One example is the real estate tax (property tax). The Ministry of Finance has wanted it for almost a decade, but many NPC delegates and local governments have serious concerns about its negative impact on property prices, land prices, and household burdens. As a result, as of early 2023, no property tax legislation of any kind has made it onto the NPC agenda.

Because of the system of indirect election, a delegate of a province may be nominated by the central government to represent a province he or she does not live in. For example, one of my colleagues, an expert in environmental protection and water resources, was nominated for the National People's Congress. He was born in Beijing and lives in Beijing, so naturally he should have been a delegate for Beijing. However, there are many people with similar qualifications from Beijing, so he was instead nominated to represent the province of Yunnan, to which he has virtually no connection. Knowing that this person is an expert in environmental protection, the Yunnan delegates did not mind electing him, since he could become a new channel for Yunnan to make its case for the allocation of more resources for its use on relevant projects.

THE CHINESE PEOPLE'S POLITICAL CONSULTATIVE CONFERENCE (CPPCC)

The Chinese People's Political Consultative Conference, or CPPCC, can be loosely understood as the House of Lords of the UK. The 2,200 members at the national level of the CPPCC are invited. If they are party members, they are invited by the Department of Organization of the Central Committee. Nonparty members are invited by the United Front Work Department of the Central Committee of the Communist Party. In contrast to the House of Lords, there is a five-year term, and usually the term limit is three terms.

The purpose of the CPPCC is to gather advice from a spectrum of elites before the party makes major decisions. CPPCC members are academics, scientists, writers, journalists, artists, movie stars, business executives, entrepreneurs, and so on, and—very importantly—retired government officials. The national CPPCC gathers once a year in early March for about ten days, jointly with the NPC, during the meetings known as the Two Sessions. At the Two Sessions, the CPPCC and NPC hear and discuss the reports by the premier, chief justice, and chief prosecutor.

Before the premier submits the Government Work Report at the Two Sessions in March, he always convenes several rounds of consultation meetings involving academics, entrepreneurs, government officials, and even peasants. This is another avenue for the Chinese government to seek input from social groups beyond the appointed leaders and delegates. I have attended some of the consultation meetings myself, and I've found that they can be very open and interactive. In one session, I proposed that the government issue more debt, and Premier Li Keqiang instantly asked, "Doesn't that mean I will have to incur a greater deficit for the central government?" He was reluctant to do this since he had promised at the beginning of his term that he would not increase the government deficit. I quickly replied that debt for infrastructure construction is classified as capital expenditure and is different from debt issued to pay for government expenses. Therefore, it would not be counted toward any deficits. I think he understood, but my advice was not taken, likely due to pressure from senior colleagues and retired top-tier officials, who still unofficially check the power of current leaders.

Meetings of the CPPCC are usually very lively since members are typically well-educated and free-minded elites. Following the major plenary meetings in the Great Hall of the People, the CPPCC members are divided into groups of thirty to forty to discuss the premier's report along with other social and policy issues. In my group at the CPPCC, we had a diverse set of members who are senior academics, painters, artists, actors, and screenplay writers. For example, one member is China's leading calligrapher, and he proposed that the government implement a policy to require primary schools to teach calligraphy, arguing that calligraphy is an integral part of China's classical culture. His proposal later turned into a central government policy of the Ministry of Education. Another member, who is a very famous news anchorman akin to Anderson Cooper in the United States, openly criticized the Chinese government's policy of allowing Western, especially American, genetically modified food to be imported into China. He claimed that foreign companies have bribed Chinese scientists to argue that genetically modified grain is safe. His view was seriously taken into account by the Chinese Ministry of Agriculture.

The Courts and Law Enforcement

The next section of the Chinese government is made up of the courts and law enforcement. Usually, at the level of the central government, these agencies are under the management of one person in the Politburo Standing Committee.

The police force is rather decentralized, similar to the situation in the United States. More specifically, each province and municipality has its own police force that reports primarily to the local leader rather than a national authority. At the highest level, the national police force is mostly responsible for nationwide cases that stretch across provincial or even international borders.

The court is more hierarchical and centralized. That is, local courts in counties and provinces are responsible to courts in the level above them. At the very top of the hierarchy, China's Supreme Court is similar to those in other countries. This court carefully chooses which cases to try, with a focus on those with the potential to have a demonstrative impact on future similar cases. In recent years, the Supreme Court has also presided over each death penalty case, since China has been moving toward reducing its death penalty sentences. The procuratorate—that is, the office of the attorney general—is also very centralized. In recent years, the amount of violent crime in China has dropped drastically, whereas white-collar crime has increased. In line with this change, the procuratorate has become more discretionary in its punishments.

MASS ORGANIZATIONS

The next category of government agency is unique to China: the so-called mass organizations. In the United States, large organizations such as unions, YMCA, and United Way are independent. But in China, as previously explained, the party manages everything. Thus, in reality, these nongovernment agencies are managed as government entities under the party, sometimes labeled with the oxymoron "government-organized non-governmental organizations," or GONGOs. The party is responsible for providing the budget of these organizations as well as approving and appointing all key leaders.

In China, if one wants to establish a new organization or association, he or she must seek a ministry-level agency to act as a sponsor. Sometimes these organizations are led by retired government officials. For example, China once had a Ministry of the Textile Industry, which was abolished during reform and opening up because of the change to leaving industries to the market. Thus, the Ministry of the Textile Industry was replaced by the Association of the Textile Industry. The chairman of this agency is usually a retired deputy minister of the Ministry of Industry and Information.

The Communist Youth League (CYL) is a unique organization with branches in high schools, universities, and most enterprises. In a remote way, it is similar to the YMCA or YWCA in the United States, but the CYL is political. The purpose of the CYL is to cultivate young people who may aspire to join the party in the future. Yet the CYL can be very apolitical in many ways. For example, branches of the CYL often organize spring outings and fall excursions, as well as more serious activities like seminars on the sociopolitical issues in the country. The process of joining the league is relatively easy: submit an application statement and be approved by the league's local branch. In many cases, the local branches are not very strict, and therefore most students are members of the CYL. Although members of the Communist Youth League may not be very politically motivated, the branch officials above a certain level are senior party officials who can be as old as forty-five or fifty. At the highest level of the Communist Youth League is the Central Committee of the CYL, whose first secretary is ranked at the level of a minister or provincial governor. In the 1990s and early 2000s, the practice was for senior officials of the Central Committee of the Communist Youth League to be promoted to senior officials of the entire country, with two examples being Premier Li Keqiang and former general secretary Hu Jintao. In the era of Xi Jinping, this practice was phased out.

THE MILITARY

Unlike in the West, the Chinese military is managed by the party, as stipulated in both the Party Constitution and State Constitution. In practice, this means that China has one Central Military Commission (CMC) for both the country and the party, and the chairman of the CMC is always the highest-ranking person in the party, who is now General Secretary Xi Jinping. The Central Military Commission also includes generals who serve as deputy chairmen.

Under Xi Jinping, the structure of the Chinese military was fundamentally reformed. The Chinese military force was formerly organized into seven military area commands across the country plus the air force and navy, whereas now there are five theater commands with an emphasis on joint operations across military departments. Another focus of these reforms was to clean up widespread corruption in the military by severely punishing corrupt officials and greatly enhancing the pay of generals.

An often neglected fact is that China is the only major country that has not engaged in any warfare in the past four decades. Xi Jinping has said that in order to reach the goal of national revival, China will be tested. It is not clear exactly what he means by "tested," but some people believe China's big test will come from being challenged militarily and that China will eventually be involved in military action. While China's leader has consistently emphasized that the Chinese military should be modernized and ready for combat, in actuality, the Chinese military is perhaps the least experienced among the largest powerful military forces in the world.

How Does the Government Work?

Again, the simple principle is that the party manages everything. All key decisions are discussed and decided by the Politburo Standing Committee before being implemented by government agencies. Besides the general secretary, each of the other six Standing Committee members is in charge of one area. The premier and the executive vice premier are mostly concerned with the economy, while another member is in charge of media for the entire country, and yet another leads the work of cleaning out corrupt party officials (that is, discipline inspection). The heads of the NPC and CPPCC are also members of the Standing Committee.

The Chinese government does have internal checks and balances, though in a different way from traditional Western governments. For example, top leaders in China often seek inputs from retired leaders on critical issues, and this practice injects some continuity into Chinese government decision making. Furthermore, as detailed in Chapter 2, Chinese leaders are always extremely conscious of how history will judge them, which pushes them to be cautious and consult with numerous experts before enacting consequential policies.

To illustrate the internal mechanism of checks and balances, take the example of legislation. When it comes to passing a law, a draft is usually proposed by a ministry and must go through numerous debates within the government as well as consultations with scholars and enterprise managers. In this regard, China is much more interactive and democratic than some people may assume. Take a specific example, the Labor Contract Law, which was enacted right before the global financial crisis in 2008. The group that led the charge for this law was the All-China Federation of Trade Unions (ACFTU), a ministry-level mass organization. After drafting this law, the ACFTU proposed it to the National People's Congress, which then organized many field trips to conduct research in regions where labor-intensive industries are concentrated, such as Guangdong province. After at least three rounds of formal discussion, with countless negotiations, debates, and consultations with academics in between, the law was passed. However, numerous complaints have since been leveled against the Labor Contract Law, and the NPC is expected to revise the law in the coming years.

PROMOTIONS AND TERM LIMITS

One key area that cements the primacy of the party in governance is that of promotions and personnel decisions. Promotions or demotions are first discussed by a branch of the Communist Party called the Organization Department. This department is similar to a human resources department, always monitoring vacancies, key issues, and potential candidates. The head of the Organization Department suggests candidates for senior-level positions to the Standing Committee, which makes decisions on the proposals. However, the Standing Committee generally approves the proposed promotions, since much of the research and background work has already been done by the Organization Department. Of course, the Central Committee Organization Department only presides over personnel decisions relating to the ranks of provincial governor and minister. Lower-rank personnel decisions are made by the Organization Departments of local party committees.

The Organization Department is also in charge of training officials. Officials are trained in a manner similar to what corporation leaders get, only more formally. The party has its own training schools for this, which increase in importance all the way up to the Central Party School, which trains top officials. All officials must undergo training before being promoted, and they must also meet three basic criteria. First, they must have sufficient relevant experience and rise through the government hierarchy level by level. For example, Xi Jinping gained experience through leadership positions in counties, cities, and provinces, working his way up step by step. He also received training throughout his career. The second important requirement is that the person must have a clean record. A candidate with any outstanding issues about discipline—for example, expensive consumption habits—will not be promoted. The third criterion is age. For example, a person older than fifty-eight will not be considered for promotion to the role of minister or provincial governor, who is normally required to retire before sixty-five.

Age limits and term limits were established by Deng Xiaoping in the early 1980s as he reflected upon the problems of Mao Zedong in his later days, especially the Cultural Revolution. It was very clear to Deng Xiaoping and many people in China that if Mao had retired twenty years prior to his death, many of his mistakes could have been avoided. The implicit assumption, with which most people agree, is that when someone is in a political position for too long, he loses touch. George Washington, for instance, was wise to step down after two terms as president. In this regard, he is highly respected, even in China.

Although positions beneath the Politburo Standing Committee level do not have term limits, there are age limits acting as de facto term limits, ensuring that no official stays in one position for too long. There are now age limits pertaining to each governmental body. For example, a minister or ministerial-level official must retire at sixty-five. The director of a department of a ministry must step down by sixty. A person older than fifty-eight is passed over as a candidate to be a minister. A vice premier must be under sixty-eight at the time of appointment, and must retire before the age of seventy-two. All these age-dependent rules are clearly considered discriminatory against the elderly in Western politics. But in China, they have been designed by Deng Xiaoping to rejuvenate the otherwise conservative bureaucracy.

How is the top leader of the party and country such as Xi Jinping selected? And in principle, how is the top leader different from a US president? First, the candidate must have already been a member of the politburo or its standing committee. That is, jumping ranks does not happen. Second, the person must be younger than sixty-eight and must have been a top leader of a major province and worked in the central government in charge of an important issue. Third, and most importantly, the Organization Department conducts surveys with a few key groups. One group is the two-hundred-member Central Committee. Another group is retired officials, especially retired Standing Committee members. Finally, the members of the Politburo Standing Committee have a final say in choosing the top leader.

An old practice that seems to have become less significant in recent years is that each August, top leaders, including retired ones, would retreat to an oceanfront resort called Bei Dai He. This conclave served as a valuable opportunity to gather opinions on upcoming promotions. Even in years without a Party Congress, top current and retired leaders gather annually in Bei Dai He to unofficially discuss major issues facing the country. The uniqueness of the meetings is the involvement of retired officials.

Though the meetings are generally quite secretive, given their importance, any information about the meetings is meticulously sniffed out and dissected by political analysts outside China.

As a result of the selection process, China's top leader is usually much more experienced with national issues than his US counterpart. Another implication is that, compared to Western leaders, it is less likely for a Chinese leader to make drastically revolutionary decisions. Continuity is maintained in China. For issues like commitments to or agreements with the world on targets of climate change, continuity is essential.

A Chinese proverb says: "When the mountains are high, the emperor is far away." This refers to the independent behavior of local government officials. Despite the powerful influence of the party reaching all the way from the highest levels to the lowest, local governments have the most direct effect on the average person's day-to-day life, and as such, there is both more demand and more space for grassroots input at the local level. In the next chapter I explain the unique characteristics of Chinese local governments, since they matter critically in today's China.

CHAPTER 5

Local
Governments

C HINESE LOCAL GOVERNMENT OFFICIALS ARE
very different from their Western counterparts in three
respects. First, they have a much wider scope of operations,
behaving like parents of local residents. Second, they act as the
CEO of the local economy. Third, they need to interact closely
with higher-level officials, and they compete against their peers
for promotions that are decided by higher officials. In general,
they are often very autonomous and active, as they are "far away
from the emperor." I explain these three things in this chapter.

THE SIMPLEST AND BEST Chinese phrase explaining the
relationship between the Chinese people and local governments is that local officials are like "parent-officials." That is,
they closely manage issues of their local residents. These officials are not elected, but are appointed by their superiors, who
are like grandparents. Thus, local officials have no need for election campaigns—instead, they compete among their peers to be
promoted by the grandparent officials. For better or for worse,
this has been the Chinese tradition for thousands of years. For
the local residents, there is almost an implicit contract with local
officials: *You take care of my problems, and in exchange, I accept some of
your intrusions.*

What do the local officials do in their role as parents of local residents? They plan for local social and economic development, relocate occupants of land to make room for development, guide the operation of schools, build new roads and railway stations, guard against traffic accidents, and in some cases even organize events like pop concerts or international forums to boost their city's publicity. Importantly, they also make sure there are no widespread protests due to conflicts between business owners and workers. When such conflicts arise, either the party secretary of the city or the mayor is usually the first one to mitigate them. Just as children may blame many problems on their parents, local citizens blame many of their problems on the local government. For example, in China, pensioners and elderly people often make bad financial investment decisions which cause them to lose money. As a result, it is not uncommon for them to organize a protest at the door of a government complex. The government then has to find a way to appease these people, sometimes even going so far as to force the financial institutions to return the investors' money. In extreme cases, the government itself has to provide compensation.

To provide another example, when inflation was at peak levels in 1994, the central government tasked provincial governors and mayors with the challenge of stabilizing local prices. During that time, it was said that mayors and governors were "caretakers of the vegetable baskets" of local residents. Each province was responsible for ensuring there would be a sufficient supply of vegetables at a reasonably low price. In 2012, pork prices doubled within the span of a few months due to farmers' miscalculations based on the extremely low prices in the previous year, which prompted them to eliminate many female pigs. The central governments then issued mandates to local governments to subsidize pork farmers, ensuring that pigs would reproduce as quickly as possible. At that time, families of single children were also subsidized for following the government's one-child population policy. A joke quickly spread on China's internet: In order to receive the most government subsidies, it is much better to have many female pigs than a single child.

With greater involvement in their constituents' affairs also comes more power for Chinese local governments and their officials. Local governments in China consist of the administrative, legislative, and judicial branches. In the United States, these branches are separate, forming checks and balances, but in China, all three are under the authority of the party leader. This is a key point to keep in mind as we explore the topic of local governments, although it is true that political reforms in China are increasingly calling for more independent local courts. In addition to the three branches, the local government also has tremendous control over local media: Senior executives in the local media are appointed and are overseen by the local government. This is akin to New York City mayor Bill de Blasio's having the power to appoint the editor-in-chief of the *New York Times* or at least the *New York Post*.

On a darker note, the huge concentration of power in the hands of local officials helps to explain corruption at the local level. As a result, a recent reform was implemented calling for the Central Commission for Discipline Inspection to supervise subordinate agencies, rather than for the Discipline Inspection Commission of a province to supervise the officials of the same province.

PERHAPS THE BEST WAY to understand local Chinese officials is to spend a day in their shoes. This is exactly what students at Tsinghua University's Schwarzman College do in a mini-course called a "deep dive." They have found it extremely revealing.

Let us meet Mr. Chen, former party secretary of a top-five city in China.[1] An eloquent and handsome man, quick to the point, his speech peppered with metaphors and famous quotes, he was a charismatic leader.

1 "Mr. Chen" is a pseudonym.

To be fair, Mr. Chen has done a great job transforming his city. Historically, his city has been regarded as a "sleepy" city where people used to leisurely chat the day away in the city's famous teahouses. Now, under Mr. Chen, it has become one of the most glamorous cities in China for great food, good taste in consumption, and leisurely living. Mr. Chen himself was not a native of the area—he is from northern China where people are known to be more expressive, eloquent, and aggressive. In an effort to avoid nepotism, in Chinese politics, a city's leader is usually not from the area. This has been the practice for thousands of years, ever since the first emperors ruled China.

In 2010, a typical day for Mr. Chen went something like this: In the morning, after finishing breakfast, he would be briefed on national and international news by his assistant, who is a young man. In China, government officials are usually not allowed to have assistants of a different gender. One particular morning, he asked specifically how the internet was reacting to his speech the day before, in which he had tried to jumpstart the rebranding of his city from one of leisure to one of hard work. Mr. Chen proposed that the city be rebranded as a city of "can do" or the "city of success." His assistant responded that most netizens were enthusiastic about his proposal, although some were sarcastic, saying that the nature of a city cannot be changed by a party secretary. In all likelihood, the overly negative comments were probably deleted by his office.

At 8 a.m., Mr. Chen held his twice-a-week meeting with the Standing Committee of the city's branch of the Communist Party. Each of these meetings was attended by nine people, including the mayor and other officials responsible for the city's most critical decisions. Mr. Chen would invite various experts to present reports to the Standing Committee, solicit the views of his fellow members, and present his summary at the end. He was very effective at gathering opinions from his colleagues and encouraging them to speak up. At this particular meeting, the participants discussed plans to further attract investments to the city and take advantage of the global financial crisis, which they compared to a curve on a racetrack where many cars slow down. As a result, they agreed that this was the best chance for his city to surpass other cities.

Throughout the day, Mr. Chen would have his team frequently monitor the internet to keep their finger on the pulse of public reactions to his policies, sometimes even gathering information from journalists. This is a common practice among all effective local government officials, as is censoring the most personal attacks. For example, when Chen built an exhibition center in the city, people criticized the move, saying it was a waste of money and the city would never recoup the expenditure. In response, Mr. Chen privatized the exhibition center by allowing a private company to run it—a rare practice among Chinese cities. Now, the exhibition center is one of the few profitable ones and serves as a model for other cities.

At 10:30, Party Secretary Chen rushed to another part of the city to attend an important ceremony for a new construction project. A major multinational automobile producer was investing in a new production facility in the city, where it would eventually produce two hundred thousand family cars per year. Mr. Chen successfully wooed the company after many visits to the headquarters of the car maker, and he also coordinated with the central government officials in the National Development and Reform Commission (NDRC), which is in charge of approving huge projects of this nature in order to avoid excessive and repetitive industrial investments. One main obstacle still stood in the way—a few families were refusing to relocate to make room for the factory. Mr. Chen issued instructions that the families should be treated considerately, and that officials should persuade them to move by talking to their relatives and by increasing their compensation. Mr. Chen also emphasized that the compensation amount should be kept secret from the media because otherwise, it would encourage other households to hold out for more money in the future.

After lunch, Party Secretary Chen attended the meeting of the Communist Party's Legal Affairs Committee, where a few thorny issues emerged. The son of a former deputy mayor was involved in a property development company that had physically injured a local resident who had asked for an extremely high amount of compensation to vacate a building that was to be torn down and rebuilt. Mr. Chen listened carefully to the details and considerations of the case. Finally, he decided to change the case from a criminal case to a civil case and settle the matter outside the court in order to minimize social impact. He worried that if the case were to go to an open trial, many local residents would believe most or all developers to have close government connections, damaging public relations. In settling the case, Mr. Chen stipulated that substantial compensation should be given to the plaintiff, and efforts should be made to ensure the plaintiff's silence. Indeed, Mr. Chen was not only the leader of political affairs, he was also the leader of the legal system.

Mr. Chen had dinner at an event attended by a few philanthropists from abroad, some of the wealthiest investors in China, and influential scholars. The dinner was followed by an academic and policy forum with the theme of environmental protection and building up western China, where his city is situated. As the first speaker at the forum, Mr. Chen knew that this was not the time for him to be outspoken, as any verbal slips would be caught and amplified by the media and scholars in attendance. He opened the forum by welcoming participants to the "city of success," and then said, "I will stick to my long-time principle that when I meet scholars, I do not speak, I listen. In front of you, I am a pupil; I am learning." When the forum ended, he shook hands with all the scholars and thanked them for their insights. It was now 10 p.m., and the end of a typical day in 2010 for Mr. Chen as the party secretary of an important and rising city.

As a capable and savvy official, Mr. Chen was familiar enough with Chinese politics to know that superb job performance would not be enough to secure a promotion—he had to be associated with the right camp. Unfortunately for Mr. Chen, he was a protégé of the former party secretary of the province, of which his city is the capital (a relationship akin to that between the governor of New York and the mayor of New York City, with the major difference being that in China, the governor appoints the mayor). Mr. Chen's mentor was later sentenced to life in prison for having taken huge bribes in exchange for arranging the promotions of party and government officials.

Sadly, Mr. Chen is also now in prison. He was alleged to have bribed his mentor and his friends in order to advance his career, and he confessed to these crimes. From prison, Mr. Chen gave a very sincere and tear-jerking interview during which he expressed remorse for his corrupt behavior and admonished other government officials to remain firmly rooted in their moral principles. The interview became a masterpiece within the educational materials of the anticorruption campaign, which started in 2012 under Xi Jinping and is discussed in the next chapter. The story of Mr. Chen was exalted as a cautionary tale.

Two details may interest you. First, are most local officials men? The answer depends on the rank. The higher the rank, the higher the percentage of men. One of the reasons is that these jobs require extremely long hours, and educated Chinese women traditionally choose professional careers such as becoming doctors, accountants, and lawyers. In recent decades, there have been explicit policies, similar to affirmative action in the United States, designed to increase the percentage of women among senior government officials.

Second, what is life in prison like for formerly senior officials like Mr. Chen? I explored this issue with an official in charge of prisons. The answer: salubrious. Food, creature comforts, reading, TV time, and family visits are generously available. No banquets, no drinking, and a strict schedule mean that those in prison become healthier than before. In one case, a convicted official refused to apply for reduced time, saying that staying inside provided an easier life than being outside.

INSTEAD OF WAGING OPEN campaigns for career promotion, ambitious local officials compete with peer cities or regions for recognition from their superiors. Continuing to reference the example of Mr. Chen (prior to his conviction), let's have a closer look at the competition for promotion among local officials. The primary scoring criteria in this "tournament" are social and economic performance. In Mr. Chen's case, he was appointed by the Communist Party Organization Department of his province. The residents in his city did not have a direct say in his selection, but officials from the Organization Department did speak with local residents and gather information on Mr. Chen before making their decision. Overwhelmingly good views from the residents do not matter, but sharp complaints from key groups (such as retired officials or key opinion leaders) will lead to further investigations and may ruin a promotion.

Mr. Chen's city is often compared with a coastal city in Shandong province and a star city in Yunnan province. As such, the party secretaries of these cities are all candidates to become governor of a major province. As the party secretary of his city, Mr. Chen needed to satisfy three criteria in order to compete seriously with his peers and improve his chances for promotion.

The first criterion is economic growth. If an official such as Mr. Chen is successful in promoting economic development, he will most likely either be promoted to the next rank or sent to another, more important region. When Mr. Chen worked in Liaoning, and later in his current city, his region's economies achieved higher economic growth rates, greater tax revenue growth rates, and more foreign investment than peer cities. His success drew the attention of higher-level party officials, setting him apart from his peers and making him an appealing choice for promotion.

The second criterion is to enact noteworthy initiatives and improvements. One of Chen's initiatives was to implement integrated development of urban and rural areas, in which farmers were recognized as residents of the city and there was no difference between rural and urban residency. Farmers were welcomed to move to cities, buy houses, and send their children to urban centers. This was a pioneering movement in Chinese cities.

The third criterion is to prevent any major incidents. For example, Mr. Chen had to avert any mass protests in front of the party secretary's office and ensure that no more than five people from his city made grievance cases to the Ministry of Civil Affairs in Beijing against policies in his city. The grievance process is often a way for local residents to voice complaints about local governance. In Chinese history, appealing grievances to higher levels of government, rather than bringing lawsuits, was a means for ordinary people to seek justice against local officials.

When a "troublemaker" goes to Beijing to present a letter of grievance in front of a central government agency, that person is quickly detained and investigated to determine which region the person is from. This is part of the so-called social stability maintenance system. During high-profile events such as the National People's Congress meetings in March, the Olympic Games, or national celebrations, every local government is responsible for preventing any local troublemakers from coming to Beijing. Police from local regions usually have already been stationed in Beijing and will drive the troublemaker home in a hired car. This does not mean that local officials should silence all protests, but they take care not to disrupt important events in the capital.

If Mr. Chen had satisfied all three of these criteria—spurring economic growth, enacting noteworthy initiatives, and preventing troublemakers from going to Beijing—plus having zero strong complaints from key subgroups of local residents, his next promotion would probably have been to either the governor of his own province or party secretary of a smaller province. Of the two, party secretary is the more coveted position for the simple reason that the party secretary is the number one official of the region.

CHINESE LOCAL OFFICIALS OFTEN behave like the CEO of the holding company of all local corporations. This means that they advocate for the interests of local corporations and solve problems for the corporations. Their schedules are brimming with banquets and investment forums, events that help them build relationships with businesses that might invest in their region. In China, a local government official who is promoted must have the spirit of an entrepreneur. What is the spirit of entrepreneurship? To me, the most important element is the desire and ability to solve problems, identify a market niche, and find a way to bypass existing regulations. Regulations are like laws, and good entrepreneurs in China have to behave like good lawyers, reinterpreting regulations while behaving like a businessperson as they actively search for solutions.

When I meet local officials, the most common question they have for me is, "Which sector or industry should the local economy develop?" As an example, Guizhou is one of the poorest provinces in China, but its officials argue that it has an abundance of hydraulic power and numerous mountains, so the province can build data-storage facilities in the mountains as backup centers. Officials also point out that Guizhou is cool in the summer, so companies can save on air conditioning costs. In this case, the officials think like the CEOs of data service companies such as IBM or EMC. When I visit the city of Baotou, the world capital of rare earth deposits, local officials often ask how they can make the best economic use of this valuable resource. My response is that they may consider aggressively promoting the MRI equipment production business, since MRI machines require the use of magnetic materials, and rare earth elements are a key ingredient in these materials. When I visit the city of Guangzhou, local officials want to know how their city can develop a financial center, since Guangzhou has become a leading manufacturing center for home appliances, motorcycles, tiles for home construction and decoration, and many other items. All in all, Chinese local government officials behave like CEOs of large holding companies with many business lines.

One consequence of the local Chinese government's pro-business and pro-investment behavior is that since 1992, China has been either the number one or number two destination for foreign direct investment, taking turns with the United States. Foreign direct investments are mostly investments to start new businesses. Although I cannot think of a single company or project that is being wooed by both China and the United States, I do come across many government officials from both countries who are trying to attract businesses to their local regions. In the years before Donald Trump became president, US officials constantly took provincial tours in China to lure Chinese investment to America. In 2006, I met the then-governor of South Carolina, Republican Mark Sanford, in Beijing. We had dinner together with a few Chinese businesspeople, during which the governor shared that his goal was to attract Chinese investors to his state. When I asked him to tell me the biggest single competitive advantage of his state, he surprised me by saying that power is much cheaper in South Carolina than in China. He impressed me as a very sincere person who did not use the dinner as an opportunity to give his tablemates a lecture on ideological matters. I came away from the evening with the strong impression that at least some US government officials act like their counterparts in China.

The competition for direct investment explains the puzzle of why Chinese regulations appear extremely complicated on paper—making it look almost impossible to do business in China—and yet deals are finalized rather quickly. Local governments are in a race against each other to help companies, especially multinational companies, bypass these regulations. For example, the central government often requires foreign investors to pay 25 percent in corporate profit tax, but local officials usually promise that in the first two years, the profit tax will be waived, and in the next three years only one-half of the profit tax has to be paid.

The intense focus on GDP growth does have bad consequences. Prior to 2012, when Xi Jinping became the party secretary general, many cultural and historical legacies were thrown by the wayside in the name of economic development. In the city of Jinan, the capital of Shandong province, there was once a beautiful train station still standing from the time when Germany controlled the province prior to World War I. The station was a classic structure, built in the European style in the early 1910s, and served as a landmark until the mayor of Jinan ordered its controversial demolition in 1992. He pushed forward despite numerous objections from citizens who wanted to save the historic structure, setting his sights on one singular goal—economic opportunity. He tore down the station to make room for a huge square that could house a newer, bigger, better station. From a purely economic perspective, the mayor was correct, as it was much easier to entice developers with an empty lot. However, many people in Jinan continue to criticize the mayor to this day for the demolition, mourning the historical treasure that has been lost. This is similar to the time when New York City's old Penn Station was demolished to make room for Madison Square Garden, but in China, such cases are more frequently observed.

After coming to power in 2012, Xi Jinping pushed to reverse this trend of economic development at the expense of all else. Before becoming the top leader, he had already shown an innate preference for preserving the environment and cultural heritage. In the mid-1990s, Xi was the head of the city of Fuzhou, Fujian, and later the entire province of Fujian. At this time, the city of Fuzhou had given Hong Kong business tycoon Li Kaishing the most valuable land in the inner city in the hopes that he would renovate a historic, thousand-year-old block called San Fang Qi Xiang (meaning three lanes and seven streets). However, Li carried out a lengthy, ten-year project to demolish the historic buildings and roads, building skyscrapers in their place. Furthermore, he was known to drag his feet on projects in the hope that China's quickly rising land prices would result in a higher value for his buildings upon their delayed completion. Under Xi Jinping, the city terminated the contract in protest of these business practices and the disrespect they conveyed for historical and cultural heritage. Later, when Xi was promoted to the head of the province of Zhejiang, he famously said that green mountains and clear rivers are more valuable than gold mountains and silver rivers. Today, with Xi being the top leader, local government officials are evaluated by their efforts in cultural and environmental preservation in addition to local economic performance.

As a result of the active role played by Chinese governments, central and local, corruption has become a prominent political issue, detrimental to the ruling party's credibility and legitimacy. Since assuming power in 2012, General Secretary Xi Jinping has made it his top priority to clean up corruption, which has had complicated implications for the country. The next chapter is devoted to this complex issue.

CHAPTER 6

Corruption

Corruption is an important social topic in China, and in this chapter, I explain several noteworthy things about it. First, in daily life, such as clearing customs at the border, being checked by traffic police, and applying for a passport, China is pretty much free of corruption, and relevant officials are under very tight monitoring. Second, corruption was formerly widespread, mostly in business dealings, and in some cases even in the promotion of government officials. In business dealings, it was an effective means for getting around cumbersome bureaucracy, which is now much less restrictive. Third, fighting corruption has been Xi Jinping's signature move since assuming power in 2012, and his efforts have been very successful, although there are significant side effects, including shirking and lack of initiative by many government officials.

For at least two decades, petty corruption, such as bribe solicitation by traffic police or border customs officials, has not been a problem. This is unlike the case in many poorly governed countries, where a police officer may stop a car to check for drunk driving and then accept cash in exchange for not issuing a ticket. Why does this not occur in China? The technical reason is that all on-duty government officials are closely monitored. All police must carry a video recorder and are heavily scrutinized. Also, they would face severe discipline if caught engaging in petty corruption. Public locations such as the border control and customs offices have numerous monitoring cameras. A more fundamental reason is that as a growing economy, China has been rich in public finance, and generally speaking, low-level government officials have been paid well relative to their peers in other vocations. Senior officials of course are paid much lower than business executives, an economic fact sowing the seeds for corruption of higher-level officials. Another important fact for China's relatively untainted low-ranking police is that in the early 2000s, Zhou Yongkang, as a tough top police officer, implemented an effective anticorruption campaign and cleaned up bad police behavior. Ironically, fifteen years later, he was sentenced to lifetime imprisonment as a highly corrupt official.

Though there is relatively little low-level corruption, until 2012, when Xi Jinping assumed power, there had been two forms of severe corruption in China. One was for economic benefits. The other was for political benefits, mostly for those seeking to be promoted, become a delegate to the People's Congress, or be selected as a member of the CPPCC. In 2011 and 2013, for example, widespread bribery related to selecting provincial leaders and delegates, as well as CPPCC delegates, occurred in Liaoning province. A major investigation into this case was carried out, and many officials were sentenced.

Economic corruption comes into play mostly because people doing business often have to bypass existing government policies or regulations, many of which have been gradually reformed or removed, but pioneering entrepreneurs still enjoy clear advantages. One example relates to Initial Public Offerings (IPOs), as there used to be a quota placed on the number of IPOs permitted per year. The rationale is to protect investors who buy poorly performing stock. I further discuss this issue in the chapter on the Chinese model of governance. Within the China Securities Regulatory Commission (CSRC), committee meetings are held to approve enterprises and add them to a queue of pending IPOs, and enterprises commonly lobby individuals within the CSRC to win a spot on this coveted list. In 2015, two CSRC deputy chairmen came under investigation and were later convicted. It was revealed that enterprises, through a chain of agents, would lobby and bribe them for permission to execute IPOs. Considering the life-changing effects of an IPO that allows a founder of a corporation to quickly turn years of hard work into cash, it is no wonder why this is a major source of corruption in China. Nowadays, many of the regulations for IPOs have been reformed, and given the very tight policies against corruption, bypassing the remaining regulations has become very difficult.

In contrast, an IPO rollout in a mature market economy is purely market-based. Investment banks work with enterprises to design an IPO plan. In principle, investors who end up buying a bad IPO stock have to blame themselves for not having done enough careful homework. Occasionally, the unlucky investors may file a legal case against the company. The government is not involved.

Another subcategory of economic corruption involves influencing a decision of a government official. One example is the case of Mr. Zheng Xiaoyu, the former head of the National Food and Drug Monitoring Bureau, which is in charge of approving or rejecting applications for new drugs and is also responsible for periodically reevaluating existing drugs. Before his downfall, Mr. Zheng Xiaoyu was an individual of great promise. He graduated from Fudan University, a top university based in Shanghai, as a biology major in 1968, when there were relatively few college graduates in China. He was considered an expert in the Chinese pharmaceutical industry. In 1988, he was appointed as the head of the newly established State Drug Administration, which became the National Food and Drug Monitoring Bureau in 2003. Zheng was the first bureau director and was named a "model laborer," an honor equivalent to a knighthood in Britain.

Between 1997 and 2006, Zheng and his family took bribes from eight drug and pharma companies amounting to 6.5 million RMB (about 1 million USD). In return, all of these companies received quick approvals from the bureau. In 2000, one company submitted an application for a new drug and received approval within one week. In exchange, the company's CEO invited Zheng Xiaoyu's son on a vacation to Hong Kong and gave him a check for 1 million HKD, equal to approximately $130,000. This is only one of many bribes Zheng's son is known to have accepted over the years. In one case, he received an Audi, which he sold for cash. In other cases, he received free shares in companies, which he also sold for cash. Furthermore, he received various gifts that he applied to a down payment on his apartment. Another company regularly sent him about 10,000 RMB a month. The amount of bribes Mr. Zheng and his family received may not have been as large as those accepted by others, but the fact that he took these bribes as the head of China's National Food and Drug Monitoring Bureau ignited public anger, prompting China's premier Wen Jiabao to take a special interest in his case and ensure it was pursued by prosecutors. In July 2007, Zheng was executed on orders from the highest court in China.

A much more prevalent form of economic corruption than that in the drug and pharma industry involves business contracts, land acquisition, and mining rights. With the property market booming over the past two decades, economic stakes in the Chinese property market have risen dramatically. The same is also true for corruption involving mining rights, as the price of coal and other mineral resources skyrocketed between 2000 and 2012. About five hundred kilometers from Beijing is the capital of the province of Shanxi, where China's greatest concentration of coal mines can be found. Arguably, one can find the world's greatest concentration of expensive Land Rovers and Hummers in Shanxi. It should not come as a surprise that Shanxi was formerly the most corrupt province in China until many of the province's senior officials were purged between 2013 and 2016.

The second category, political corruption, can best be illustrated by Minister Liu Zhijun and Ms. Ding. Minister Liu is still remembered as the hero of Chinese rapid rail. He was the minister of the former Ministry of Railways, a fervent believer in rapid rail, and a workaholic determined to see his plans for the rapid rail system come to fruition. As a politically ambitious official, he had been frustrated that he was not promoted fast enough. Then along came Ms. Ding. When China was building its first high-speed train from July 2005 to December 2007 (the first train began operation on August 1, 2008), companies competed for the right to manufacture the train's toilets. These companies included one owned by Ding Shumiao, known as the "Queen of Toilets" and somewhat of a legendary figure in China. She was not well educated, having finished only primary school, but was a genuine entrepreneur who worked extremely hard and recognized the importance of knowing the right people. Ding started her business in international trade but gradually realized that railroads were big business. Hailing from the aforementioned Shanxi province, she knew that transporting coal outside of Shanxi faced bottlenecks, and whoever controlled the railroad freight routes (not the rapid rail system for passengers) would have access to an abundance of power and money. Ding thus began to cultivate her relationship with the railways, including the then-minister of railways, Mr. Liu Zhijun. Using this relationship, she directly and indirectly bribed ministers for business contracts, including high-speed rail projects ranging from supplying toilets and signal lights to constructing various parts of the track and other infrastructure.

A main reason why Liu Zhijun took bribes from businesspeople like Ms. Ding Shumiao was that he needed money to pay his own bribes, or "promotion fees." Liu was an extremely capable government official and was largely responsible for the tremendous rise of China's rapid rail. However, he was frustrated to watch many of his less capable and less accomplished peers earn promotions ahead of him. Eventually, he decided to cozy up to party officials such as Ling Jihua, then chief of staff to Hu Jintao, the general secretary of the CCP at the time. Ling Jihua also happened to be from Shanxi province. With the money and connections provided by his relationship with Ding, Minister Liu was able to pay bribes to officials like Ling Jihua, allowing him to rise through the ranks. In 2013, Minister Liu was given a death sentence with delayed execution (in practice, this means life imprisonment). In December 2014, Ms. Ding was sentenced to twenty years of imprisonment. Both cases attracted widespread attention.

Perhaps the most egregious case of political corruption involved two former military leaders, Guo Boxiong and Xu Caihou, who were so senior that they were outranked in the Chinese military hierarchy only by the president of the nation. They served as vice chairmen of China's Central Military Committee, which is headed by the president and is the highest decision-making body in the Chinese military. Perhaps their most significant power was the ability to influence decisions about promoting generals. According to a report from the *South China Morning Post* that cited a book written by a former subordinate of Guo, Guo had delineated an explicit price for each position. For a promotion to major general, he was asking for 5 to 10 million RMB. To become a lieutenant general, he was demanding 10 to 30 million RMB. In one case, a major general from the Nanjing Military District who wanted to be promoted to lieutenant general gave Guo 10 million RMB. Guo agreed to the promotion, but a few days later, when another major general offered 20 million RMB for the same position, Guo Boxiong awarded the promotion to the higher bidder.

The cases of Guo and Xu were by far the biggest corruption scandals in the history of the Communist Party. Not only were these men corrupt, but they were also discovered to have kept multiple mistresses. The Chinese military formerly had its own performing arts troupes, much like that of the Soviet Union and North Korea. Thus, it was very convenient for these two officials

to find friendship with beautiful young artists in these troupes.
Again, Xi Jinping's reforms did away with many Chinese military
performing arts troupes in order to focus the military on its mission: national defense.

The most corrupt subordinate promoted by Guo Boxiong was
Gu Junshan, the head of the former General Logistics Department of the Chinese military. He was in charge of military pro-
curement as well as building apartments for military officials. Gu
was found to have accepted numerous bribes, and he also issued
bribes to Guo Boxiong and his relatives. In one instance, Gu gave
Guo's daughter 20 million RMB, which Guo shipped in part to
his brother's house in a village. His brother then built a thirty-
meter-long vault to store Guo's loot from years of bribery—a
vault which was so full of liquor, wine, and art that it took multiple days and four trucks for anticorruption officials to empty it
upon Guo's downfall. In 2015, Guo Boxiong received a life sentence and Gu Junshan was given a death sentence with a two-year
delayed execution, which was later waived in exchange for a life
sentence in prison.

CORRUPTION IN CHINA IS perhaps among the most economically "efficient" forms of corruption in the world, which
makes it all the more damaging. That is, in China, an unscrupu-
lous individual needs only to bribe a few key decision makers—
and often just one—with one-stop payments to get what they
want. In countries like India, for instance, corruption is less coordinated, meaning that one has to bribe many officials, and in the
end things may not be done. Thus, Indian corruption is less efficient at getting desired results than in China.

Because of the highly efficient nature of Chinese corruption,
it causes more damage to the political regime than to economic
performance. In doing business, government officials can be
motivated by bribery to make exceptions and give the green light

to otherwise impossible business deals. Politically, however, this directly exposes key decision makers to mistrust by the population. In the Chinese case, the fruits of corruption fall largely into the pockets of a few powerful people, whereas in India, petty corruption could be perceived as routine income for low-level government officials. This also explains why key decision makers get nervous when China launches a large anticorruption campaign.

More generally, the biggest cost of corruption is that it runs directly against the Communist Party's mission to serve the people. The party claims to represent the interests of all people in China, whereas corruption embodies the diametrical opposite of this goal by serving only the interests of the most powerful. Therefore, corruption is despised by the general populace and undermines the party's reputation. Whenever negative news comes to light, the internet is always abuzz with comments blaming corruption.

Beyond sowing seeds of distrust among the general public, corruption with regard to promotions also compromises the principle of meritocracy, which is held in high esteem by the party and is rooted in thousands of years of Chinese civil service culture. Corruption encourages the promotion of individuals who would not otherwise be competent enough to earn their positions in a competition of skill. In some local governments, you can see that the people in key positions are often the best social drinkers and connection-builders, or those with the most prestigious family backgrounds. In recent years, when corruption was in high gear, many of my students told me that it was impossible for poor, hardworking, well-qualified university graduates to earn senior positions or other highly coveted posts in the business sector, such as in large investment banks and even some foreign banks. Without a reference letter or introductory message from an individual with strong connections to the company, most candidates found it impossible to get even a first interview. Connections remained very important through the final stages of the interview process. Naturally, students detested this situation. Fortunately, this problem is not as severe regarding entry-level government positions, since regulations in China stipulate that all entry-level civil servant job offers must be based on the results of written exams.

Most ordinary people in China credit Xi Jinping for cleaning up Chinese corruption with his massive anticorruption campaign, although educated elites often voice their concerns about the side effects. The claimed side effects include the unchecked power of the anticorruption agency, which often leads to the blending of politics and anticorruption efforts. Another side effect is that many officials choose to be hesitant in their work for fear of making enemies who may provoke anticorruption investigations of an official's historical cases.

Why does most of the population regard the anticorruption campaign as a success? It is hard to come up with precise supporting evidence. Two observations perhaps are relevant. First, during the first decade since Xi has been in power, as many as 17 percent of senior officials positioned as ministers, provincial governors, or above, were disciplined (in most cases sentenced) for corruption.[1] This amounted to about 210 officials, while in previous decades, the number was less than 20! Second, by 2021, anticorruption investigations had become the number one worry of almost all government officials, making overt forms of corruption few and far between. The side effect, of course, has been overly cautious behavior by government officials.

What is the key instrument of the massive anticorruption campaign? It is the tough and elevated role of the party's discipline inspection committees, which coexist with the party committee at each level of the government and had been rather sleepy

1 This is an estimate based on my collected data published on the website of the Communist Party's Central Discipline Inspection Committee around May 2022.

until the ascendency of Xi. The discipline inspection committees function side by side and often above the system of government attorneys or the procuratorates. The discipline inspection
committees initiate and complete each corruption case before
sending it to the procuratorates, who then take over and finish
the formalities.

How do the party's discipline inspection committees find
clues to tip them off about a corruption case? In most cases, they
rely on whistleblowers, broadly defined. Tradition in China provides for people to bring their grievances against corrupt officials
to senior government agencies rather than the court. Interestingly, it is quite common for a grievance to come from the disen-
chanted lover of a corrupt official. When a lover brings personal
or emotional grievances to the commission, the official in question is placed under full investigation, and both the lover and
official are almost always convicted. This is because lovers are
often directly involved in demanding cash and benefits from
businesspeople who are trying to gain favor with the officials. In
China, the joke is that lovers are the most effective weapon in the
anticorruption campaign.

Throughout the anticorruption campaign, President Xi's right-
hand man and the so-called czar of the campaign has been Wang
Qishan, one of the seven most powerful officials in China on the
Standing Committee from 2013 to 2018. Perhaps the best way
to describe his personality is as a combination of Vladimir Putin
and Bill Clinton. Like Clinton, Wang is extremely intellectual and
articulate. An avid reader, especially of history, he can speak on
various subjects for hours. Wang is a "tough guy." He is known to
be a straight-talker, always quick to the point, and is more outspoken than many of his peers.

At a large banquet that I attended around 2015, everyone
stood up and moved to Wang's table to toast to him, which is
a Chinese way of showing respect. One of the Americans mentioned that Larry Summers, the former treasury secretary under

President Clinton, had recently visited Beijing, and Wang took the opportunity to share a good-natured story about him and Larry Summers. Wang said that when he met Summers for the first time at the China-US Strategic Dialogue,[1] he told him, "You are smart, but I can outsmart you in our negotiations because I read all the books you wrote, but you don't read all of the books in Chinese that I read." When Summers asked Wang for a book suggestion, he responded, "论语," which is the *Analects of Confucius*. Wang told Summers, "If you can understand this one book, then you can rule the world." Summers said, "I will read the English translation," to which Wang joked that there would be no way for Summers, or any Westerner, to fully understand this book in its true meaning, since the essence of the book cannot be translated. Such a personality makes Wang Qishan stand out among Chinese officials, who are usually polite and reserved, while Wang is outspoken and often boastful in a joking way.

The anticorruption campaign requires a person with an impeccable reputation and no possible connection to corruption to lead it, and Wang Qishan fits this profile perfectly. He has no children, and his wife is a descendant of senior officials who were upright revolutionary veterans. Wang's family situation is expedient, as it is often wives and children who demand bribes, sometimes even without the knowledge of the official. Wang is also a problem solver and implementer—absolutely essential attributes for an anticorruption chief. I do not think that people had any idea he would make anticorruption one of the most impactful features of Xi Jinping's leadership when he was first assigned the job.

Many people in China are concerned with the side effects of the massive anticorruption campaign. The first side effect is that

---

1 This annual meeting between China and US cabinet members was initiated by President George W. Bush and then continued under President Obama. President Trump terminated it.

government officials, especially those dealing with economic affairs, have now become inert. The reason is that active officials almost surely create enemies or grumbling groups, such as through the demolition of an old building to make room for new investments. These groups would bring their cases, and perhaps even historical cases, to the party discipline committee. On their path to promotion and their current positions, most officials have either intentionally or unintentionally engaged in practices that are not in compliance with today's tighter government rules. In the Chinese reform process, laws and regulations are gradually implemented and then tightened. The anticorruption campaign is using today's tighter regulations to judge the past conduct of officials, which occurred when the rules were either looser or entirely unclear. As a result, officials today are extremely hesitant to take any action that would make them stand out or draw extra attention, even if those actions are in the best interests of the locale or department they serve.

How much has the anticorruption campaign impacted economic growth? According to studies by Bank of America Merrill Lynch, the anticorruption campaign caused a decline of 1 percent in GDP growth in 2014, while BNP Paribas estimated the slowdown to be in the range of 1–1.5 percent. Fortunately, the long-term outlook is brighter, since doing business might be easier with less corruption. According to a survey of seventeen economists by Bloomberg, the anticorruption campaign was expected to boost China's GDP growth by 0.1 percent to 0.5 percent per year by 2020. Of course, it is very hard to confirm such predictions, as the COVID-19 pandemic hit the world in 2020. The overall sentiment is that the anticorruption campaign is good for long-term growth.

Another side effect is more subtle than the first one. That is, as many people have argued, the anticorruption campaign has become rather arbitrary and driven by politics. The ability to retroactively prosecute past behavior using today's new standards has resulted in rather flexible interpretations of corruption. A common pattern is the sale of shares in a bankrupt state-owned enterprise to an official, who later becomes CEO and turns the enterprise profitable. By today's standards, such behavior could easily be labeled as corruption since the price of the transaction is deemed too low given the high profit today, but whether such an official is investigated or not ultimately comes down to politics: for example, whether they have personal ties to allegedly bad officials or good ones.

WHAT ARE THE FUTURE prospects for corruption in China? Most likely, corruption as a widespread social phenomenon and source of discontent will give way to other social problems such as the high cost of childcare and health care. Following through with the immense progress made under the CCP's fierce anticorruption campaign, the party is now following the strategies of Singapore and Hong Kong to institutionalize anticorruption practices.

The experiences of Hong Kong and Singapore are the most revealing and are carefully studied on the mainland. In the 1960s and 1970s, Hong Kong police and civil servants were extremely corrupt. However, the city was able to reverse this situation through the establishment of the Independent Commission Against Corruption (ICAC). From the Singaporean experience, China has learned that in order to avoid corruption, the salaries of officials must be greatly increased. In Singapore, the pay for senior government officials is on par with the salary of a senior executive of a large corporation. Of course, with these high salaries come extremely high standards regarding the conduct and integrity of the officials. Eventually, this will become the practice of the Chinese government: high pay, high standards, and high expectations, along with stringent institutions and regulations to prevent and monitor possible corruption. China and Singapore share the same Confucian tradition of civil service.

A typical Chinese minister is now paid around 200,000 RMB a year (around 30,000 USD) and is provided with a 150 square meter (1,650 square foot) apartment and a chauffeured car. The apartment is granted to the minister for his entire life and may or may not be inherited by his children. This is a significant job perk, as the value of such an apartment in Beijing can easily reach half a million USD. Ministers also hold a very high social status, on which a monetary value cannot be placed. However, bureau chiefs, general directors of departments of ministries, and other sub-ministerial-level positions are different in this regard. Unless you pay these officials well, they may not be very dedicated to their job, or they may simply use their position as a stepping stone to other jobs or as a way to boost the careers of their children. To ameliorate these concerns, I expect officials will ultimately receive substantial salary increases, especially at the sub-ministerial level. In many other countries, such as the United States, officials such as cabinet members are not very well paid compared to what they could earn in the private sector. Still, this situation is sustainable because these people enjoy high social status, in many cases have already made good money in the private sector, and can switch to the private sector following their term of service.

In 2018, China established the State Supervisory Commission to phase out the anticorruption campaign while maintaining the battle. The State Supervisory Commission is essentially the Party Discipline Inspection Committee but now also functions as a state anticorruption agency. It also monitors corruption cases involving non-Communist Party members.

Most people in China seem to believe that the level of corruption in China will certainly continue to decline. The reason is that once the above-mentioned policies are implemented, officials will maintain their influential social status while also being well compensated and held to correspondingly high standards. Government posts will be regarded as stable and prestigious positions due to Confucius tradition, and young people will still consider a government career appealing.

After discussing the all-important topic of the Chinese Communist Party and how it coordinates the operations of the central and local governments, as well as the issue of corruption, we are ready to move on and discuss the Chinese economy. How does it work and why has it been growing so fast with seemingly non-standard market economic institutions? As a transition, I begin this discussion with an analysis of government in the economy in the next chapter.

CHAPTER 7

Government in
the Economy

I N ORDER TO UNDERSTAND HOW THE CHINESE
economy operates, it is essential to understand the relationship
between the economy and the government. Government intervention is pervasive in many aspects of the Chinese economy,
which Westerners commonly believe to be a defect. However, if
this were truly a flaw, the Chinese economy would not have been
able to grow so rapidly for such a long period of time. Moreover,
in the past four decades of rapid growth, China has successfully
avoided a financial crisis, which accompanied each of the historical episodes of rapid economic growth in the United States, Japan,
Germany, and Korea.

The relationship between the government and the market has
been undergoing gradual changes during the past four decades,
mostly moving toward letting the market play a more important role, with the government standing by when the market
fails. China is a great laboratory in this regard, and its experiences hold lessons for many countries, including Western market economies. Even today, the consensus in Chinese society is
that the government-market relationship still needs rebalanc-
ing. To understand the general picture, I start by explaining
the rationale behind the Chinese government's intervention in
the economy.

WHY DOES CHINA'S GOVERNMENT, in contrast to governments in most other countries, intervene extensively in the economy and society? There are fundamental and philosophical reasons for this. The first can be summarized as all-responsible government, which means that the government believes that it should behave like a parent, with the general public regarded as children who expect to be taken care of. This philosophy can be traced back to Confucianism—Confucius argued that subjects should be loyal to their emperor, and, in return, the emperor must be benevolent toward his subjects.

The mentality of the all-responsible government is vividly illustrated by the fact that each level of Chinese government includes a department called the grievance agency. When people believe they have been mistreated either by lower-level governments, local enterprises, other individuals, or society in general, they can line up at the agency's door to have their voices heard. These individuals often write lengthy statements detailing how they have been wronged, and sometimes even cut their fingers to sign them in their own blood. This is different from a court, where the adversary system exists. Even though China does have a court system, many still believe in the grievance system, where the government is the final renderer of justice.

As an implication of the philosophy of all-responsible government, the government tends to intervene more in areas where it feels a large number of households or citizens might be wounded. For example, the government intervenes much more in the commercial banking sector than in the private equity sector. This is because many households place their money in a bank, whereas investors in the private equity market comprise a relatively low proportion of the population. Furthermore, a person must prove that they have significant assets in order to invest in private equity. Therefore, if a problem were to occur with a large commercial bank, it would negatively affect a large number of households, many without much net worth outside of their bank savings. In contrast, private equity firms usually involve a small number of high-net-worth individuals with less of a need for government protection.

Consistent with the philosophy of all-responsible government is that often, government intervention is directly motivated by the desire to avert massive protests or demonstrations. The government worries that if a large number of people lose money or jobs, they will take to the streets in protest. Such events would never occur if only a handful of high-net-worth people were to lose money. In that instance, they might go to the government to conduct closed-door negotiations. This would be a more comfortable scenario for the government than mass demonstrations.

The second philosophy regarding extensive government intervention is based on the belief that the good of society takes priority over an individual's welfare. Again, this concept can be traced back to Confucius's political philosophy. On the global stage, the American political philosophy sits at one extreme, placing great emphasis on individual liberty. This concept can be traced back to English and Scottish philosophers. In contrast, some continental European philosophers have historically placed relatively more emphasis on social order than individual liberty. The Chinese government goes one step beyond that idea: When it comes to making major decisions, effecting social stability and economic prosperity are more important than ensuring individual rights.

China's policies regarding motorcycle ownership and usage provide a good example of the prioritization of social order over individual liberty, forming a sharp contrast to those in the United States, where, for example, gun ownership is largely legalized. Since the early 1990s, all major cities in China have either completely banned motorcycles or strictly limited the issuance of motorcycle registration licenses. Moreover, most highways prohibit motorcycles from entering. Why? The reasons given by the government are that motorcycles are unsafe for the riders, are

intrusive for pedestrians and other vehicles on the road, and—
most importantly—are oftentimes used by criminals. Therefore,
in the interest of the general public, motorcycles are banned in
almost all cities. The city of Beijing is relatively more friendly to
motorcycles: Instead of having a complete ban, only about ten
thousand class A motorcycle registration licenses are allowed,
whose market value had gone up as high as 60,000 US dollars
each by early 2023. As a fan of motorcycles, I have been arguing
for and proposing the elimination of restrictions on motorcycles
and have written many policy proposals for this. So far, I have not
been successful. Considering that in the United States, gun ownership is legal, many of my friends agree that both countries have
gone to extremes.

NO SINGLE GOVERNMENT AGENCY in China more vividly
illustrates how the Chinese government works with the economy
than the NDRC, the National Development and Reform Commission. The NDRC is easily China's busiest central government
agency. Most of the one-thousand-plus officials work overtime
perennially, and one of my former schoolmates had a stroke at
the age of fifty due to overwork there. The NDRC boasts thirteen
directors and deputy directors. The first of the NDRC's major
functions is to monitor China's macroeconomic operations. Semi-
annually, the NDRC produces an analysis of the macroeconomy
and forms policy responses and suggestions for China's top leadership. I am occasionally invited to meet with NDRC directors,
deputy directors, and, on occasion, directors of individual NDRC
departments to discuss how to best analyze the macroeconomy,
how to carry out policies, and how to decide which measures will
best facilitate the smooth operation of the economy.

In economic and many other social affairs, the NDRC wields
a significant amount of power. In fact, the head of the NDRC is
a half-step above the heads of other ministries. The structure of

the NDRC includes several major departments that are responsible for tasks such as monitoring the Chinese macroeconomy (much like the US Department of the Treasury), formulating policies in various industries, and keeping tabs on the markets for resources such as electricity, gas, and coal to prevent any shortages. The NDRC also has a large economic research complex, a department in charge of approving and managing super-large investment projects, and a department working on issues related to global warming.

The NDRC is well known among many economists across the world and has won praise by liberal (as opposed to free-market) economists. I recall that in 2010, after walking out of a high-level workshop on the world economy at the International Monetary Fund headquarters, a world-renowned US economist told me: "You are from China and your comments just now were the most optimistic among everyone in the room because you have an NDRC. I wish the US had thirteen NDRCs!"

The directors and deputy directors of the NDRC often boast rich experiences in local or other government agencies, but are usually modest in personality and adept at synthesizing different views and coordinating conflicting interests. Former director Mr. Zhang Ping is a prime example. In the winter of 2012, I was in an NDRC conference room with about twenty people. Seated across the table facing me was Mr. Zhang, the director at the time, along with two deputy directors and his chief of staff. Seated next to me were seven fellow academics. I had already finished my presentation, which analyzed the macroeconomic situation and included my policy proposal. The last speaker was a professor from Renmin University. He gave a long lecture, citing Keynes, Milton Friedman, and so on. He spoke for twenty minutes without coming close to analyzing the Chinese economy. The chief of staff clearly grew very impatient, as did the other academics. The chief of staff stood up and interjected, asking the speaker to please make his points and finish as quickly as possible, saying that it was time for us to have lunch and that the director needed to take a nap after lunch. Mr. Zhang patiently waved his hand to his assistant and said to the professor, "Take your time, professor. Please continue." Mr. Zhang is a polite, mild-mannered, and modest person who pays close attention to details. This apparently is the style of all NDRC directors. Mr. Zhang's predecessor, Mr. Ma Kai, who later became the vice premier of China in charge of finance, possesses the same style, as do most of the others. They are all experts at coordinating various interests and views on the economy.

Each ministry has its own culture of behavior, and that of the NDRC is surely modesty and caution. This is because the NDRC, as a powerful and coordinating agency, often has to play the role of the "bad guy," rejecting lobbying from other agencies. For example, the Ministry of Industry and Information may push for government investments in the high-tech industry, while the Ministry of Hydraulic Engineering and Water Management pushes for investments in building and repairing reservoirs. Being pulled in many different directions, the NDRC must remain firmly in the middle, balancing all competing requirements. NDRC officials must be mild-mannered and ensure that they can politely reject requests without damaging relationships. Imagine if the situation were reversed—if the director of the NDRC, which is by far China's most powerful agency—wielded its power to eliminate many projects. People would complain, the director would draw the enmity of the other ministries, and sooner or later, the minister would be forced out of politics. The recent mild-mannered and modest directors have all received promotions, later becoming either a vice premier or deputy chairman of the CPPCC, a political body similar to Britain's House of Lords.

Young talents compete to get into the NDRC, and its young staff members have a very active, proud, and studious culture. I was once invited to sit on the jury for an annual economic essay and speech competition for young NDRC staff. I found this experience highly interesting because the young staff members were all tremendously enthusiastic and hardworking. They came up with numerous thought-provoking ideas regarding economic regulation, and I could tell their opinions were valued, as all of the NDRC directors were in attendance when the finalists gave their presentations. As a jury member, I provided feedback to the essayists and then voted for the best. During this experience, I found the young people at the NDRC to be extremely ambitious, perceiving themselves as the managers of the entire economy (and possibly as future premiers). Many of them have master's or even PhD degrees in economics or business. They passionately discuss and often criticize China's policies pertaining to population and land, as well as other major issues, and truly feel they can effect change.

WHAT ARE THE MAJOR areas of the economy that are still under extensive government intervention, either directly or indirectly? The first area is **prices of goods and services that are socially sensitive,** ranging from household electricity and gasoline, to school tuition, to medical surgery. This is especially the case during economically and politically sensitive periods. For example, gasoline, diesel, and natural gas prices are government-regulated, which is under the purview of the NDRC. The government has published a formula linking the average international price of crude oil over the previous ten days, in addition to other variables, to the announced gasoline price. However, they do not always strictly follow this formula, so there are still surprises. Chinese gasoline prices are among the lowest in the world, only slightly higher than those in the United States. There are sound political reasons for the government to keep prices low: China is now the world's largest automobile market in terms of sales (around twenty-seven million) and ownership (around 270 million by June 2022) and is still growing. For comparison, US annual sales fluctuate around thirteen million to eighteen million units, and total ownership is at 260 million. Any call to potentially raise gasoline taxes will ignite public complaints against the government. In this regard, China and the United States are the same. However, economists generally disagree with the practice of gas price regulation as it encourages overreliance on fossil energy.

The tuition for executive MBA programs is also regulated by the NDRC. An executive MBA is a part-time MBA program offered to business executives. Of course, EMBA (Executive MBA) programs are also offered by US and European business schools. Chinese business schools have found that EMBA programs are very useful not only in boosting the schools' revenue but also in adding some of the country's most successful business-people to their alumni network. But since the tuition fees are quite high—around 100,000 USD for a two-year program—an uproar erupted on social media and the internet at large, saying that elite universities were being too greedy. As a result, the NDRC stepped in and began regulating tuition prices. The rationale for regulation is political: The government does not want to be accused of allowing state-owned universities to collect what are perceived to be exorbitant fees. Again, most economists and elites disagree with the NDRC in regulating tuition, arguing that this is a subsidy for high-income executives.

Large investment projects are also under NDRC control, which is perhaps one of the most unique aspects of the Chinese economy. The rationale for controlling or promoting major investments is to prevent the economy from becoming too cool or too hot. In recent years, this practice was also intended to prevent overcapacity in production—a problem that plagues China's aluminum, iron, steel, and power-generation industries. When prices of iron and steel drop very low, many enterprises in this field are unprofitable. Yet, there are still entrepreneurs willing to gamble by building factories in these sectors. They believe they have either unique technologies or superior operating models. The entrepreneurs may well be rational based on their own interest, since when their projects work, they benefit, and when their projects fail, it is workers, local governments, and banks that suffer. Also, existing enterprises, including foreign producers, suffer due to lower prices caused by the new projects. Therefore, the central government issues a ban on new projects in certain sectors when prices are too low or when the government believes the production capacity is already too high. Such bans can be very tough. In 2003, for instance, a private entrepreneur was imprisoned for violating the central government's ban on building new iron and steel plants.

Because of the practice of restricting large investment projects, it is said that the drawers in the NDRC offices are filled with applications from local governments and private entrepreneurs seeking to make investments in various sectors. One implication is that the NDRC can quickly jumpstart the economy by loosening its control of projects. For example, subway construction requires approval from the NDRC to prevent local governments from becoming overly burdened by debt. Around 2012, cities with a population of at least three million could successfully apply for a subway, but now, when the economy slows down, projects in some cities with a population of less than three million are being approved.

You may think that multinationals hate the NDRC for its policy of controlling new projects. The fact is often the opposite! This is because multinationals usually have higher thresholds of profitability and environmental impact, so their projects usually pass the NDRC quickly. They are grateful to the NDRC for stopping other projects by domestic players, since they often complain about Chinese private investors' aggressive investment in relevant sectors, which causes industrial prices to drop exceptionally low.

Product standards are another area under extensive government regulation, usually supervised by China's Ministry of Industry and Information. In this regard, China and the United States follow opposite philosophies. In China, to sell a product on the market, the producer often must first gain approval from the government by passing a standard. In the United States, producers can often begin selling immediately without approval, but if the product is later believed to be unsafe, the producer may face lawsuits, which often result in paying extremely high compensation, and ultimately in bankruptcy. In China, when a product is unsafe, consumers will go after the government (rather than the producer) via the grievance protocol. Not aware of the difference between China and the United States, in 2022, many Chinese electric vehicle producers were considering entering the US market, and I often suggested they be cautious and well prepared before making any commitments.

Partly to avoid problems of product liability, China often has very high technical thresholds for consumer products, at least on paper. China's product standards are often among the world's highest, similar to those of the United States and Europe. However, the implementation and enforcement of these standards is the problem. I was told by a friend that only about 30 percent of China's motorcycles meet national emission standards because manufacturers, seeking to reduce costs, send their best samples for inspection, later assembling substandard products for volume production. In the United States and Europe, random checking by the government curbs this practice.

The property market is another area with which the Chinese government is deeply concerned. In places like the United States, Hong Kong, or the UK, when property prices are very high, the government raises interest rates, and banks might also take some measures to tighten their supply of credit. Unfortunately, the United States did not take such actions before the financial crisis, allowing the property market to spin out of control. In the Chinese case, all of these measures have been attempted, but they are often not sufficient, and as a result, property prices have kept rising. By 2011, the central government urged local governments to take the drastic step of rationing the purchase of apartments. For example, each household in Beijing can now purchase only two pieces of property. In order to buy property, households must demonstrate that in the past two years, they have been legally residing in Beijing and paying their taxes. Foreigners can only buy property in Beijing after living in the city and paying local taxes for at least five years. The policy has helped stabilize Beijing's housing prices, but of course, such a draconian policy often draws attacks by economists for being antimarket.

Stock prices are another area subject to active government intervention. Whenever stock prices were extremely high during the past two decades, the *People's Daily*, China's official newspaper, published editorials urging investors to be cautious, consistent with the philosophy of all-responsible government. Such editorials would often be seen as countersignals for many smart investors who used them as indicators that the market was not only currently hot, but would also remain hot for some time, making "now" a good time to invest. Thus, the government failed to sufficiently persuade people, and more cash was pumped into the stock market. When market prices are high, the government encourages IPOs in order to cool down market prices. Conversely, when the stock market is low, the government tends to ban IPOs. In most countries, investment banks and enterprises decide when to pursue an IPO, but in China, this decision is under government regulation. The government feels that addressing the excesses of the stock market is the government's responsibility.

IS GOVERNMENT INTERVENTION IN the economy ultimately successful in China? This is a very difficult and controversial question. My simple answer is that intervention has been successful for the purpose of preventing drastic economic crises, including financial crises. However, for the purpose of developing individual industries, government intervention has been much less successful. This is why there have been conscious efforts to gradually let market forces play a larger role in the economy.

One major reason for successfully avoiding a major economic crisis is that the premier's office is very much focused on China's macroeconomic operation and market fluctuations. In most countries, these issues are the responsibility of entities akin to the Central Bank and the Ministry of Finance, while in China they reach much higher in the leadership, and are personally overseen by the premier. Every six months, the premier convenes meetings with academic and business experts to discuss the macroeconomy. I have attended many of these meetings, during which the premier usually asks each expert to speak for about ten minutes and then responds and explains his ideas regarding managing the economy. At one of these meetings in July 2014, the concern was the economic slowdown. I proposed that China follow the practice of the World Bank by setting up investment funds and issuing debt to support long-term infrastructure investment. The practice at that time was to have commercial banks support long-term projects, thus crowding out enterprises from the credit market. The premier immediately asked whether this would invoke a larger government deficit. Apparently, the premier is very concerned with the budget deficit because every March he faces the scrutiny of the National People's Congress.

At the level of individual industries, intervention by the central government, as well as by many local governments, has mixed results. When governments see too much production in an industry or when they try to promote an industry, they tend to choose some individual enterprises to cut or subsidize. That is, they are like an NBA general manager picking the basketball players in a draft. Although there are successful stories, in many cases they choose the wrong enterprises. Most of today's industry champions were not chosen by governments but instead emerged as the victors through competition. For example, China's home appliance producer Haier was on the verge of being forced to close down by the central government in the late 1990s, when the home appliance industry was plagued by overproduction. Fortunately,

Haier fought hard to stay in the industry and excelled, while many chosen producers failed and later were liquidated. Some good local governments know this well and behave like an organizer of a sports tournament to stimulate firms to compete and then hand the trophy to the winner. China's Huawei, Xiaomi, Alibaba, and so forth, all follow this model. Local governments such as those of Shenzhen, Guangzhou, or Hangzhou function as tournament managers.

After understanding the motivation and behavior of government in the economy, in the next chapters, we move closer to the economy by examining different types of Chinese enterprises in order to understand why Chinese industries have been growing rapidly over the past decades. We start with state-owned enterprises, whose existence and behavior have aroused many questions outside China.

CHAPTER 8

State-Owned
Enterprises

CHINA'S STATE-OWNED ENTERPRISES (SOEs) often stand out in discussions of the Chinese economy and require an in-depth analysis. Their existence is the main reason why China has not been accepted as a market economy in many international trade and investment treaties, since SOEs are blamed for violating market principles. In this chapter, I make two simple points. First, except for a small number of national monopolies, the majority of SOEs operate and compete in the marketplace just as private enterprises do. Second, SOEs are undergoing continuous reforms, and most of them will be transformed into modern corporations similar to IBM or Bosch. Instead of directly controlling SOEs, the Chinese government will mostly hold shares of various corporations, as pension fund managers do. The Chinese economy will be subject to diminishing direct control from various levels of government.

STATE-OWNED ENTERPRISES ARE enterprises in which the government holds the largest number of shares. This gives the government the authority to appoint the chairman of the board, fill top management positions, and approve key decisions. An SOE may be managed by the central government or by a provincial or subprovincial government. There are three main types of SOEs.

The first type of SOEs is large monopolies managed mostly by the central government. They exist in such sectors as natural resources, commercial banking, telecommunications, commercial jet manufacturing, and power transmission. PetroChina, one of the top ten national oil companies in the world, is a state-owned enterprise that was listed on the New York Stock Exchange between 2000 and 2022. Its output of crude oil ranks among the top five globally, and it has more than five hundred thousand employees, making it one of the largest employers in the world. No reason was given for its 2022 retreat from the New York Stock Exchange, but many believed the move was made to prevent US investors from demanding national secrets from China's energy sector. About 130 state-owned enterprises similar to PetroChina are under the direct control of the central government. However, just twenty of them account for 50 percent of the total profits of all SOEs. These SOEs include China Mobile, Bank of China, China Unicom, China Telecom, Construction Bank of China, Agricultural Bank of China, and the Industrial and Commercial Bank of China (ICBC)—the most profitable commercial bank in the world. These star SOEs are all listed in the top half of the world's Fortune 500 list.

The second type of SOEs are enterprises in competitive industries. They are supervised mostly by provincial or sub-provincial governments. One cluster of these SOEs consists of joint ventures in automobile industries, including the Shanghai Automobile Industry (with joint-venture partners GM, VW, and so forth) and the Beijing Automobile Corporation (with joint-venture partners Hyundai and Mercedes Benz). They exist because, as in many other developing countries, the government used to require companies like BMW to form joint ventures in order to produce in the country. However, this regulation is gradually phasing out.

Many surprising cases are among the second type of SOEs.

While McDonald's represents a quintessential symbol of American capitalism, in the city of Beijing, McDonald's restaurants are all SOEs that have franchise agreements with the McDonald's corporation. They are actually owned by the Beijing Capital Agricultural Group. Why? When McDonald's entered China in the late 1980s, the municipal government was the largest landlord, so it was easiest for McDonald's to let a Beijing SOE figure out the tricky job of renting store space. McDonald's has been very profitable, so the city of Beijing has not allowed it to privatize.

Similar to McDonald's, Quanjude Peking Duck, the most famous restaurant in Beijing, is an example of a Beijing SOE that persists for historical reasons. Quanjude is an "old-brand" restaurant, which means it specializes in cuisine from a particular city—in this case, Beijing. In China, every city boasts its own brands of restaurants. Quanjude was originally founded in 1846 and has become the most famous brand of Peking Duck. After the Chinese Revolution in 1949, it was gradually collectivized and then eventually transformed into a state-owned enterprise under the Beijing municipal government. It is now a listed company on the Shanghai Stock Exchange. The Beijing municipal government, through the Beijing Tourism Group, owns majority shares in Quanjude.

The third type of SOE, which is still emerging, is that of investment funds. Almost all levels of government in China have such funds. A successful example is an investment fund of the city of Hefei, the capital of Anhui province. In 2019, the Hefei investment fund provided cash to the electric car producer NIO when its New York share price dropped to as low as 1 US dollar. In exchange for this investment, the city of Hefei required NIO to build a production plant in Hefei. By 2021, NIO's share price went up to around 50 US dollars, and its production plant was working overtime, not only producing NIO cars but also paying taxes to the city of Hefei. The Hefei government won not only by getting higher share prices but also by collecting tax revenue from NIO's production. Of course, not all government funds are as successful as Hefei's.

WHY DO SOEs EXIST? The simplest answer to this question is "history." That is, many SOEs are legacies of the command economy era before China's reform and opening up. At the founding of the People's Republic of China in 1949, the original view was that enterprises and production assets must be owned by the government—a defining feature of a socialist economy. When the Communist Party assumed power, its initial plan called for the nationalization of Western-controlled companies, which the party called "imperialist companies." That is precisely what happened, for instance, with commercial banks such as Citibank and HSBC. This is no different from what occurred in many other countries in the past, such as those in Latin America and Africa, following their independence from colonial rule. The Chinese Communist Party initially decided that it was necessary to make a gradual transition from the capitalist economy that had existed under the Nationalist government to a socialist economy, and intended to take fifteen to twenty years to gradually nationalize or collectivize enterprises.

Mao drastically sped up this plan of gradually nationalizing capital through the Great Leap Forward in 1958. Farms were collectivized, and ownership of individual household land was centralized into people's communes. Assets in commerce, service, and industry were quickly nationalized. In the early 1930s, my mother's parents owned and managed many pieces of property in the city of Nanjing, which was the capital of the Nationalist government. Their property was confiscated by the Communist government during the Great Leap Forward. In exchange, my grandparents were given some cash and relocated to a distant suburb of Nanjing, where they built a small house and lived off the remainder of their government payment. The extended family used to consist of over fifty members, and when it was time for lunch or dinner, the head of the family had to ring a bell to call everybody to the dining hall. However, in the suburbs, the extended family no longer lived together. It was only my grandparents, and their living standards suffered a huge decline—they found it very difficult to survive. Fortunately, my mother was already working, and I remember that every month she would send one-third of her salary home to support her parents.

In the reform era starting in 1978, the Chinese government began to gradually privatize SOEs because many SOEs had become unprofitable and ineffective. For example, the city of Shenyang, China's industrial stronghold, used to have six thousand industrial SOEs; by 2021, fewer than twenty still existed. It was a painful process for Shenyang, and the most difficult period was the late 1990s, when as many as sixty thousand SOE workers lost their jobs. The city gradually recovered with the help of the central government and a joint-venture plant with BMW, which now contributes about one-third of the city's fiscal revenue.

The process of privatization can be summarized as "let go of the small and hold on to the large." That is, small and unprofitable SOEs were either sold to individual private owners or liquidated. Meanwhile, the government has maintained its ownership of the largest enterprises, partly because the large ones are often monopolies and are profitable.

The second reason for the existence of SOEs is to stabilize public finance. Although tax revenue tends to fluctuate with the macroeconomy, in an economic crisis, if the government already owns assets—even minority shares—it can use these assets as collateral to issue debt or simply sell some of the shares to help balance the budget. This is the logic underpinning the sovereign wealth funds found in many other countries. For example, the Singaporean government owns several large investment funds, holding many assets in China and the United States, including industrial parks in China and stock-issuing companies all over the world.

The third reason why SOEs exist is that they can help the government implement certain policies that private enterprises may not. An obvious example is the Beijing Olympics in 2008, which was conducted on a grander scale than any Olympics in history—particularly the opening and closing ceremonies. Recent Olympics have proven to be enormously unprofitable and can burden a city with debt for many years. However, in the case of Beijing, the municipal government was actually able to turn a small profit. How was this possible? The simple answer is that the Beijing municipal government, with the help of the central government, made numerous requests to state-owned enterprises—such as to build a special power plant near the Olympic Park. In addition, SOEs were asked to rush deadlines for building facilities and roads, and were even requested to assist in ceremony rehearsals.

The fourth reason for the existence of SOEs in China is ideological, though this may well change over time. This ideological view holds that China is a socialist economy and the Communist Party is the party in power, so SOEs should be the cornerstones of the political regime. On its surface, this argument is logical, but in reality, it does not hold water. It is simply overkill for the government to directly own so many assets for maintaining political governance. The reason is that the government collects taxes on all enterprises, and the taxes for an average enterprise can easily amount to at least 20 percent of total sales. As a result, the government is already a huge stakeholder in every enterprise, not just SOEs. All enterprises are the basis of political governance..

Do SOEs behave differently from other types of enterprises, such as private ones or multinationals? The answer is no, in general. Because of decades of tough market competition and selection, the overwhelming majority of SOEs are competitive and owned by local governments. Most of them are listed on the stock market. Unprofitable ones have already been privatized, since Chinese governments do not want to be burdened by subsidies. Moreover, most of the remaining SOEs have very strong and independent senior executives who are often respected and revered by local government heads.

The leading example is Gree Electric, which is one of the world's leading home appliance producers. It boasts an extremely capable and charismatic CEO in Dong Mingzhu, perhaps even more powerful than Carly Fiorina, the former CEO of HP. Dong is popular, articulate, and most importantly, powerful. She has even appeared in commercials for her company on China's national TV, saying that there is no need to hire expensive movie stars like Jackie Chan to serve as advertising spokespeople for Gree when she can do the commercials for free. Gree Electric is one of the star companies on the Chinese stock exchange and boasts prominent investors such as the Yale University Endowment Fund and TEMASEK, an investment fund run by the Singaporean government. It might surprise you to learn that Gree Electric is a state-owned enterprise owned by the city of Zhuhai, which has been designated a special economic zone. In a TV panel with Dong Mingzhu, I joked that she should acknowledge an important factor of her success: that she has a nonmeddling "mother-in-law." By mother-in-law, I refer to the government of Zhuhai. Usually an argumentative person, she readily agreed, adding that the Zhuhai government had indeed acted in an extremely laissez faire manner in her case.

There are quite a large number of local SOEs like Gree, each having a powerful leader like Dong Mingzhu. They include Weichai Power in Shandong, Conch Cement in Anhui, and XCMG in Jiangsu. When I attend public events with the senior executives of such companies, I often joke with them by asking whether they would trade places with the CEO of a central government-owned enterprise. The answer is always "Never."

In the case of one to two dozen super-large SOEs of the central government, the top executives are appointed by the central government, and they may be promoted or rotated to a government position at any moment. Therefore, such state enterprises need to pay more attention to central government policies and social responsibilities, such as supporting the Beijing Olympics. But the senior executives' daily responsibility is to make their company competitive in the marketplace. Most of them are very capable. I come across the senior executives of these SOEs often. One occasion was the annual meeting of the World Economic Forum in Davos, Switzerland. Walking out of a closed-door session, the top executive of a top-five world mining company stopped me to ask: "David, please explain to me why that guy from Chinalco (China's largest aluminum firm) is really on top of his business and knows everything, much better than many executives from Western companies. How come?" My answer was that his top priority is profitability, and he was chosen for that when Chinalco was doing very bad financially, although he also has to be watchful of politics.

Another example is ICBC, the world's largest and for many years most profitable commercial bank. Mr. Jiang Jianqing, the former chairman of the board, is the longest-serving commercial banker in China. He comes from southern China and has an extremely sharp mind regarding finance and management. At one point, Mr. Jiang's salary was around 1 million RMB, but it is now limited to 600,000 RMB, which translates to approximately $100,000—a number hardly on par with the importance of Mr. Jiang's job. As in effect a political appointee, he had no choice but to accept this.

TWO SIGNIFICANT SOE REFORMS are under way that will make SOEs function like other companies, moving the Chinese economy closer to a mature market economy. The first reform is to transform most SOEs into mixed-ownership companies with majority shares held by nongovernment entities, greatly reducing the direct influence of the government. Consistent with the first reform, the second reform is for central and local governments to hold investment funds instead of directly managing SOEs. The government-owned investment funds invest in all kinds of individual companies.

These reforms were openly declared by the government. They were first announced in November 2013, when the Central Committee of the Communist Party held its Third Plenary Session, which approved an elaborate document outlining the full economic reform program for the next eight years. Again, in November 2017, the same reforms were affirmed by the Nineteenth Party Congress. The documents state that transitioning to mixed-ownership is the goal—that is, converting many of the existing solely owned SOEs into enterprises with partial private ownership. The other component mentioned is the intention to encourage SOEs to hire senior executives from the marketplace rather than having them appointed by the government.

Why the reforms? A major reason is that with the progress of the market, Chinese governments find it increasingly unnecessary to own SOEs to help solve their problems. Directly purchasing services from nonstate enterprises is becoming a more attractive solution than owning an SOE to provide the same service. One simple example is that many local governments no longer own a fleet of cars or buses—instead, they sign a long-term service contract with a private transportation company. This allows the government to avoid details like the hiring and firing of drivers and provision of their pensions. Another example is the case of dining services in government buildings, which used to be run by the government. Now, most government branches outsource their dining services to private food service companies.

Another reason for SOE reform is international. Xi Jinping is very ambitious, aiming to become one of the world's most progressive leaders. This was demonstrated in his aggressive carbon-reduction goals. More importantly, against the trend of antiglobalization, he has demonstrated that China under his leadership wants to be a leader in globalization. In January 2018, he made such a proclamation in his speech at the annual meeting of the World Economic Forum. To be a leader in globalization, Chinese SOEs have to become like other enterprises competing in the market. Thus, SOEs have to become independent of direct government influence.

Practically, in the future, it is highly conceivable that there will be several TEMASEK-type funds in every city. TEMASEK, an investment fund run by the Singaporean government, is managed almost entirely with open market principles, with the main purpose of making a profit. Local government funds will invest in individual enterprises, so at the grassroots level, it will be difficult to identify which enterprises are state-owned and which are private. All enterprises will have shares owned by the local government. For the city of Beijing, I have specifically proposed that Beijing's municipal government should own three to five large funds. Each fund would invest not only in enterprises with significant government ownership but also in private and foreign enterprises. These funds would compete with each other and would be reported annually to the local People's Congress. To me, this would be an effective way to enhance the efficiency of enterprises while greatly reducing government interference in the overall economy. Most importantly, once these funds are properly managed, the Beijing municipal government's public finances will become more stable. In the event of another global financial crisis, Beijing will be able to use some of its shares to issue bonds in the financial market.

What is the most important piece of evidence that SOE reforms will come to fruition so that nonstate enterprises, including foreign companies, will have easier access to the Chinese market? In November 2020, President Xi Jinping made a formal speech in front of the leaders of APEC (Asian-Pacific Economic Cooperation) countries, including the United States and Japan, stating

that China is willing to join the CPTPP (Comprehensive and Progressive Agreement for Trans-Pacific Partnership). The CPTPP
is a more demanding version of the TPP (Trans-Pacific Partnership) proposed by President Obama. The TPP was designed to
exclude China by essentially disallowing SOEs. Therefore, China's announced desire to join means that substantial reform must
occur so that SOEs will behave in the same way as non-SOEs.
Otherwise, countries like Japan would never give the green light
to China's application to join.

As interesting and unique as SOEs are, the dynamism of the
Chinese economy has not been due to their existence. Rather, this
dynamism stems mostly from China's emerging private enterprises and entrepreneurs, who come from all parts of Chinese
society. Next, we analyze in detail China's private enterprises
and entrepreneurs.

CHAPTER 9

Private
Entrepreneurs:
Heroes or Villains?

Private businesses are the most dynamic forces behind China's economic growth, accounting for over 75 percent of the country's economic output and 90 percent of nongovernment employment. This is why it is essential to understand the workings of private businesses and their creators, private entrepreneurs. In this chapter, I first explain that during the past four decades of rapid growth, the Chinese economy has benefited from several distinct generations of entrepreneurs. Second, Chinese entrepreneurs have to successfully deal with two important issues: They need to overcome two thousand years of prejudice against businessmen and to work closely with the government. Third, although the government has established special institutions for private entrepreneurs to participate in politics, since 2021, it has grown wary of some of the entrepreneurs interfering in politics and policymaking. As a result, the government has waged a so-called campaign against the disorderly expansion of capital. This campaign is expected to ease off before long since Chinese economic growth is critically dependent on active entrepreneurs.

THE ERA OF CHINA'S rapid economic growth, starting in the early 1980s, has seen several generations of private entrepreneurs.

The first generation, about thirty years ago, consisted of poorly educated but extremely competent peasants. For various reasons, these motivated individuals could not receive a formal education or become senior government officials or scholars. This left entre- preneurship as their only remaining option to make money and improve both their material comfort and social standing.

Mr. Cao Mingfang, who was born in a small village not too far from Shanghai in the 1930s, received only a primary school edu- cation. He was the party secretary of the small Communist Party branch in his township. Mr. Cao knew very well that it would be impossible for him to become an important party or government official or a scholar. The only way to establish himself would be to become successful in business, and in the process to generate income for his fellow villagers.

In the mid-1980s, Mr. Cao found a perfect opportunity in China's emerging automobile industry. Automobiles were in extremely short supply in China. In order to stimulate economic growth, up until the 1980s, the Chinese government followed the Stalinist development strategy of investing in heavy industries, including capital goods such as trucks. Unfortunately, the result was that the heavy industries mostly did business with each other rather than serving the real economy as intended. This caused China to experience an acute shortage of consumption goods, ranging from watches to automobiles. One response was that around 1984, Shanghai Automobile Industrial Company (SAIC) and Volkswagen (VW) of Germany formed a joint venture. How- ever, as a prerequisite for entering the Chinese market, the gov- ernment required VW to achieve a sequence of goals pertaining to the percentage of parts produced locally, known as the "local content requirement." The purpose of this policy was to increase Chinese employment and accelerate technology transfer.

Mr. Cao quickly found that providing parts for VW Shanghai was a golden opportunity. At the beginning, VW officials were stumped by the problem of local supply. Mr. Cao was the head of his township-owned enterprise, which at the time was involved in the production of export goods like toys and Christmas candles. In an extremely bold move, Mr. Cao knocked on the door of a Shanghai VW executive without any appointment or introduction and proposed that his enterprise be involved in production. The VW executive regarded Mr. Cao as a lowly peasant and did not take him seriously, politely rejecting him by presenting an apparently impossible task: to come back within thirty days with a model of the bumper for the VW Santana. However, the executive underestimated Mr. Cao, who returned to his village and literally hammered out a model bumper. When Mr. Cao returned to VW, the person who received him had long forgotten about his assignment, that is, until he saw the bumper model. Ultimately, Mr. Cao was awarded a contract to produce fifty thousand bumpers—too small a number to attract any investment in the project. He met his target by cutting costs and borrowing money from banks, and his township enterprise ultimately lost money on the deal. Mr. Cao knew this would happen from the beginning, but he chose to make the deal anyway because he had bigger future deals in mind. Indeed, Mr. Cao's company grew into Jiangnan Mould & Plastic Technology Co., LTD, which has developed into the major supplier for not only VW, but also BMW, GM, and Mercedes Benz. The company is even expanding internationally into Mexico to produce bumpers for BMW's Mexican plant.

Mr. Cao has a motto for his son and his whole company: "Work a little bit harder than everyone else, don't fear hardship, and don't fear short run losses." After rising to success, Mr. Cao realized the importance of education and sent his eighteen-year-old son, Robert, to live with his business partner in a small town in Germany. Initially, Robert spoke nothing but Chinese, but he returned to China speaking fluent German. However, Mr. Cao realized that Robert could not successfully function in China with only German business experience and knowledge, so he sent Robert to the business school at Tsinghua University in Beijing. This enabled him not only to receive China's foremost business education, but also to accumulate social connections through his classmates and faculty members. Robert is now the CEO of the family-owned company, which is listed on the Shanghai Stock Exchange. I have known Robert for many years now, and he has introduced me to a number of German business executives who wish to learn about the Chinese economy. As a result of his well-rounded education, Robert has been able to help his family expand its business into wind-power equipment production, hospitals, and equipment leasing. Robert, who was born and raised in China and college-educated in Germany, is now a rare crossbreed of the two cultures. He established the Dusseldorf China Center, an exchange hub for economic, cultural, political, athletic, and media cooperation between China and Germany. In March 2013, President Xi Jinping even visited the center (I was also there as a member of the Sino-German Economic Advisory Council). At no small cost, Robert arranged to have meals delivered to the Chinese delegation after the official banquet, as Chinese officials and businessmen often feel ill when they do not eat a Chinese meal for a few days. In China, people often say that good relationships start with a good meal, so Robert was very wise to provide this much-needed service. He has become a trusted partner of many government agencies.

The second generation of entrepreneurs consisted of former government employees—some being retired soldiers or junior military officials—who were highly disciplined and had beneficial business connections. In the mid-1990s, as the saying goes, a wave of government officials took the "leap into the ocean," quitting their government jobs and entering the business world. In over 90 percent of the cases, the husband leapt while his wife "stayed dry," keeping her government job as backup.

A prominent figure in this generation is Wang Jianlin, the chairman of Dalian Wanda Group, which has become one of the world's largest property developers and owns the world's largest cinema chain operator (including AMC Entertainment). Mr. Wang used to be known as the "Bill Gates of China," boasting the nation's highest personal net worth of over $20 billion for a few years in the mid-2010s. As a developer, Dalian Wanda Group was highly profitable and is already listed on the global Fortune 500 list, easily overshadowing the Trump Organization by more than one hundred times.

Two main factors in Mr. Wang's background have helped him achieve this enormous success. First, Mr. Wang joined the army in 1970, when he was sixteen. This was considered a privilege at the time, since it exempted him from laboring as a peasant. Undergoing military training at such a young age shaped him into a person of discipline, adopting the succinct and precise speech so often seen in people with military backgrounds in China. In fact, I have appeared on television discussion panels with Wang Jianlin on a number of occasions, and I was very impressed by his ability to get to the point quickly (which TV moderators love) thanks to his military training.

The other key factor in Wang Jianlin's background is that he was the director of the office of the mayor in a district of the city of Dalian, a beautiful coastal city in China with Russian influence. The director of the mayor's office must be socially adept, as the position requires serving as a liaison between many other departments of the government as well as a wide spectrum of society. A useful skill is to be able to drink, because drinking with friends at business functions relaxes the atmosphere and enhances the prospects for closing deals. Indeed, in China, liquor serves as a lubricant in business. Sitting at a banquet table, a person seeking a business or personal relationship should propose a drink to the hoped-for friend. This practice is called "respect liquor" (Jing Jiu), and it is impolite for the receiving party to refuse. If both sides eventually get drunk, the relationship is sealed or at least enhanced. Being able to propose "respect liquor" and still remain physically functional is an important skill in the business environment. Wang Jianlin's time in the mayor's office undoubt-edly trained him not only to hold his liquor but also to cultivate strong business relationships and serve as a bridge across sectors.

The second generation of entrepreneurs built a bridge between two backgrounds and environments: government and the emerg-ing business world. A key to their business success was possessing the skills required to deal with the government, often aided by the discipline acquired through their military or government back-grounds. In addition, this generation was also defined by their technological or entrepreneurial sense. They represent a transi-tional group—in the future, we will not see many of their kind because the second generation emerged at a stage when the Chi-nese economy was half-market, half-government. Considering that the Chinese government was gradually loosening control of the economy during the height of the second generation, they fit perfectly into this transitional stage.

The third generation of entrepreneurs emerged in the late 1990s, consisting mainly of young people who were educated abroad or acutely knowledgeable about the West. That was the honeymoon period between China and the West. Many of these entrepreneurs were educated in America. One example is Charles Zhang, the founder of Sohu.com, who started as a bright Tsing-hua University student majoring in physics, one of the most pop-ular majors at that time. During his undergraduate days, Charles was already displaying qualities that made him stand out from his classmates. For example, he would go swimming in the icy open-air swimming pool during the winter to enhance his ability to resist cold and to demonstrate his strength and fortitude.

After graduation, Mr. Zhang was admitted to the PhD pro-gram in physics at MIT. The most sought-after goal among Chi-nese graduates in the 1980s was to go to the United States and pursue a PhD, and at that time, MIT was regarded in China as the American Tsinghua. (However, a foreign guest making this refer-ence today would surely offend the president of Tsinghua, who is seeking to make Tsinghua the Harvard-plus-MIT of China.) Once in America, Charles quickly realized that academics may not offer the same influence or fame as the business sector. Thus, when he returned to China, Charles followed the example of Yahoo.com and established his own portal website called Sohu.com, which is now a top portal in China. His US experience and education clearly proved beneficial in his business ventures.

I was not at all surprised to witness Charles's success, as we were both at Tsinghua and Cambridge, Massachusetts, at the same time, and he has always been effortlessly cool. During weekend parties at MIT, Charles displayed the best dance moves among the Chinese students. He also once appeared on a dating show on Chinese Central TV, demonstrating his roller-skating skills, among other talents. After his resounding success with Sohu.com, Charles decided to shun business and social events for a few years, instead studying philosophy and religion. After a few years as a recluse, he returned to the public scene, teaching quantum physics on the internet, staying young and staying cool—a goal of many entrepreneurs. In the spirit of staying young and staying cool, in many respects Charles Zhang is not too different from Steve Jobs. However, in Chinese culture, such unusually talented people often have a much harder time becoming truly influential since they are often regarded with suspicion.

Jack Ma, the founder of Alibaba.com, also belongs to the third generation of entrepreneurs but appears to be Charles Zhang's opposite. Ma's path to success proved to be very rocky. In fact, it took him three attempts to pass the college entrance examination, and his embarrassingly low score in mathematics is still widely discussed today. Ma may not realize that this difficulty was partially influenced by his family background, as his parents are professional opera performers, and arts and math are not easily integrated into Chinese education. If Jack were in the United States, he would have been admitted by an elite college on his unique talents, without considering mathematics, and would have started his business career in college. But in China, he faced the formidable obstacle of the college entrance exam, which serves as the gatekeeper for all opportunities in higher education. Furthermore, forgoing college was not an option, as a young person in 1980s China who did not attend college would have been laughed out of any professional environment. After his third attempt at the exam, Ma was eventually able to attend a small college in China, which at that time was approximately equivalent to a community college in the United States, but now is very famous, partly because of Jack Ma.

All the while, Ma kept an eye on ideas and trends from abroad. He worked hard to develop his English language skills, taking opportunities to speak with foreign tourists in his hometown, and was among the few Chinese business figures to recognize the importance of the internet early on. Ma initially wanted to replace the Chinese Yellow Book with his portal but later realized that there was a great need to establish a network linking Chinese producers with US wholesalers. He ultimately realized that he could establish an online superstore in which individual retailers could operate. Thus, Alibaba was born, which in China set up a website, Taobao.com. Alibaba serves as a platform for individual businesses in which capital is provided and risks are assumed by individual store owners rather than by the host company, which only charges fees for listing on the website. This endeavor has made Jack Ma into one of the richest and most influential business leaders in China. I come across him quite frequently, mostly when giving talks to an audience. I readily confess that it is a nightmare to speak either before or after him. He is the most argumentative, hilarious, and incendiary speaker I have ever known of.

In all of these entrepreneurs' experiences, learning from the West, and from the United States in particular, proved to be a key element in their success. Of course, they were often able to innovate and go beyond the business models they observed abroad, building something new and uniquely suitable for the Chinese market. For example, the business of bicycles for rent originated in Chinese cities because the business model requires high population density and ubiquitous coverage of cell phone signals.

CHINESE ENTREPRENEURS HAVE HAD to fight social prejudice more than the American tycoons of the early 1900s. The reason is that Confucian values place businessmen among society's lowest classes. In many ancient civilizations around the world, merchants and businesspeople were not held in high esteem within the social hierarchy. In fact, most were subjected to severe discrimination, as in Shakespeare's *The Merchant of Venice*. This attitude was particularly prevalent in China, where Confucianism designated the king and his relatives as the highest class, followed by government officials, scholars, and peasants. Artisans and merchants were ranked the lowest. Even today, this tradition remains deeply embedded in peoples' psyches. This could explain why many private entrepreneurs, after becoming successful, seek to establish close relationships with academics.

When Mr. Wang Shi, one of the most successful real estate developers in China, was in his sixties, he spent two years at Harvard University attending classes, getting acquainted with professors, and simply enjoying spending time around academics. He took great pride in this experience and still loves to participate in university events. In this regard, Mr. Wang Shi is not alone. When I was engaging in fund-raising for the Schwarzman Scholars program at Tsinghua University, I encountered an extremely generous potential donor. Money was not an issue as long as he could be granted the title of professor. This request was rejected by Tsinghua, an elite university that values its academic reputation. However, not all universities in China are so principled, and some may grant such a request.

For Chinese entrepreneurs, an even more difficult problem than overcoming social prejudice is discerning how to work with the government and navigate politics in general. Since the founding of modern China, the government has had control over many key decisions in the business world, as previously discussed. In the chapter about local government, I explained that local government officials are like the CEOs of the holding company of the region. Therefore, private entrepreneurs must interact closely with local government as well as other government agencies.

The Wanda group provides a good illustration of how important it is to work with the government. For example, when you travel through most capital cities of Chinese provinces, you will likely find similarly designed structures composed of shopping malls, office buildings, hotels, and high-end residential compounds. These complexes are all called Wanda Plaza or Wanda Center, developed by the above-mentioned Dalian Wanda Group. The Wanda Center typically sits in the new center of a city (in China, many cities have built new city centers) and a good distance from the old city. Like the UN building in New York, the centers resemble a matchbox with several buildings thirty to forty stories high. They are usually light brown in color, in a modern style, and anchored by a five-star hotel—sometimes a Sofitel, sometimes a Marriott. They usually include an upscale store like Saks Fifth Avenue, an office building, a complex of high-end condos, and a cinema (after all, Wanda owns AMC theaters).

The key to Wanda's success has been its ability to negotiate with local governments better than many other entrepreneurs. Take the example of the city of Baotou, known as China's capital of rare earth metals. Rare earth metals are a type of refined material that can be blended into steel to create powerful magnets, which are an extremely important component of most high-tech products. By 2013, the city of Baotou realized that it needed to have a diversified economy rather than relying mostly upon rare earth elements. Wanda offered to help the city diversify. The company built a business complex in Baotou to help attract non-rare-earth firms. This was possible because a Wanda complex is known to raise the stature of any city. Wanda promised that within eighteen months, with Wanda's experience and expertise, it could build a huge complex comparable to two blocks of Manhattan office space and hotels. The city government, eager to promote local GDP growth, granted Wanda a piece of land at the center of the city. Of course, this land was already occupied, so the government compensated the existing occupants and found other places for them to live, and then turned the land over to Wanda. Wanda delivered on its promise, and the Wanda Plaza is now a landmark in Baotou.

In contrast to this process, when real estate entrepreneurs like Donald Trump want to develop a piece of land, they must deal with the local zoning board. However, an even more imposing obstacle may come from negotiating with existing landowners. Developing a two-block business complex within eighteen months would never be possible in the United States. This example reinforces the point that in order for Wanda to succeed, it is imperative for it to work closely with the government.

Such a business model would not work outside China. While attending the World Economic Forum in Davos, I occasionally come across Wang Jianlin. Frustrated by the small, crowded hotels in Switzerland, he considered building his own hotel, with the main purpose of providing him and other participants a good hotel to stay at when attending the WEF. Unfortunately for Wanda, the process did not move as smoothly in Davos as it does in China, as the Davos local government does not have the same amount of authority to coordinate with local residents.

A much less fortunate example than Wanda is that of Dai Guo-fang. Mr. Dai, an outstanding entrepreneur, began his career as a poor mason. By 2004 he had earned a place on the list of the four hundred richest Chinese entrepreneurs. Mr. Dai sought to realize his dream of becoming the Chinese version of Andrew Carnegie by building a huge iron and steel complex in the coastal province of Jiangsu. However, with his masonry background, he did not understand how harsh the government's macroeconomic policies could be. This lack of knowledge and attention proved to be disastrous.

In the middle of 2003, Mr. Dai embarked on his dream of building one of the world's largest single steel mills, which quickly ended in disaster and sent him to prison. Mr. Dai's dream project ran directly against the central government ban on new iron and steel, since China was facing the problem of overproduction. The Chinese central government worried that if investments in steel plants were to continue, steel supply in the marketplace would far outpace demand. Meanwhile, antidumping lawsuits had been filed against Chinese exporters in the United States and Europe. Under these conditions, there would be a domestic decline in the price of steel, and many loans rendered to these enterprises would default, creating a serious economic problem. Usually, when the central government issues a policy, some people act contrary to its edicts because they believe that the government is incapable of controlling the trend. In response, the central government apprehends a few high-profile offenders to exert its authority and emphasize that it is still in control. Before the Chinese New Year on January 22, 2004, the central government sent eight groups of investigators to various locations to halt investments in steel, aluminum, and cement. By April, they arrived in Changzhou, and Mr. Dai's enterprise fell victim. The investigators shut down the project on the spot, and major investors, including Mr. Dai, were placed under house arrest. After a brief trial, Mr. Dai was imprisoned for counterfeiting sales bills and evading taxes.

On becoming successful, private entrepreneurs everywhere in the world tend to develop strong opinions and oftentimes desire to participate in politics. The United States has plenty of examples: Andrew Carnegie, Ross Perot, Mitt Romney, and Donald Trump. In China, there is also no dearth of private entrepreneurs who wish to express their opinions through participation in politics.

That entrepreneurs often have a strong urge to join politics

PRIVATE ENTREPRENEURS: HEROES OR VILLAINS? 135

is well understood by the Chinese Communist Party, which has established special institutions to accommodate this. Moreover, as mentioned previously, Party Secretary Jiang Zemin reformed the party's charter to encourage entrepreneurs to join the party. In addition, each level of the party committee has a Department of United Front Work serving as a liaison between the party and influential individuals outside the party, including private business owners. Private entrepreneurs also have their own organization, the All-China Federation of Industry and Commerce (ACFIC). The leadership of this federation is selected through close coordination between private entrepreneurs and the Communist Party. There are also provincial and city-level ACFICs. At each level (central, provincial, and municipal), top leaders in the federation are recommended by the Chinese Communist Party to become delegates to the National People's Congress or members of the Chinese People's Political Consultative Conference (CPPCC)— China's national legislature and political advisory body, respectively. In addition, several times a year, leaders of the Communist Party at each level hold consultation meetings with leaders of the ACFIC. At such meetings, the private entrepreneurs are not as confrontational or direct in their speeches as, for instance, members of the British Parliament.

Nowadays, most successful private entrepreneurs in China hold some kind of political position. A leadership position in the ACFIC is one channel, while another is a senior position in one of the nine political parties approved by the Communist Party. As explained above, such positions are usually an important means to create close ties with the government. At the same time, any entrepreneur who has succeeded in business is actively sought out by the Communist Party to become active in these formal channels.

In all countries, entrepreneurs trying to enter the political realm must follow certain rules, and interfering in politics by violating these rules is not welcome. China is not an exception. In the United States, when Donald Trump became president, he had to step aside from managing his businesses. Before that, when making donations to his favorite politicians, he had to follow relevant laws.

In China, the government encourages private entrepreneurs to join politics through the established institutions, but they are very much prohibited from interfering in politics. The most severely punished behavior is interference in the appointment or promotion of a government official.

Mr. Huang Guangyu, founder of Guomei, China's largest home appliance seller, similar to Best Buy in the United States, ended up in prison for seven years as a result of allegedly having tried to help a senior official of the city of Beijing to get a promotion in exchange for business favors. Mr. Huang grew up in a small fishing village in the coastal province of Fujian, and he did not seem to have any interest or ambition in politics. Rather, he just wanted to grow his business as quickly as possible. In his home electronics business, Huang needed land for warehouses and logistics infrastructure. Even though land was essentially given to him free of charge because his business could generate revenue for the city, relocating the incumbent residents is always costly. Mr. Huang was alleged to have gotten help from a senior official in the city of Beijing so that he could aggressively evict people from the land. In exchange, Mr. Huang was believed to have helped the senior official bribe other officials for promotion.

As we've seen in the previous examples, the relationship between entrepreneurs and politics in China can be tricky to navigate. Of all the private entrepreneurs in China, Wang Jianlin might have the most valuable insight into this relationship. In 2014, Wang came to Tsinghua University and delivered a remarkable speech, saying that to do business in China, get close to the government, but stay away from politics. What a perceptive point!

BEGINNING IN LATE 2020, the Chinese government started a campaign to control monopolies of internet platforms and the disorderly expansion of capital. Internet platform companies such as Alibaba (retail), Baidu (search engine), JD.com (retail), and Tencent (social network and games) were fined for behavior such as forbidding suppliers from working with other platforms and for not properly reporting merger and acquisition deals in the past. Moreover, internet platform companies were placed under government restrictions when expanding into banking and media businesses. This campaign was costly for the internet platform companies—by mid-2022, on average, the market value of each of these companies decreased by around 50 percent. As a result, China's unicorn companies (highly valued start-up companies destined for listing on the stock market) greatly shrank in number and value, since the platform companies are usually major investors in the unicorns. Before the campaign, China easily had twenty of the world's top one hundred unicorns. After the campaign, the number shrunk to less than five.

What is the fundamental goal of the campaign to control monopolies and the disorderly expansion of capital? It is not simply economics. Many believe that the government is worried that the extensive and expanding influence of the internet platform companies will erode the government's control of social and political affairs.

Many believe the government is wary about the big tech platform, and they cite the case of Jack Ma and Alibaba to support their views. The huge influence of Alibaba has made Jack Ma an iconic hero among the young Chinese. Each year, Jack would organize a huge rally in a stadium, in which he would come out wearing a cool outfit or sporting a tai chi move much like Michael Jackson in his live music and dance shows. He would give bombastic speeches stating, for example, that if the inefficient banking industry refused to change, his internet company would change it. In a stunning speech given in November 2020, he announced that his financial platform Ant Finance would do exactly that, having lined up almost all the important investors to support him. His speech came one week before the IPO of Ant Finance. The government immediately suspended the IPO. It is unclear whether Jack Ma's passionate speech caused the government to cancel the IPO, or whether he was already aware of the decision and took the opportunity to vent his anger through his speech. Either way, this example shows Jack's audacity in China. In fact, four years before that, in late 2016, Jack flew to New York City and had meetings and took photos with president-elect Trump, promising to create two million new jobs for the United States through Alibaba, a move beyond any plan or imagination of any top government official!

It seems that China and the United States are remarkably similar in worrying that internet platforms and their founders, like Jack Ma and Mark Zuckerberg, have too much influence in politics and society. While many men and women in the US Congress and politicians are currently deliberating about how to best set up new regulations and laws to resolve the issue, China's approach has been to first rein in the influence of big names in tech, and then, once they are in the domain of the government, to settle on new policies via rounds of debate. The Chinese approach is much more precautionary than the US one, for better or for worse.

Does this mean the end of the dynamism in Chinese internet industries, and more broadly, the whole community of private entrepreneurs? Many inside and outside China seem to hold this view. I disagree. Since the policy wave of reining in the internet platforms, I have been arguing that the internet and private entrepreneurship are essential for a healthy and dynamic Chinese economy, without which the Chinese government will not be able to accomplish its grand goal of national revival. Currently, the Chinese government is playing it safe. After carefully watching the US and European experiences when it comes to regulating internet platforms, the Chinese government will likely issue specific regulations and loosen up its currently tight control on these companies. Indeed, by early 2023, the Chinese central government began to issue policies to encourage internet companies to grow faster.

In these three chapters about the Chinese economy, I have tried to paint a general picture of how the Chinese economy works. That is, private enterprises and private entrepreneurs have been the primary driving force for the economy's dynamism, while SOEs exist mainly for historical reasons and have been through extensive reforms. More importantly, Chinese local governments and many central government branches function as helping hands for the market economy by trying to remove obstacles to the market. In contrast, in most Western countries, governments are much less active in helping the market economy except in the event of a grave crisis.

Next, we move on to discuss Chinese society, in which the economy is embedded. Many aspects of society, such as education and population, are closely related to the economy.

CHAPTER 10

Education

EDUCATION IS PERHAPS THE SINGLE MOST REVEAL-ing window to gain an inside look and deeper understanding of Chinese culture and society. Indeed, the state of education provides clues as to a society's future trajectory of development. In this chapter, I first explain why many, if not most, Chinese families have a religious enthusiasm and anxiety about the education of their children. Meanwhile, exams stand at the center stage of the Chinese education system, aggravating the anxiety of the students and parents. Although major reforms are likely to be implemented in China's education system, it is probable that the system will continue producing a huge contingent of highly disciplined and skilled laborers. At the same time, highly creative talents will have to be imported from outside or cultivated with international collaboration.

TO MANY WESTERNERS, Chinese parents seem to have an incredible craze for their children's education. In fact, the number one priority and anxiety of most middle-income parents is their children's school performance. Until recently, on any given weekend, you would find a very crowded scene at the site of any after-school tutoring center or "cram school." The business of after-school tutoring was easily the most prosperous among all service businesses in China. Building after building in cities across the country forced out tenants like restaurants, bakeries, or stores to accommodate tutoring centers. Economics works here: The tutoring centers were able to pay higher rent than all other businesses, including popular restaurants. This situation got the attention of China's top decision makers, and so in early 2021, a stern ban was issued on after-school tutoring, causing tutoring businesses to stall suddenly. However, it is widely believed that underground one-on-one tutoring has taken over.

Why are Chinese parents so crazy about their children's education? The reason for this is deeply rooted in Confucian doctrine: parents and children are bonded for life. I often joke that in Western countries, children are limited subsidiaries of their parent companies, becoming spin-offs when they reach independence at age eighteen to twenty. In contrast, Chinese kids are lifetime unlimited subsidiaries of their parents, never spinning off from their parents' balance sheets. Practically, this means that a successful child is obliged to take care of their parents and grandparents when the parents and grandparents grow older. This is why many Chinese parents believe that their children's education is the most important investment a family can make to ensure long-term prosperity. Poor families know this even better, since a well-educated child will lift up the whole family economically and socially. Such beliefs are even reflected in the goals of local governments.

Responding to the concerns for education of local residents, local government officials also take education as one of their key performance indicators. When welcoming a visitor, the mayor of a city may report on the performance of local students in recent years pertaining to their admission rate to either Tsinghua or Peking University. It is almost like the mayor of Detroit, Michigan, talking about how well the local professional sports team has been doing in recent seasons.

With almost all parents extremely anxious about making investments in their children's schooling, education has inevitably become a "tournament" with exams as the key battleground. Exams are almost the sole determinant used to sort out students for admissions to schools of the next level. This is well under-stood by Chinese parents and schools. The mother of all exams is the set of college entrance exams called the *gaokao*. For three and sometimes four straight days in early June each year, over ten million students in China sit for this exam to determine their future. As almost the sole criterion for entry into most Chinese universities, the exams are extremely high-stakes. In many ways, the *gaokao* is treated as the most important exam of a person's life.[1]

China's college entrance exams are perhaps the most rigorously organized exams in the world. A few days before the exams, the exam papers are guarded as closely as bankers guard their cash, and satellite tracking is employed to monitor the movement of each box of the exam papers. Occasionally, news surfaces that the contents of the exams were leaked by accident. Whenever this happens, it becomes a nationwide scandal because exams are considered the most sacred and equitable form of competition in China. New exams will be given in such cases. Before the test, all who were involved in designing the exam questions are secluded in a hotel until the exams conclude. After the exam, a large con-tingent of graders, numbered in the tens of thousands, are also secluded while doing the grading. All answer sheets are supposed to be anonymous. Any answer sheets with a possibility of disclos-ing the identity of the student would be voided.

The primacy of exams in China stems from a long historical tradition. For over 1,400 years, China has maintained a history of using written examinations for selecting civil servants. The earliest exams covered literature, history, and nonfiction writing, sometimes concluding with finalists being interviewed by the emperor. Today, some historians praise such a system as merito-cratic, as the exams gave any bright and hardworking youngster the chance to become a government official up to the level of the

---

1 For sports or arts talents, Chinese universities require a minimum score of the gaokao. However, there are exams for such talents.

prime minister. Others criticized this exam system for channeling most young talents to serve the emperor rather than pursuing independent academic research and therefore causing China to lag behind the West in science and technology for most of the past five hundred years.

In the Chinese education system, schools and teachers are also evaluated based on the exam grades of their students. Starting in primary school, each class, typically numbering thirty to fifty students, is assigned a director, the teacher who usually provides instruction in Chinese, math, or occasionally, English. The director is evaluated mainly on the test performance of their class, and thus they typically pay particular attention to top students who are doing well on their class exams and are projected to succeed on the college entrance exams or exams for high school admissions. Therefore, starting at a very young age, children are often subjected to intellectual discrimination: Those who mature early and demonstrate impressive cognitive skills are favored and are often appointed as the leader of the class or head of a subject (such as math); lower-achieving students are often teased and ostracized by schoolmates or even teachers, since usually these students need the teachers' extra efforts to improve grades and the teachers would rather help the high achievers. The situation is similar to that in a sports team, in which the coach favors the stars and the supporting cast are not treated as well as the stars.

In China, the pressure of the college entrance examinations is felt mainly by students from the countryside. For them, a college degree is the only path to a white-collar job, allowing them to escape the fate of becoming a migrant worker in a big city. In recent years, there has been an emergence of "super schools" in China that essentially "lock up" their students, putting them through drill after drill and treating them almost like medieval monks. These schools are not expensive in comparison with many private (often called international) schools but are selective and tend to enroll hardworking students. The students become machines programmed to succeed on exams. This process does indeed help students excel on the exams, and the exercise questions used during the test preparation drills have become a sort of Bible for all students in China. As a result, books on test preparation are in great demand.

One such school is in the city of Hengshui in Hebei province, neighboring Beijing. The school is known for its boarding system in which students are required to go to bed at 10 p.m. and wake up at 6 a.m. for exercise. The entire day is spent in classrooms, memorizing facts and undergoing repetitive exam drills. No weekends! No mobile phones! (Except for one day a month.) Students from Hengshui High School consistently produce the highest average test scores in the province, and the champion of the Hebei college entrance exam often comes from Hengshui. Each province has high schools like Hengshui, which are popular for economically disadvantaged students. At one school, the principal holds a ceremony thirty days before the college entrance exams to boost the morale of the students. He has the students line up and then rides past them in a World War II–style Jeep. Standing in the back seat, he waves to the students as if in a military parade. The students shout "Hooah!" and other military-style slogans. Indeed, for poor kids, the college exam is akin to war because it determines their fate.

In contrast, elite schools in large cities, especially provincial capitals, do not often produce the champions of the college entrance exam. Instead, they take pride in preparing students to attend overseas universities such as those in the Ivy League in the United States.

As one may have guessed, top scorers on the exams may not actually be the best students. Chinese leading universities like Tsinghua and Peking University provide good illustrations of this, as they attract the provincial champions of the college entrance examinations. After excelling on the national college entrance examination, some of these students continue to succeed, but there are many cases in which the exam champions flunk out after one year due to poor academic performance. This is because unlike in high school, there are no teachers or tutors to push them with drills. In 2010, I came across a student from Peking University wishing to apply to my university's PhD program. He later failed to be admitted because of a lack of academic potential. But I learned that he had been a college entrance examination "champion" and entered Peking University, only to flunk out because he played too many computer games. One year later, he retook the entrance exam, and again he achieved splendid scores, forcing Peking University to readmit him, as the admissions system only relies on the total score of all exams. This story illustrates that there are special talents in achieving high scores in the Chinese education system, but such talents may not be the same as academic excellence.

Another reason for the decline of top test performers after entering college is that they have studied too hard preparing for the entrance exams and are simply burned out upon entering college. The Chinese society has yet to pay due attention to the phenomenon of burned-out students. My wife teaches a compulsory course in biology for undergraduates, and each year, among the 250 students in her class, there are always a dozen students who simply refuse to show up for classes or exams. Such students have lost interest in studying and chosen to stay in their dormitories. In such cases, their parents usually would plead for mercy by going after the professor or the student coordinator of the academic school to let their kid pass exams—recall that I explained how Chinese children are unlimited lifetime subsidiaries of their parents.

Virtually everyone in China is an expert when it comes to criticizing the ensuing problems of the exam-centered education system. Why not reform away the exams and follow the US college admissions system, for example? The answer is very simple: Any alternatives will likely involve massive cheating and are much worse and less fair. Imagine that instead of written exams, China utilized only recommendation letters and interviews to determine college admissions. Then, personal connections would be prominently involved, and, because economically disadvantaged students lack those connections, they would be greatly disadvantaged. In this regard, I have always found it miraculous that the US system of college admissions is mostly devoid of large-scale cases of corruption. It relies principally on grades, but reference letters and interviews, which are subject to many types of possible manipulation and interference, are also important. Yet, in the United States in 2019 there were news reports alleging that some actresses had falsified credentials so that their kids could get into their desired colleges. I am surprised that these cases are seemingly rare, but they still cause a great stir in the national news when they are uncovered.

Problems with the education system have long been focused on in Chinese society and therefore, various reforms have been implemented. One strand of reform is to dilute the importance of exams. For example, about one hundred prominent high schools have been chosen to let their principals each recommend a dozen students to top Chinese universities. The list of the recommended students is published on the internet in order to be scrutinized by the general public. In order not to be alleged to have been nepotistic, the principals usually choose students who are well-rounded and have consistently great grades, rather than controversial genius. The latest reform came in March 2021. The Chinese central government issued an urgent and sweeping policy, which was widely guessed to be requested by the office of China's top leadership, to resolve the problem of too much outside-class tutoring among primary and high school students. As a result, out of the blue, all the formerly extremely busy and profitable tutoring services were banned. Many such agencies are listed companies in New York, and their share prices drastically declined. Hundreds of thousands of teachers in the tutoring industry lost their jobs.

Of course, many of them switched to private sessions with individual families on the side. Such a reform was no doubt meant well. However, the long-term impact has yet to be observed and analyzed. Many claim that after the reform, students from high-income families have benefited since tutoring became much more expensive than before. The root problem is the college entrance exam system, which still prompts students and parents to seek tutoring services.

Perhaps the biggest impact on the Chinese education system has come from openness to the world. Many Chinese primary schools in large cities, as well as high schools all over China, participate in foreign exchange programs. Through these exchanges, Chinese schools and students increasingly understand that education is more than exams and there are many more things to learn about than just academics. For example, in my daughter's primary school, many of her classmates had opportunities to visit countries such as Australia, South Korea, the United States, and the UK. Two of her teachers also spent a year in Australia teaching Chinese. In addition, they have had foreign students visit their classes for as long as several weeks. At the college level, Tsinghua University conducts a program that allows undergraduate students to spend one semester in a foreign country, mostly in the United States or Europe. About a third of the students in the School of Economics and Management have taken advantage of these opportunities. In my undergraduate class, which is a required course that I teach in English, out of three hundred students, usually about thirty are exchange students from the United States, Europe, South Korea, and Japan, among other countries.

The increasing openness of the Chinese education system has provided a stimulus for reform, much to the benefit of students. Schools have begun to introduce new curricula such as critical and moral thinking and to pay more attention to writing and in-class presentations in addition to written exams as requirements of teaching. One of my former PhD students is a good illustration. Her home is in a small city in southern China. She attended the International Program of Economics and Law at Nankai University, which is near Beijing and is one of China's elite universities. Many courses in her program were comparable to those in the West. After leaving the program, she came to Tsinghua, where she worked diligently as a student and earned financial support from the government to spend a year at MIT, whose economics program is one of the best in the world. That one year at MIT helped her tremendously, improving her English language proficiency, and more importantly, expanding her perspectives. After returning to China, she worked as an intern at the World Bank, and following her graduation from Tsinghua, she earned a coveted position with the Economist Program of the International Monetary Fund. The program usually only recruits graduates from top US and UK PhD programs. She was one of the first graduates accepted from a PhD program in China. Her example provides evidence that opening up to the world education system is substantially transforming the capabilities and proficiencies of Chinese students. This gives me confidence that China's educational system will gradually become capable of regularly producing students who are prepared to succeed in international settings, especially students from China's elite programs.

THERE ARE MANY IMPLICATIONS of the Chinese education system for the future of China. The first one is relatively lighthearted. Because the future of students is determined by exams, parents usually do not allow their children enough time to play sports unless their kid can become a professional player. Thus, China does well in sports where talents can be easily identified early on. For example, children who become very tall at a young age are persuaded to specialize in basketball or volleyball. Yao Ming, the basketball star, is one example of this. In the sport of diving, China has been very competitive. This is because the potential for talent can be identified at a young age through various measures like bone size. Once identified as a candidate for athletic success, these kids bypass academics and concentrate on training for their respective sports. Once they are successful, the whole family gets lifted up economically. However, there are sports where talent is latent and takes years of competition to reveal. One of the greatest illustrations of this phenomenon in Chinese sports is soccer. In soccer, unlike diving or basketball, future stars are very difficult to identify at a young age. To a parent, letting their kids play soccer is a lousy investment, as the return is too low in comparison to academic work at school. No wonder the Chinese national soccer team performs so badly in international competitions! The potential future soccer stars are forced to study for their exams, which are a more reliable path to a successful future. I often joke that in China, those beer-bellied middle-aged men watching TV broadcasts of Chinese soccer and then complaining bitterly about the performance of the national soccer team should blame themselves, since they would not allow their school-aged kids to play soccer at the cost of academics. Facing the shortage of domestic stars, the Chinese professional soccer league has been very successful in acquiring the best soccer players from foreign countries, often offering the world's highest salary.

On the more serious side, the Chinese education system is adept at producing a large quantity of highly disciplined and well-trained laborers and knowledge workers such as mobile phone assemblers and computer programmers. For subjects such as math and physics, Chinese primary schools, high schools, and universities subject students to drill after drill. As a result, Chinese students are among the world's top achievers when it comes to these subjects. According to the mother of the US-born Chinese Olympian superstar in free skiing, gold medalist Eileen Gu, just ten days of summer training in a Chinese math tutoring program would keep Eileen at the top of her math class in the US high school for the ensuing academic year. The Organization for Economic Cooperation and Development (OECD), an international agency based in Paris, has conducted several rounds of universal tests for high school students in Europe, the United States, China, and beyond. In such tests, Chinese students outperform their peers from other countries by far. There is also another study comparing US workers on the factory floor with their counterparts in China, which found that the Chinese workers are much more skilled at reading and understanding machine manuals than US workers. To me, this is not surprising at all. As a result, China will maintain the advantage of a huge pool of well-trained and highly disciplined laborers.

However, there is certainly a downside to the Chinese education system. It is not the most effective in nurturing young students with raw talent into geniuses. At least, the Chinese system is not producing such individuals in a large quantity. Many geniuses like Edison, Einstein, Bill Gates, and Steve Jobs have a unique type of intelligence that is not well measured by traditional metrics of academic success. In fact, by such standards they may be completely overlooked! In the Chinese education system, such young talents often cannot survive. They are often scolded by teachers, laughed at by peers, or even discouraged by their parents. The Chinese education system rewards students who succeed based on a rigid academic rubric early on, while a good education system often places tolerance for errors and individual character as top priorities, giving students room to learn from their mistakes and thus fostering creativity. From this perspective, it will take some time for China to be truly a world leader in groundbreaking scientific research, as this requires a good number of geniuses.

Another implication of the Chinese education system is that China will face a shortage of graduates with international skills. The Chinese education system does not encourage students to express and argue for their views as much as those in the United States or India. Rather, Chinese students are mostly rewarded for perfecting the skills taught by their teachers, and therefore it is common for Chinese students and young professionals to appear submissive and passive. This is regarded as a merit in Chinese culture for a student or young person. However, in international conferences, multilateral organizations, and multinational corporations, this is a drawback. In these contexts, a young professional is encouraged to respectfully dissent and to express their own ideas. As a result, China faces a shortage of talents who are trained to speak up and play a leadership role outside of China. This is almost the opposite of the Indian situation. Increasingly, many multinational companies and international organizations have top executives born and educated in India, while this has not been the case for Chinese businesspeople.

From my illustrations and analysis above, it is obvious that education is an intense and hot topic in Chinese society, on the level of racial or gender equity and associated policies in the United States, on which everyone has an opinion and tangible interest. Another socially important topic is media and the internet, to which I turn in the coming chapter.

CHAPTER 11

The Media and
the Internet

PERHAPS THE BIGGEST MISPERCEPTION THAT OUT-
siders have about China is that Chinese media and the
Chinese internet are wastelands of boring content, given that
Facebook and Google are blocked in China. On the contrary, the
Chinese internet ecosystem is a buzzing marketplace of 1.3 billion internet users exchanging ideas, creating content, and buying
products. It is a universe of its own. Every day the Chinese internet gives rise to a number of new hot topics, viral videos, or slang
terms. Even my ninety-eight-year-old mother is glued to WeChat
(a chat program, social media app, and payment platform all in
one). Meanwhile, Douyin (the Chinese version of Tik Tok) is wildly
popular for memes, exchanging ideas, and e-commerce. Most of
my friends have a habit of checking their mobile phones for news
and WeChat posts every five minutes. People discuss everything
on the Chinese internet, and some even sell their insights by putting their news, analysis, and courses up for purchase. Meanwhile,
influencers broadcast at all hours of the day recommending products for sale. China's top influencer (as inferred from a case of tax
evasion) earns around 250 million USD a year, about twice that of
the world's best athletes like LeBron James or Messi.[1]

1 Her internet name is Weiya and in December 2021, she was found to have
evaded personal income tax for 2019 and 2020 and was ordered to pay as much
as 1.34 billion RMB in late payments and penalties. There was much conjec-

In this chapter, I explain that the Chinese internet and media have two interesting features beyond the well-known phenomenon of tight government control. That is, there is an onion structure to the internet and media, with the inner layers being much more open than the outside. Also, there are coded ways to express one's opinions. After this, I explain that, given the mounting pressure for more openness, China's internet and media will see significant reforms, with the effect of softening control.

THERE ARE THREE FEATURES of the Chinese approach to news media and the internet, as well as freedom of speech in general. One of them is obvious, while the other two are less noticeable or even unknown. One needs to understand all of them in order to comprehend the whole picture and the underlying factors of the Chinese approach.

The first feature is rather obvious. That is, the Chinese news media and internet are under careful management. If you push an inappropriate post, it will be blacked out in a few minutes. If you want to send out an inappropriate picture or file through WeChat, your friend will not receive it. WeChat seems to have sophisticated programs to do this in order to fulfill the monumental task of ensuring users abide by government guidelines. Meanwhile, inappropriate foreign websites are not accessible from inside China. If you want to visit the website of Google or the *New York Times*, you will either wait forever as the page perpetually loads, or you will receive a message saying that the link is broken. Some people have ways to get around this, for example, by using a Virtual Private Network (VPN).

What contents on the internet are regarded as inappropriate?

---

ture on the Chinese internet as to how much her actual annual income was. Most estimates were higher than those of the world's top athletes, the cap of which are around 100 million USD.

To begin with, personal attacks on individual political leaders are not appropriate, including jokes about their accent or appearance. In addition, comments and articles criticizing the political regime are prohibited. Interestingly, discussions that are clearly in favor of the Communist Party but stray from the officially accepted terminology are also blocked. For example, around 2016, one of my colleagues, Professor Daniel Bell, wrote an op-ed in the *New York Times*, praising the effectiveness of the Chinese Communist Party in recruiting and promoting good talents to join the party and the government. He said that the party will exist for a long time, but its name may change, dropping the word *communism.* As a Canadian professor teaching in China, he was treated with great respect, but the Chinese translation of this article was blocked.

The second feature of the Chinese media and internet is less known than the first. That is, China has an onion-structured media market with the inner layers being more open than the outer layers, providing specific news and media services for China's inner circle of decision makers. Senior Chinese officials are provided with a special news service called reference news. In the Mao era, a few volumes of reference news were compiled twice a day by a special branch of the Xinhua News Agency, with each volume about the size of a magazine. Such a tradition is still in practice. Only officials higher than a certain rank were allowed access to these reports, which covered not only international news, but also domestic events regarded as unfitting for the general public, such as severe damage from a natural disaster or a public demonstration in a local region. In addition to news, relevant commentary from key opinion makers was also featured in the reports. In the reform era, the same tradition has been kept, but with some added sophistication due to technological advancements. Each rank of officials has special information and opinion-gathering services. In addition, highly educated individuals often buy VPN services, which allow them to read all of the news from the outside world. A VPN is a paid service account enabling users to bypass the Chinese "great firewall." Although strictly speaking, VPN services are illegal in China, the risk of individual users being punished is close to zero so long as they do not actively use or publicize foreign news in Chinese social media. Why is there this seemingly hypocritical practice? The answer is that elites and decision makers in China need to be and are well informed on news and social opinions from around the world. As a result, it is incorrect to assume that top officials in China are deprived of true information.

The third feature is perhaps even more interesting than the second. That is, there are many ways to voice discontent, disagreement, or even clear criticism in the Chinese media and internet. There are articles, posts, and speeches in the media and on the internet, as well as in-person meetings, which convey sharp criticisms in an indirect way. This may be called the coded speech of criticism, with the end result being that relevant government officials still receive the messages intended for them. It might be a surprise to people outside of China that higher-level officials are usually willing to listen to sharp opinions and criticism in private. People used to joke that the most antigovernment and anti-Communist Party views are voiced and discussed in the Central Party School, where senior officials periodically receive training. Many China hands outside China knew this, and they took pride in having been invited to give talks at the Central Party School, where central government officials are very much willing to listen to criticisms. As a non–Communist Party scholar, I have been invited to give talks to officials on various occasions. Before my talks, the hosts often say: "We want to hear the truth; be bold, and open." Why is this? The reason is very simple: These are like intra-family talks; the audience knows that the intention of the speaker is not to undermine the regime, and they are hungry for information not conveyed in the official media, the outer layers of the onion.

The speech coded as a way to constructively criticize the government and its policies has over two thousand years of history in China and is still essential to all publications in today's media and internet. In history, ministers of a court always first praise the emperor before making suggestions. Today, all published and uncensored materials in Chinese media and on the internet fall into two categories. The first is purely praising the government and policies. They usually do not carry much readership. The second category is constructive criticism or coded speech. For example, each quarter or half year, many economic research centers publish reports on the latest news about the Chinese economy. Such reports always start with positive aspects of the economy and give credit to relevant policies. Then, much more space is devoted to the aspects that can be improved and relevant policy proposals. The wording is always positive but it does not take an expert to understand the sharp criticisms. What is most interesting is that in China top leaders pay more attention to the second category of publication and often write comments on such articles. Their comments are treated as orders to take actions by lower-level officials. Writing such comments is a major part of the work of a senior official. And being commented on by a senior official is a credit to the author of the original article and is a KPI (key performance indicator) for a think tank.

WHY DOES THE CHINESE government exercise careful control over the news media and internet? Some fundamental reasons for this delve deep into the political tradition of the Communist Party, while others can be traced through China's two thousand years of political thinking. Both of these foundations for Chinese thinking on media and the internet now face daily challenges in a modern and fast-paced Chinese society.

The Chinese Communist Party has a long tradition of carefully managing its messages to the general public, going back to its founding day in 1921. The party was established by a small number of scholars and students who absorbed the values of communism and endeavored to spread its message like evangelical believers. Of course, what motivated the young scholars and students was not just the ideals of Marxism, but also a deep concern for the decline of China as a nation. Later on, when the party faced its first monumental setback in the spring of 1927 as hundreds of party members were killed at the hands of the Nationalists, party leaders began to organize military uprisings and went to the countryside to establish military bases. The key idea was to spread the messages of the party in order to recruit believers to join the revolution.

Beginning in the fall of 1928, the Chinese Communist Party formed a two-handed revolutionary strategy: one hand for holding rifles, and the other hand for holding pens—that is, mass propaganda. Propaganda in today's Western language has a very negative connotation, but in a time of war, it is absolutely critical. It was essential that the Red Army reach out to the population at a grassroots level for material support, such as recruiting soldiers, obtaining food and clothing, and scouting for intelligence. During the most difficult days of the Communist Party's history, when the Red Army was forced to retreat from their home base, they still held on to their printing machines. The Red Army would go around and print pamphlets, passing them out to the peasants in the countryside to gain their support. As a revolutionary party, the Communist Party made propaganda its top priority a decade before realizing the importance of organizing its own military force. Mao Zedong said numerous times that mobilizing the masses was the key to winning the revolution, and the key to mobilizing the masses was conveying direct messages to them— that is, propaganda.

To summarize, the importance of public relations is rooted deep in the tradition of China's ruling party. Today, at each level of the government, one of the top five officials is solely responsible for news and media or publicity work in general. The Minister of the Department of Propaganda is regarded as one of the five most prominent figures in Communist Party committees at all levels. On a provincial or municipal level, the person in charge of propaganda is also one of the seven or nine standing committee members of the Communist Party branch.

As a result of its long revolutionary tradition, today's Chinese government more or less continues to directly control the country's news media organizations. All TV stations, as well as all official national and regional newspapers, such the *People's Daily*, *Beijing Daily*, and *Sichuan Daily*, are under the control of the party's Department of Publicity. Internet platforms such as sina.com and qq.com exist in a gray area. Officially, they do not have permission to conduct interviews or broadcast news. In reality, they do so with self-constraint, avoiding the publication of news or comments that could potentially be politically irritating. The Chinese government issues direct guidelines and policies to such organizations, rather than by law having its effect through market forces.

In addition to its revolutionary tradition, there is also a fundamental philosophical tenet behind the Chinese government's approach to news media and the internet—that is, the all-responsible thinking of Confucian political philosophy. According to this thinking, the government is like a parent, the general public is like children, and the parent must look out for the best interests of the children. Some news may cause widespread panic among the general public, while some comments and opinions may cause discomfort and anxiety. Thus, these sources of panic and distrust must be managed. This is obviously drastically different from the libertarian philosophy, which holds the belief that individuals are rational and individual freedom is of the highest value to society, and individuals should make judgments for themselves.

PRESSURES ARE MOUNTING ON the Chinese government to reform its management of media and the internet. The leading reason is very simple: China's rising middle-income population is demanding better access to information and more open expression of their opinions. As of 2020, China had as many as four hundred million middle-income citizens. By 2035, the number may go up to eight hundred million, larger than the sum of middle-income inhabitants of Europe, Japan, and the United States. This sector of the Chinese population is full of people who are well educated and enjoy increasingly comfortable living. They often travel abroad as tourists and send their children to foreign countries for education. The next thing they desire is information on various issues and freedom of expression. This does not necessarily mean that they are unhappy with the government. In fact, according to many surveys, the majority of them are not willing to accept the major political instability that would accompany a change in China's political structure.

In addition to the demand of the rising middle-income population, Chinese top leadership knows very well that they have to rise to the challenge of the media and internet. Xi Jinping has said many times in very colloquial language: If we (the ruling party) cannot respond properly to the challenge of the internet, we will not be able to govern the country for long. By this, he means that the ruling party and the Chinese government must find ways to release the pressure simmering in the internet, and more important, to make sure that competing political forces will not undermine the regime by manipulating content in the internet and media.

Another reason for the Chinese government to implement reforms of the media and internet is that with continued economic development and improvement in social management, Chinese leaders will become more confident and will be less afraid of domestic and international criticisms. Take for example the Chinese relative success in response to the global financial crisis of 2008, the Beijing Olympics of 2008, and the Beijing Winter Olympics of 2022. As confidence builds, government policies regarding the news media and internet will be gradually relaxed. This will be a very popular and welcome reform in China.

What are the possible reforms to the internet and media? Many believe that there are two dimensions. First, self-governing mechanisms among internet companies, user groups, and media organizations. The keyword is decentralization. In many countries, hate speech, false claims, and extremist views are not eliminated by any central authority. Instead, news agencies and media companies have incentives to weed out such views. For example, I have noticed that in major media websites such as that of the *New York Times*, users leave comments after each article. If other readers find the comments to be hateful, they can choose to report the comment in question. When a posting receives a large number of complaints, the posting or the writer will be blocked. In China, such practices are being followed but will certainly be more widely implemented.

The second dimension of the reform is that the government will become much more proactive in making its own case in the media and internet, competing with other views rather than restricting the opinions of the netizens directly. That is, government agencies will lower their profile and speak equally and persuasively with the population rather than proclaiming commanding messages. There is already a clear trend of government agencies appointing a spokesperson to work with the media. It used to be that such spokespersons often fell victim to controversy and widespread criticism. For example, after a crash of a high-speed train in July 2011, the spokesperson of the Chinese Ministry of Railways (now the Chinese Railway Corporation) ran into big trouble with the general public. After providing his version of the cause of the accident, he said casually in a colloquial style: "Whatever you believe, I believe it." His remarks immediately drew widespread criticism on the internet as netizens joked about the tone of the speech. Nowadays, these kinds of nonprofessional government spokespersons are diminishing in number, as they have undergone rounds of training in schools of journalism in Chinese universities. I know of colleagues who specialize in such training and teach simple principles guiding government officials who face the media and internet. Some of the principles include: Be open and friendly, publicize only information that has already been verified, and when facing challenging questions, repeat what you know and never go beyond your key messages.

The media and internet are perhaps some of the most socially divisive topics everywhere in the world, and from the descriptions above, China does not seem to be an exception. The environment and carbon emissions are another worldwide hot topic, and on this subject, Chinese society overall has seen good progress and is much less divided than on other topics. We turn to such issues in the next chapter.

CHAPTER 12

The Environment
and Climate Change

CHINA'S ENVIRONMENTAL PROTECTION, INCLUD-
ing decarbonization, is a rare social issue uniting all three
communities: the Chinese population, the Chinese government,
and the international community. This is the case primarily
because as China becomes richer, the population is increasingly
more concerned about the environment. Moreover, the Chinese
top leadership has identified environmental protection as a top
priority not only to gain popularity with the local population, but
to showcase its capacity of good governance to the world, since
China's centralized governance system gives it the ability to be
particularly effective on this issue. Finally, I explain that planting trees, pushing for investment in green technology, and phasing out polluting factories are the major means by which China
is seeking to improve the environment and reduce carbon emissions. At the current pace, China is likely to become a world leader
in improving environmental quality and fighting climate change.

THERE IS NO DOUBT that the environment, especially air
quality, has become an increasingly important social issue in
China. Around 2016, I saw a TV interview in which people were
asked how much money they would be willing to pay for significantly improved air quality. The median reply was 10,000 RMB
(1,300 USD), about two months of an average salary of a white

collar worker. In fact, some elites even choose to emigrate out of China for better air quality, literally becoming refugees of pollution. I have a senior colleague at my university who decided to have his son emigrate to Canada because of Beijing's air pollution, as his son had developed asthma. The boy's mother gave up her much-coveted job as a senior official in the Beijing municipal government to emigrate with her son to Canada.

Why have environmental issues become so important in China? One fundamental reason is that the Chinese population is becoming wealthier and enjoying a much longer life expectancy, now exceeding seventy-eight years, slightly higher than that of the United States. When people are economically better off and live longer, they devote their time and energy to quality-of-life issues. Pollution has therefore become a much greater concern among the population than it was even five years ago.

A second reason for the ascendence of China's environmental issues is international. That is, China as a nation is now attracting international attention and has become very globalized, especially cities like Beijing and Shanghai, to which increasing numbers of foreign students and visitors are coming and even settling. China's rapid development has propelled cities like Beijing and Shanghai onto the same global stage as London, Paris, and New York. As a result of this increased visibility, pollution in Chinese cities has become more of an international issue. When I was working on establishing the Schwarzman College at Tsinghua University around 2012–2017, I received many inquiries from applicants and later the parents of admitted Schwarzman scholars. They were intimidated by the fabled poor air quality of Beijing. To address their concerns, the whole College building was equipped with the most elaborate air cleaning system so that 24/7, students could enjoy air quality as good as that in any US city on the east coast. The cost of such a system comes not only from the initial equipment and the electricity consumed by the air pumps. In fact, the highest cost comes from the replacement of the air filters, which costs as much as it would to hire a dozen staff members for the College! The super high air quality of the Schwarzman College has become a local political issue. Many local Chinese citizens have attacked us for spoiling the foreign students and generating inequality among the students on campus. We have had to keep a very low profile on this issue and tend to guard this as a top secret of the College.

SINCE HE BECAME CHINA'S leader in 2012, Xi Jinping has elevated environmental protection to one of the five major areas for national progress. He has popularized his idea of environmental protection in a "two mountain" metaphor. The Chinese government's top five priority areas for national progress are politics, economic development, social welfare, cultural affairs, and environmental protection. Xi's "two mountain" metaphor goes like this: A mountain made of gold or silver is valuable, but a green mountain with clear rivers is more precious. The underlying meaning is that economic development policies must also make room for environmental protection and recovery.

One likely intention behind Xi's focus on environmental protection is to demonstrate that China can outperform both the developed West and democracies in emerging market countries like India in this regard, therefore showing that Chinese sociopolitical institutions can compete with, or even surpass, those of many democracies. President Xi has already earned a respectable international reputation, especially considering the context of the United States' retreat from the Paris Agreement on climate change under President Trump. As the United States took a backseat on climate issues, China stepped up and is positioned to work closely with Europe to develop environmental policies and solutions. China's commitments to global climate efforts grew even further in September 2020 and December 2020, when Chinese president Xi made a surprising pledge to peak China's carbon emissions by

2030 and make the country carbon neutral by 2060. I was told by Chinese experts that these goals were the most ambitious ones deliberated among all the alternative options. This shows that the Chinese top leadership has been very aggressive on the issue of global warming.

As a matter of fact, Chinese sociopolitical institutions are indeed well positioned to implement initiatives on environmental protection and climate change. This is because most projects in environmental protection and recovery require coordination and collective action, such as relocating factories and enacting policies that may sacrifice short-term profits. Such efforts also require the adoption of new technologies. Fortunately, these two areas are the forte of Chinese institutions.

Broadly speaking, there are three simultaneous approaches for China to achieve its goals in environmental protection and car-bon reduction. The first approach is oftentimes very challenging. That is, to phase out or wipe out polluting production facilities. For example, in the western section of Beijing, where the wind blows to the east in the winter, there was once a huge industrial complex called Capital Steel, which produced steel using coal and iron ore extracted not far from the plant. When I was in college, I spent one month as an intern working at Capital Steel. I still remember the horrible scene of crimson-colored water running through the factory, serving as a coolant. And then there was the sight of smoke billowing out from the chimneys—all of this at a factory only fifteen kilometers away from Tiananmen Square, the center of Beijing! In 2007, one year before the 2008 Beijing Olympics, the municipal government finally moved that factory to a new site in the province of Hebei, 250 kilometers from Bei-jing, near the oceanfront. It now uses modern technology, such as multiple cycles of water treatment, dust control, and recycling the heat produced as energy, trapping the emissions of sulfur diox-ide. This was not an easy process, and required the relocation of more than 150,000 employees. More recently, the old Capital Steel

compound was renovated and repurposed as the planning headquarters for the 2022 Beijing Winter Olympics. It also hosted a
number of Olympic events, with the big air snowboard ramp art-
fully placed among the factory's former smokestacks—a powerful symbol of urban regeneration.

China's drive to close polluting production facilities has caused
economic pains in many provinces, especially those such as Hebei,
Jiangsu, and Shandong, which are strongholds of heavy industry. I
am often invited to give talks to business executives and government officials in these regions, and one of their biggest complaints
has been the mounting pressure to either clean up or shut down.
For example, I know the founder of one of the biggest phospho-
rus firms in China. His company supplies ingredients to products
like Coca-Cola and toothpaste, and is based in Jiangsu province,
the richest province in China. This executive had to shut down
a brand-new factory because he did not obtain complete environmental approval before investment. Even though he told me
that his factory was completely compatible with all relevant regulations, nobody could save him. In the end, his company had
to default on its bank loans, causing a huge loss for many of his
friends, who had guaranteed the loans. Environmental protection
has become a must-do issue!

The second approach to improving environmental quality is
to push for the adoption of green technologies at a swift pace.
As a result of this rapid investment in green technology, cleaning up China's pollution may actually become a major engine for
generating future economic growth. This is facilitated by the fact
that China has a high-savings economy and the supply for capital investment is abundant. Once, I met a director-general of the
Chinese Ministry of Industry and Information, and I was told that
they are encouraging the rapid adoption of ten common green
technologies for industries. One example is energy-efficient water
boilers. Water boilers are widely used in manufacturing firms to
generate hot water and steam, and their energy efficiency is very

important. All over China, there is also an ongoing effort to phase out coal-fired power plants and replace them with wind and solar power. By 2022, China had become the world's leading producer of solar panels and wind turbines by far. The cost of solar power is moving downward very quickly, such that it has become cheaper than coal-fired power by 2023. The greatest challenge is storing solar energy for use in the evening, after the sun has set. To address this issue, a senior engineer of China's State Grid, the company that owns China's electricity network, showed me that they are developing low-cost and maintenance-free batteries as large as cargo containers, which will be deployed in deserts next to the solar panels.

Another example of environmental improvement technology is extra high voltage transmission, which raises the voltage from five hundred thousand to one million volts so that power can be transmitted over two thousand kilometers without much loss. This is important because most of China's energy is used in the eastern coastal areas, whereas a large amount of renewable energy, including wind and solar, is produced in western China. With this extra high voltage technology, 50 percent of the power generated in southwestern China near Vietnam—where hydro energy is mostly used—can be delivered to the province of Guangdong. In this way, Guangdong, which is an industrial stronghold, is able to greatly reduce its consumption of coal. As of 2017, there were many discussions in China regarding building an energy internet between China and its neighboring countries. The idea is to connect the countries with an extra high voltage power grid in order for countries to share energy and balance gaps in demand and supply across countries.

Automobiles and gasoline are yet another area exemplifying the rapid adoption of green technology. The current standard for the cleanliness of gasoline supplied in Beijing is as high as most US standards. Moreover, the Beijing government is aggressive in forcing old cars to stay off the road. My family bought a seven-seat minivan in 2005, and the car was still in excellent condition in 2017, with only thirty-two thousand kilometers on the odometer. However, starting in 2017, I could no longer drive it on weekdays because it was deemed too old. Furthermore, it had to be inspected every year to stay on the road at all. If I scrapped the car according to government policy, I would receive the equivalent of 700 US dollars in subsidies, intended to eliminate highly polluting cars from the road. Such government measures regarding automobiles do not make economic sense, because the main source of pollution in Beijing is clearly the surrounding iron, steel, and cement industries. In the city of Tangshan, two hundred kilometers from Beijing, row after row of steel plant chimneys can be seen. About 30 percent of China's steel production and nearly 50 percent of coke production (the process that creates the greatest amount of pollution) are concentrated near Beijing. Instead of spending money on programs like encouraging the scrapping of "old" cars, the Beijing Municipal Government should provide funds to Hebei province to reduce pollution. There is a calculation that for every Yuan spent on reducing pollution in Hebei, the impact is twice as great as when the money is spent in Beijing.

Electric vehicles have been heavily promoted, and starting in 2022 China accounted for over one-half of the world's production and sales of EVs. In the city of Beijing, drivers must enter an incredibly competitive lottery to obtain a valid license plate, and they have a much higher chance of winning if they have a purely electric car as opposed to a conventional one. In addition, each traditional energy car is prohibited from being driven one day per week, depending on the last number of the license plate, while a pure electric car can always be used. In the city of Shanghai, the license plate for a plug-in hybrid or purely electrical car is free, while that for a conventional car costs about 12,000 USD. It's no wonder that in 2020, Chinese electric car producer NIO became the third largest car company in stock market value, following Tesla and Toyota. Its share price shot up by 1,000 times in 2020.

The third approach to improving the environment is simple: Plant trees and guard with extreme diligence against forest fires. Each year in mid-March, China has a national Tree Planting Day, demonstrating the country's commitment to maintaining green spaces, even in urban areas. As the world's biggest tree planter, China is one of the very few large countries to have significantly improved its forest coverage, from 14 percent to 23 percent between 1977 and 2019. For example, Beijing is surrounded by six circular highways, or "ring roads," that emanate outward from the center of the city. The 5th Ring Road is as long as ninety-nine kilometers, and the Beijing municipal government has planted trees all along it at a width of one hundred meters of trees on the inside and two hundred meters on the outside. Along the 188-km-long 6th Ring Road, the tree regions are as wide as five hundred meters on the inside and one thousand meters on the outside. In recent years, many international experts have raised the issue of the need for diversity of the species of tree in China. To increase the variety of trees, more than thirty types of vegetation have been included in the case of Beijing.

CHINA'S COORDINATED POLICY MAKING and rapid adoption of green technologies have allowed many of China's major cities, such as Beijing, to make significant improvements in air quality over the past decade and a half. According to a study by the United Nations Environmental Protection Agency (UNEP), most airborne pollutants in China declined drastically between 1998 and 2013. Sulfur dioxide (SO_2) fell by 17 percent, nitrogen dioxide (NO_2) fell by 24 percent, PM 10 (a measure of inhalable pollutants) fell by 43 percent, and carbon dioxide (CO_2) fell by 57 percent. In the case of Beijing, from 2015 to 2020, the measure of PM2.5, sulphur dioxide (SO_2), nitrogen dioxide (NO_2), and PM10 declined by 52.9 percent, 70.4 percent, 42.0 percent and 44.8 percent, respectively. The most important contributions came from replacing coal with natural gas for winter heating and cleaning up polluting production facilities in regions near Beijing.[1] By 2023, the issue of air quality in major Chinese cities has faded away from being the top internet topic.

In recent years, the Chinese central government has further tightened its policy on environmental protection, oftentimes against the preference of local government officials and private entrepreneurs who are more concerned about economic growth. Large cities are phasing out coal for winter heating, replaced by natural gas. There is a ten-year fishing ban from 2020 to 2030 for the whole Yangtze River to allow the fish population to recoup. A number of mountain ranges, grasslands, and river areas, where the ecological systems are perceived to be very fragile, are singled out for protection from all economic investments. A few industries such as coal mining, iron and steel, nonferrous metal, and construction materials have also been given orders to cap their production, meaning that they may have to trade production permits among themselves. Such measures are economically forceful or even brutal but promise environmental benefits.

Again, the environment in China is a rare happy story, in which the population breathes cleaner air, the top leadership gets credit, and the international community has its concerns partly addressed, even though more progress is still desired. In addition, as China has become one of the world's top carbon emitters but also the world's center of solar panels and windmill manufacturing, climate change will be one of the few areas on which China and the West collaborate closely. In comparison with the issue of pollution, the issue of population policy proves to be much more complex, as there is not as much consensus in this area. Next, I discuss the issue of Chinese population policy.

1 PM2.5 is the density of very refined inhalable airborne particles that are very damaging to the human body. A high level of PM2.5 causes haze in the air. It is the most watched index of air quality in China. The Beijing statistics came from an annual report of the Beijing Bureau of Environmental Protection.

CHAPTER 13

Population and Population Policy

POPULATION IS A COMPLICATED ISSUE IN ALL countries, and in this chapter, I attempt to explain the Chinese situation in simple language. After listing a few possible reasons why China has such a huge population, I illustrate how the debate between Chairman Mao and a legendary economics professor resulted in a laissez faire population policy in the first thirty years of the current government. After this, at the beginning of the reform and opening up era, a one-child policy was implemented, reducing global population growth by possibly as many as three hundred million. The one-child policy by 2020 had been phased out. Finally, I argue that population aging is a grave social problem, but is not an insurmountable obstacle to continued economic growth.

WHY DOES CHINA HAVE such a huge population? This is a very simple question but is very difficult to answer. There are many possible reasons. As a fact, the period of largest and fastest increase in population was between 1500, the middle of the prosperous Ming Dynasty, and 1840, the beginning of the Opium War of the late Qing Dynasty. China's population grew from 102 million to 412 million during this time, increasing by about 300 percent. In comparison, during the same period, India's population grew from 110 million to 227 million, Italy's from 11 million to 23 million, and France's from 15 million to 35 million. In most European countries, the population grew by about 2 to 2.3 times.[1] Why did China experience much faster population growth than other regions in the world during this period? It might be because during this period, as a large and unified country, China was relatively stable, with significantly fewer wars than other regions. Another factor is that Confucianism as the dominant belief system has traditionally promoted the idea that a filial son should have as many children as possible. Yet another possible factor is that for whatever reason, China did not suffer from repeated pandemics like the Black Death in Europe. Some believe that the traditional Chinese medical theory and practice, with its philosophical analysis of the human body and herbs and acupuncture, has been effective not only in dealing with pandemics but also in enhancing humans' reproduction.

Population policy became one of the first major debates after the Communist Party gained national power, and provides a striking example of how Chairman Mao made critical decisions. Ma Yingchu is a legendary figure in Chinese academia. When he was in his early 20s, he passed the Qing dynasty government exams and was sent by the Qing emperor to the United States to acquire expertise in metallurgy (the study of metals) because the emperor and his ministers felt that China needed to develop the technology to produce iron and steel. Instead, Ma studied economics, obtaining a master's degree from Yale in 1910. Four years later, he earned a PhD in economics from Columbia. His dissertation on New York City's public finance was later used in a freshman textbook at Columbia. When he returned to China in the 1920s, he became a fierce critic of the government under the Nationalist Party. Chiang Kai-shek, the leader of the Nationalist Party, who happened to be one of Ma's high school students, once invited Ma to dinner through an assistant. Ma refused, saying a student

---

1 According to the Angus Maddison Data Base (2020).

should invite his teacher in person. What a proud academic! Chiang later imprisoned Ma for supporting the student protest movement against the government.

Partly due to his derision of Chiang and the Nationalist government, Ma was initially very well respected and treated by the Chinese Communist Party and Chairman Mao. In response to a personal invitation from Zhou Enlai in 1949, Ma returned from Hong Kong, a popular city for Chinese top scholars, where he had sought refuge during the Civil War from 1945 to 1949, and joined the new government. He was appointed deputy minister of finance in the central government. In 1952, he was appointed the president of Peking University. As an economist, he soon observed that the population in China was growing too rapidly and argued strongly with persuasive statistics that China needed to control its population growth in order to modernize. According to his studies, the population growth was over 2.2 percent a year. He argued that at such a rate, by 2000, China's population would be about 2.6 billion, which would be greater than the 1952 population of the entire world. Based on this, Ma wrote many articles and delivered proposals in person to Mao and Zhou. His argument was extremely compelling: dealing with population growth should be a key part of the government's central planning. Mao initially was very supportive, but by 1958, he came to believe the exaggerated reports by local officials that China was producing more grain than could be consumed. As a result, Mao reversed his position and said that human beings are valuable and therefore, the larger the population the better.

The initial tone of the debate between Mao and Ma on population policy was friendly, and Mao joked with Ma by asking, "You claim that China's peasants are having too many kids because they don't have electricity and have to go to bed early every evening. Yet you have seven kids and you have electricity every night." Soon, however, the tone turned malicious. Mao was extremely angry with the movement that saw Chinese intellectuals attacking the party. By 1958, Professor Ma was labeled a Malthusian. Thomas R. Malthus was a British economist who argued that the human race was doomed because the population was growing too quickly, and only wars and pandemics could solve the population problem. Ma was attacked and was named a public enemy of society. Already in his 80s, Ma knew that he could not win the battle and had to bend against the wind. In order to survive, he burned all his manuscripts and tried to become an ordinary citizen.

Ma was a scholar with a big heart and tremendous fortitude. He not only survived the political ordeal but also became one of the few political enemies who outlived Mao. By 1979, three years after Mao's death, China, under Deng Xiaoping, began to implement the family-planning policy and Ma became a huge hero. People said that because Ma lost his debate against Mao, at least two hundred million more babies were born in China. As an economist, Ma never proposed forced abortions or other harsh policies to control the population; instead, he proposed that every family have only two children, and should be encouraged to do so through an annual bonus. Families who had more than two children would not receive the bonus. Ma died in 1982 at the age of 101 and was perceived to be one of the extremely rare cases of a political and intellectual enemy of Mao who not only outlived Mao but also eventually reversed Mao's policy.

IN 1980, DENG XIAOPING adopted a policy of "one child per family." The idea was to control the population in China to mitigate social problems associated with a large population. The one-child policy was rigorously implemented among people who were employed by state enterprises, the government, universities, and all other local institutions. If an employee of these organizations was found to have more than one child, the person would be fired.

When the one-child policy was announced, there were two very different reactions. In 1979, cities were crowded and housing was in extremely short supply. Furthermore, the unemployment rate was extremely high, and many parents were forced to retire earlier, in their late 40s, in order for their children to be employed in the same factory or institution. In urban houses, the average living area for a family of four was sixteen square meters (170 square feet). Thus, urban residents accepted the one-child policy with relative ease. My brother, who is sixteen years my senior, does not regret having only one child. In 1978, he and his wife were struggling in Beijing after returning from a village to which they had been sent. They had to squeeze into a tiny room with his in-laws. Why would they want to have a second child?

In rural areas, however, peasants still followed the traditional Chinese belief that "the more children, the more fortune." They showed a drastically negative reaction to the one-child policy and tried various ways to evade it. Sometimes wives would get pregnant and go to other cities or villages to deliver the baby, avoiding detection by local officials who were responsible for enforcing the one-child policy only among their locality's residents. In the early 1980s, a popular comedy show called "The Guerrilla of Kids" appeared on Chinese TV. It parodied a peasant family that had so many kids, they had to wander around the countryside to avoid punishment. The show was intended to illustrate that the traditional idea of having many children was obsolete.

Many observers claim that the one-child policy spawned a significant gender imbalance beginning in the early 1980s because many couples sought abortions after ultrasonic tests, but careful study shows that such claims grossly exaggerate reality. True, the official statistic of baby boys to girls was 116 to 100 in the 1990s, while the global ratio was 106 to 100. However, careful studies in the 1990s and early 2000s show that the boy-to-girl ratio was actually normal, since peasants would choose not to register their baby girls with the local government so they could get a second chance at producing a baby boy. But when the girls were seven years old, the parents would register them to attend school. Thus, by age seven, the population began to balance out gender-wise and the ratio moved close to 106–100 as parents began to register their young daughters who were not registered at birth.[1] The failure of hospitals to register these births can most likely be attributed to bribery on the part of the parents during this period of time.

In reality, how tightly was the one-child policy implemented? I have a habit of doing my own small-scale field research on this. When I go to restaurants in China, I often find a friendly way to ask the waitress where she's from, and in almost every case she comes from a rural area. I then ask whether she has a brother or sister, and over 80 percent of the time, she says she does. In fact, the national average is 1.7 to 1.8 children for each Chinese adult female. Also, whenever I take a taxi in China, I choose to sit in the front row and try to get friendly with the driver and conduct an easygoing conversation. After a few questions, I often ask the driver how many kids they have. Taxi drivers in large Chinese cities are usually from the suburbs and were farmers until the early 2000s. In most cases they reply "two," and then I ask how they got around the one-child policy. They tell me that they paid fines, usually amounting to one or two years of an average villager's annual income. In cities, government or state-owned enterprise employees did not have this option, since the one-child policy was strictly enforced in cities. My administrative assistant was her family's second child due to an accidental pregnancy. She has often said that her father blamed her for his inability to get a promotion as a high school teacher because of his violation of the family-planning policy.

The one-child policy has been an emotional issue both inside and outside China. Many politicians, academics, and activists in

---

1 Such studies include Zeng et al. (1993), Liu (2005), Croll (2000), and Cai & Lavely (2003).

the West argue that the one-child policy was a blatant violation of human rights and that families should have the freedom to choose whether to have children, and how many to have. Former president Jimmy Carter held the same view against China's one-child policy. In 1979, he hosted Deng Xiaoping on Deng's official visit to America. This was a historic meeting, the first visit by a Chinese leader after the two countries resumed normal diplomatic relations. At the top of President Carter's agenda was hopefully to persuade China to abolish the one-child policy. President Carter supposedly gave long lectures to Deng Xiaoping on how horrible the policy was. In his usual concise and dry style, Deng Xiaoping replied by saying, "Mr. President, I have a proposal for you: We abolish the one-child policy, but the US agrees to accept ten million immigrants from China each year." At that, the discussion on the one-child policy abruptly ended.

There are different demographic, philosophical, and religious views with any population policy, especially in China. Environmentalists tend to agree that, given China's huge population, without an initial curb on population growth, the world would have been burdened by an even larger and increasingly unsustainable population. However, people holding certain religious or philosophical views may argue fervently, as did President Carter, that childbearing is the ultimate human right and the government should not interfere.

Regardless of its moral implications, China's one-child policy was arguably the world's largest carbon-reduction or save-the-earth program, if not by intention, since it resulted in hundreds of millions of fewer births during three and one-half decades. There is a wide range of estimates on the exact number. China's Family Planning Commission, which now exists, stated, as might be expected, a high-end number in order to highlight its achievements: four hundred million. Meanwhile, some population scholars in China argue that even if there had not been a family planning policy, China would still have had approximately two hundred million fewer births since income increased rapidly during the same period, and the general rule is that the higher the income, the lower the birth rate. Interestingly, Steven Mosher, an American demographer who is the director of the American Population Institute, agreed with China's official number of four hundred million.

One can calculate how much extra carbon dioxide would have been produced without the one-child policy. With the rapid increases in China's living standards, energy consumption, and longevity, roughly speaking, China will save the equivalent of half of the European Union's carbon emissions between 2000 and 2060, when China aims to reach carbon neutrality.

It should be emphasized that the one-child policy has caused a huge sacrifice for one generation of the Chinese people who were born between 1950 and 1980, since the one-child policy was implemented between 1980 and 2016, when most of them got married and gave birth to their children. The pain of this generation comes in three ways. The first is obvious: They had to forgo the freedom to have as many children as they desired.

The second pain of this generation will come when they get old, as there will be proportionately fewer young people to take care of them. This also means that elderly care will be increasingly expensive. It is widely agreed that China's population is rapidly aging, with three stages to this trend. The first stage extends from 2001 to 2020. It is estimated that by 2020, 17 percent of the population was sixty-five or older, while 12 percent was eighty or older. The second stage, covering 2021 to 2050, will be the accelerated aging period. By 2050, 30 percent of the population will be sixty-five or older, while 22 percent will be over eighty. During the third stage, between 2051 and 2100, it is predicted that the population will stabilize, with 31 percent being sixty or older and 25–30 percent being eighty or older. Even assuming that China will implement a flexible retirement age, more than 20 percent of the population will consist of retirees who will have to be supported by the younger generations. The impact will be enormous: It is estimated that China will have to spend over 20 percent of its GDP supporting the elderly.

Yet there is a third type of pain for the generation impacted by the one-child policy. That is, the assets they have saved may lose value as the population ages. Some economists have argued that by the middle of the 2020s, housing prices will collapse because many elderly people will sell their housing stock to young people, who are much fewer in number. Such predictions have not been realized, but indeed there are signs that increases in housing prices began to slow down by 2019.

THE ONE-CHILD POLICY HAS now been phased out. In fact, when Deng Xiaoping announced the one-child policy, he said it would only last for thirty years. By the end of 2015, all families were allowed to have two children, and in 2021, the policy was relaxed to three children. In reality, most families can have as many children as they want.

Given the relatively low consensus forecasts of the Chinese population, before long, China will implement policies to encourage childbearing, since most young families have a decreased desire to have children. This is almost a universal phenomenon across countries of different cultures and religious beliefs. The reason for this is simple and economic in nature. That is, with social and economic development, women are more likely to be employed, greatly increasing the costs of childbearing. The key to help stabilize the age structure of the population is to reduce the cost of childbearing and child care as much as possible.

Indeed, the Chinese population has already peaked with a minor probability of rebound. The Chinese government announced in early 2023 that the Chinese population decreased by 850 thousand in 2022 and the population at the end of 2022 was 1.411 billion. It is possible that after the COVID pandemic, young couples may have a higher desire to give birth to babies. However, the consensus among demographers is that the Chinese population more or less has peaked at around 1.411 billion. This also means that by 2022, India surpassed China as the world's most populous country.

Many analysts have long argued that the Chinese economy, like Japan's, will soon run into a state of very low growth due to population aging and the decrease of the population. Their argument is very simple: There will be more and more retired people to be taken care of by the young, and therefore there will be pressure to tax young people at a higher rate to pay for retiree care, thus reducing their work incentives. Professor Cai Fang, a former vice president of the Chinese Academy of Social Sciences, one of China's government-established think tanks, has argued that because of the one-child policy, the labor supply in China already peaked by 2015 and China's economic growth will slow down significantly. According to him, the Chinese growth rate will decrease from almost 10 percent between 1978 and 2018 to around 4 percent by 2035, not much higher than that of the United States.

Based on very careful analysis, I do not believe the above pessimistic view holds water. In 2022, my colleagues and I published a research report on this. We found that due to the improvements in health and education, partly thanks to the one-child policy, the effective total labor supply will continue to increase until 2050. Labor supply is defined as the population between sixteen and sixty-five. However, effective labor supply is the product of the healthy population above sixteen multiplied by their labor skills as measured by education. We found that between 2022 and 2050, there will be a 17 percent increase in the effective labor supply, which means that China will have an effective labor supply in 2050 that is equivalent to having a population of 1.644 billion that has the same level of public health and education as the population of 2020. This is because the average education level of the population has been rapidly increasing, with about 50 percent of young people attending college by 2022. Therefore, the quality of the labor force will make up for the loss of quantity. In addition, the average health measured by the proportion of healthy and active people is improving for each adult age cohort. As a result, older members of the population will be increasingly willing and able to work given flexible retirement policies. The reform of flexible retirement will be extremely important in mitigating the aging issue in the Chinese case. As of 2022, there had already been extensive discussions of such reforms, and most likely they will be implemented before long.

Given that population aging is unlikely to be an insurmountable challenge to China's continued economic growth and ability to catch up with the West, will there be other critical problems stalling China's development? Will the rapid rise of China turn out to be a super bubble that will burst before long? In the next chapter, we address these very important questions.

CHAPTER 14

Is China a Super Bubble?

THE VERY REASON YOU TAKE AN INTEREST IN this book is likely that you were surprised or alarmed or impressed by the rapid rise of China over the past few decades. But is China headed for a big collapse, making everything you have read irrelevant? In other words, is the rise of China a super bubble that will burst, as was the case with the Soviet Union and Japan? In this chapter, I explain that China is different from the former Soviet Union and Japan, and its rise will most likely continue. There are three reasons for this. First, the market economy has taken root in China. Second, the average income level is still only about 20 percent of that in the United States, and yet the average levels of education and health of the population are not too far away from those in the United States. And third, the political regime does enjoy popular support from the population, if not all of the educated elites.

MOSCOW IS AN IMPRESSIVE city by any standard and to me, the most fascinating place is the subway. Many stations are absolutely gorgeous and too splendid artistically to merely be called subway stations; they are more like museums, with beautiful marble domes, paintings, and sculptures, each station in the town center being unique in style. In comparison, New York subway stations are grimy and run-down, often in various stages of disrepair. During my first visit to Moscow, I asked my Russian host to take me and my Chinese colleagues on a subway tour, and I still vividly recall being stunned by the elegance.

The Moscow subway, built in 1933, was a symbol of the Soviet Union's triumph over the capitalist West; the Soviet economy was growing vigorously and was positioned to overtake the West. Indeed, it was during the Great Depression that the Soviet Union experienced its extraordinarily rapid economic emergence, and many economists wrote that central planning was not only working but superior to a market economy. This was the period when some economists from Austria began to establish their careers by claiming that the Soviet system was doomed to fail.

An even more potent symbolic Soviet achievement was Sputnik, the first manmade satellite. When it was successfully launched in 1957, the entire Western world was shocked and embarrassed. After all, the United States was supposed to be the leader in science and technology, yet it was the Soviet Union that launched the first satellite and later sent the first human into orbit. Wasn't this clear evidence of the Soviets' economic and political superiority?

Yet, by 1992, the Soviet Union had collapsed. The faltering Soviet economy simply could not support its expansive military empire. Long before the collapse, the Soviet economy had shown clear signs of fatigue. The best days of the economy in the 1930s were long gone. Although the debate over the Soviet Union's central planning and free-market economy was long settled by the late 1980s, very few, if any, experts studying the Soviet system were predicting the imminent collapse of the Soviet Union and its entire Eastern European bloc.

IN THE LATE 1980s, there were unmistakable signs of "Japan as No. 1," the title of a popular book by the late Harvard sociologist Ezra Vogel. The most visible signs were the ubiquitous electronics such as the Walkman and the extremely reliable, fuel-efficient automobiles made in Japan. They were so superior in reliability, functionality, and design that American consumers were willing to pay even higher prices when the Japanese were forced to restrict their exports to the United States (the so-called voluntary export restriction plan, or VER).

Yet just a decade after the feared Japan as No. 1, Japanese asset prices began to plunge and this led to decades of slow economic growth. Within three months, from January 7 to April 1, 1990, the stock index dropped by 22 percent, from 37,517 to 29,279. By early 2023, thirty-three years later, when the United States and many European stock markets had set many new record highs, the Japanese stock price still hovered significantly below 30,000. The drastic fall in asset prices pushed many Japanese companies into delinquency. Businesses shrank. Between 1990 and 2019, the Japanese average annual growth rate was just around 1 percent.

While everyone spoke of the threat to the United States posed by Japan's economic emergence in the late 1980s, very few people realized that a devastating collapse of the Japanese housing and financial markets was imminent. And even fewer people predicted that in the following twenty-plus years, the Japanese economy would either shrink or grow at a rate not even one-half of that of the US economy.

Although many people claim that Japan is more livable now with fewer traffic jams, lower housing prices, and less congested streets, it is an undeniable fact that Japan did not become the threat to the United States that people feared in the 1990s.

Both the Soviet Union and Japan were formidable economic forces in their times and collapsed in dramatic fashion. Both cases illustrate how cataclysmic social events can occur quite quickly, and experts and social scientists have a very poor record in predicting "bubble" collapses. This leads us to the key questions of this chapter: Is today's China another 1980s Japan or 1930s Soviet Union? Is the Chinese economy headed for collapse the same way that those economies were? Is China a "super bubble" waiting to burst?

The Chinese economy is indeed facing substantial challenges. The GDP growth rate in 2010 was 11 percent. Since then, it has been steadily declining, from 11 percent, to 9.7 percent, to 7.8 percent, to 7.4 percent, and finally to 6.1 percent in 2019 just before the COVID-19 pandemic. This slowdown happened despite several rounds of mini-stimulus packages implemented by the central government, consisting of measures including relaxing bank loans, moderately increasing fiscal deficits, and pushing for large infrastructure projects, such as high-speed railways. This slowdown has spurred talk of whether the Chinese economy will replicate the "super bubble" that burst in Japan.

Despite its economic slowdown, the first and most fundamental reason why China is not the former Soviet Union is that the Chinese economy is mostly market-based, dominated by private enterprises, and substantially more dynamic and innovative than the Soviet Union's. Over 70 percent of the Chinese economy by output and 90 percent by employment is private and market-based, while almost 100 percent of the former Soviet economy was state-owned and government-controlled. Thus, the Chinese economy is much better equipped to respond to the market and provide proper incentives.

Take the example of Sany Heavy Industry. I happen to know the company and its founders very well. In December 2008, during the global financial crisis, I was invited to Sany to meet the founders. I told them the impending 4 trillion RMB stimulus package would mostly be in infrastructure investment, and Sany would be the first to benefit, so they should speed up and expand their production ASAP! Seven months later, I brought my high school–age son with me to visit Changsha, where Sany's headquarters are located. I was curious how they were doing and paid a private visit to their campus. I found that they were operating twenty-four hours a day, and their leading product was a special machine used to install high-speed railroads, which they had developed in anticipation of China's high-speed rail boom.

The reason why Sany was able to respond to the market so effectively and involve itself in R&D so intensely is that it is a publicly listed company founded and run by four schoolmates with a rich history together. The leader and now the largest shareholder is Mr. Liang Wengen, who long dreamed of success and recruited his friends to join him in what would become the wildly successful business venture of Sany. By 2018, Sany, which means "three one" as a nod to Liang and his three classmates, had become a top Fortune 500 firm and a top-five manufacturer of construction equipment worldwide.

It might come as a surprise to a non-Chinese person that Mr. Liang, a private entrepreneur, is a model Communist Party member. He was elected as one of the three thousand delegates to several rounds of the National Congress of the Communist Party. The two roles—entrepreneur and party member—do not conflict: Li founded a major company, provided jobs to thousands of people nationwide, and paid hundreds of millions of RMB in taxes. Although he rides in a luxurious car called the Maybach (the former high-end branch of Mercedes Benz), he works day and night and lives on the company's campus. The Charter of the Chinese Communist Party does not require that he should give up his shares or his Maybach. Mr. Liang and I meet at least once a year to exchange notes on the macroeconomy. Sany now has manufacturing operations in Africa, India, Germany, and the United States.

Sany does not stand alone as a non-state-owned leader of an economic sector in China. There is Huawei in communications and mobile phones, DJI in the manufacturing of nonmilitary drones, Geely in automobiles, Lenovo in PCs, and more.

The second reason why China is very different from the Soviet Union is that China's top decision makers have been extremely cautious or even paranoid about maintaining regime security when it comes to issues of mass grievances. Therefore, the government takes cautious actions to mitigate such issues. This was not the case in the former Soviet Union. In fact, it might be surprising to people outside China that mass protests do occur in China, all concerning specific social or economic issues. For example, up to mid-2018, there were constant and widespread protests by retired soldiers seeking better pensions and other benefits. Thousands of these veterans would suddenly appear at popular tourist sites, extremely well organized. They would line up military-style, singing military songs, and always strived to remain nonviolent. They would assign a few comrades to record the events on smartphones, especially the episodes where the police resorted to violent force to expel them. Almost all such protests ended up being peacefully dispersed, not only because the government did not want to escalate the situation, but, more importantly, because policy negotiations were in the works to accommodate protestors' demands. These protests by veterans occurred so frequently that by March 2018, the central government established a new ministry, the Ministry of Veteran Affairs, to deal with the issue. After 2018, protests by retired soldiers had stopped.

The third reason why China is not the former Soviet Union is too obvious to be mentioned in many discussions. That is, the former Soviet Union was committed to playing the role of a superpower and was managing if not colonizing many parts of the world. It was closely managing the Eastern European bloc and part of the Middle East, and even had influence reaching as far as Cuba. It had a military presence in most of these countries and sent tanks and armies to Prague in Czechoslovakia to crack down on street protests, and to Afghanistan to take over the regime. The USSR was way too overextended in relation to its economic and military capacity. In contrast, China has no overseas military bases in any conventional sense (with the exception of a leased supply base in Djibouti, where many other countries including the United States also have a military presence). China's Belt and Road Initiative and projects in Africa are in essence economic endeavors of limited scale relative to the size of the Chinese economy (the total outstanding stock of such investments is around

15 percent of the Chinese GDP, while the annual national savings is around 30 percent of GDP). Furthermore, China's claims of sovereignty over a few dozen islands in the South China Sea would have been regarded as child's play in the eyes of former Soviet leaders. All in all, China's geopolitical burden is minimal in comparison with that of the former USSR.

Is CHINA ON THE path to replicate Japan's twenty-plus years of anemic growth? In many ways, China indeed resembles the Japan of the 1990s. Like Japan, China's consumption ratio as a share of GDP is low, making China dependent on domestic investment and foreign markets to absorb the tremendous amount of savings each year. Like Japan, China's enterprises have borrowed a huge amount of debt, and China's property prices are extremely high. In large cities like Beijing, an average person must save twenty years of their salary to purchase a small apartment. Property market prices have risen to such a high level that the total value of property as of the end of 2019 was four times China's GDP, larger both in ratio and absolute value than that of the US economy. All these factors are similar to those seen in the Japanese economy immediately before its crisis.

However, today's China is fundamentally different from Japan in the late 1980s. Firstly and most obviously, China is a much poorer economy than Japan was, and still has space to outgrow its problems. As of 2020, China's average income was around 20 percent that of the United States, while by the late 1980s Japan had an average income as high as 80 percent of that of the United States. A country with lower income has much more room to grow and can still outgrow many economic problems. (Another argument, with which I partly agree, is that Japan's economic collapse was a deliberate outcome of US economic policies, and today's China is much more independent of the US and therefore will not repeat the failure of Japan.)

An example of how relatively low income translates into rapid growth is urbanization. Only about 60 percent of Chinese people live in cities, while Japanese urbanization in 1990 was over 75 percent. Rural populations in China have been pouring into cities, becoming wealthy, and beginning to live and consume like typical urban residents. Meet Mrs. Wang, my family's domestic helper for over ten years. She was a poor farmer who was widowed at a young age, remarried, and later got divorced. She has two sons, and we have paid her above the market rate at around 900 USD a month plus her rent. She used to live in a dormitory in the basement of our residential complex. With little extra living expenses since she eats her meals with us, she has saved so much money that she bought a nice apartment in a city near her hometown for 50,000 USD, around five years of her income. She has extra savings and often asks my advice on investments. She now has retired and remarried and stays at her own apartment in her hometown. She should have easily saved around 20,000 USD in addition to her apartment and still is able to work some odd jobs and continue to live her urban lifestyle.

There are about three hundred million former farmers like Mrs. Wang. They are the future consumers who will be purchasing and/ or renovating apartments. And when they return to their hometowns to live, they will drive up the local economy. Some cities anticipate this and are beefing up their investments in roads, airports, and railroads. When the residents return home, they will buy appliances, furniture, and maybe even their first cars. They personify the forces of growth represented by a formerly poor population and the source of savings of the Chinese economy. This was definitely not the case with Japan in the 1990s, when even farmers were already wealthy.

The second reason that today's China is not Japan of the 1990s is the enormity of China's domestic market. China's population is about eleven times greater than Japan's and the labor force about thirteen times larger, due to China's younger population and higher ratio of labor participation among women. In addition, China's land area is twenty-five times greater than Japan's. All this means that China has the potential to develop a huge domestic market. The poorer western parts of China can trade with the richer eastern parts just as Japan would trade with Africa, only with much lower logistical costs and trade barriers.

The property market illustrates why today's China is different from Japan in the 1980s. China's high-priced property has been a top concern about China among many Western observers. However, China is fundamentally different from Japan, and the Chinese property market is unlikely to be a detonating cord for the economy.

To begin with, as explained, China is still a growing and urbanizing economy. Only 61 percent of the Chinese population was living in cities as of 2020, and furthermore, not all people living in cities are recognized as residents of those cities or own property in the city where they work. Across China, as many as two hundred million people will migrate to cities in the next two decades. This means the demand for urban housing is still growing.

Another reason is that China has been a high savings economy. Chinese households borrow less from banks to buy their apartments than people in other countries. On aggregate, fewer than 50 percent of Chinese housing investments come through bank loans, while in the United States, this number is at least 70–80 percent. Furthermore, Chinese households have high savings rates—more than 30 percent of their disposable income. And finally, Chinese households have a strong attachment to their housing. Together, these factors mean that the holding power of families—in other words, the ability to maintain a property without defaulting—is categorically much higher in China than in the United States.

The final and most interesting reason is that there have been enough calls that the wolf is coming that many draconian policies have been put in place to prevent significant price increases in the housing market. In 2012, the central government implemented a policy restricting the purchase of new properties. Under this policy, people without local residency in a city are prohibited from purchasing property there unless they can provide evidence that they have paid local taxes for the past five years. Additionally, local residents cannot purchase more than two units of property. This policy has proven to be extremely effective in lowering speculative demand for housing, although many free-market economists are very critical of it.

TODAY'S CHINA FACES TWO critical social issues that were not faced by the Soviet Union or Japan. The first is huge economic inequality. A significant amount of research shows that China's income inequality is at least as great as that of the United States, which is among the highest in the developed world. There is a measure of inequity, called the Gini coefficient, which is zero if everyone has the same share of income, and is equal to one if a single person receives all the society's income. Most economists agree that a Gini coefficient below 0.3 is good, while one approaching 0.4 is dangerous. The US number currently stands at 0.45, but there is no definitive agreement on the Chinese Gini coefficient. Some estimates place the current figure at 0.47, while others place it as high as 0.5. Besides a high Gini coefficient, another clear indication of inequality is the urban/rural disparity. In China, the average income of a rural resident is about 30 percent of that of an urban resident—one of the largest rural/urban disparities in the world.

Why might China's huge economic inequality drag down economic growth? Those who study the Latin American experience would point out that a country with high income inequality can spawn increasing social divisions, causing those with low incomes to fight for policies of redistribution, leading to higher taxes for high-income groups, and thus diminishing that group's incentive to work hard. Based on the Latin American example, China will soon find itself in a crisis: For high-income groups, taxes will be high and incentives low. The free market–style reforms featuring low tax rates will be reversed.

In the Chinese case, vast economic inequality is indeed an issue but is perhaps less damaging than in other countries. To begin with, China is unlikely to adopt a political system of popular voting, in which the effects of economic inequality can create the most damage. In this system, low-income voters, larger in number, would often support populist policies and vote for the candidates who espouse them. If these candidates emerged victorious and their policies were implemented, the financial transfer from high-income and economically dynamic earners to low-income earners would drag down the country's economic dynamism. In China, policy makers are very much aware of these tendencies and potential consequences. I have heard many Chinese government ministers, including a former finance minister and two central bank governors, discuss guarding against such possibilities. Local officials share the same concern. Around 2009, I was invited to attend a consultation meeting with the mayor of Beijing regarding the city's next five-year plan. The mayor said something shocking: Beijing is rich enough in public finance to afford making all buses free for everyone. But he added that he would never implement such a policy because it would set a bad example of pleasing the poor at the expense of long-term public investment, and it would attract an unsustainable number of additional people to Beijing.

Another reason why China's vast economic inequality is less damaging than in many other countries is that China's inequality is largely due to regional differences, which are gradually being targeted for improvement by the central government. That is, an individual living in a city in the east is very likely to be far better off than someone living in a rural area in the west. For example, my brother is a retired manual worker in Beijing and my sister is a college-educated retiree in the western city of Chengdu. My brother is much better off economically than my sister. His pension is easily 50 percent higher than my sister's, with much better medical benefits, and, as a senior citizen, he receives a free bus card. The reason for this disparity is that Beijing's municipal government is much wealthier than Chengdu's. At our family gatherings, my brother has said many times, with theatrical exaggeration, that he is grateful to the Chinese government and the Communist Party. On the other hand, my sister, being more educated, often complains about government policies. The central government is fully aware of these regional disparities. For decades, there has been a national policy to encourage investors to invest in western and rural areas. In 2000, the ratio between the wealthiest and poorest provinces in per capita income was 4 times; by 2018, it was 3.5. Economic convergence has been occurring all across provinces. Provinces and municipalities have been gradually pooling their pension funds and creating a situation where retirees are increasingly receiving, or will eventually receive, equal pension payments.

The other critical social problem that today's China faces is the fast-growing middle-income class, which has become increasingly anxious and vocal regarding politics and public policies. The most critical internet postings against the government emanate from this community, which comprises roughly four hundred million people. As discussed before in the chapter on internet and media, the middle-income group desires more freedom of expression and better access to information, and there will be relevant reforms in the future. Meanwhile, a careful analysis reveals that the middle-income class is still mostly concerned with specific social and economic issues rather than seeking a change in political regime, since they worry that a regime change would bring huge and unpredictable social turmoil. Their most prominent areas of concern are, in descending order: the intense competition in precollege education, high housing prices, and expensive medical services. Since these concerns do not constitute a desire for or attempts at regime-changing, the Chinese government should be able to respond by specific reforms.

———

TO SUMMARIZE WHAT HAS been discussed above, it is unlikely for China to suddenly collapse like a bursting bubble. There are two reasons for this. The first is that China's top policy makers are extremely cautious. Among them, there is a constant sense of crisis and urgency. In fact, this sense can even be described as paranoia. Every six months, all agencies through every layer of the government, especially the central government, hold policy consultative meetings. As an economist, I have attended a dozen of these meetings in the past decade, including ones with the president and the premier. The meetings with the president are usually very formal. They begin with the premier giving an overall review of the macroeconomy, followed by each speaker reading from prepared notes, and finally the president providing a summary in which he occasionally refers to the points made by the previous speakers. The president's summary usually serves as a directive for the policies to be implemented in the coming months. The meetings with the premier are much less formal and intended to be of an advice-gathering nature. In my experience, Premiers Wen Jiabao and Li Keqiang behave like professors at a university seminar, often intervening in the presentations and arguing with the speakers. The premiers invite not only academic economists to attend, but also business executives and farmers. The invitations often arrive a few days before the meeting so as to provide no preparation time for the speakers, who therefore talk about issues that they care about the most.

There is a simple rationale behind the intense consultation meetings and frequent field visits organized by China's top decision makers: Key policy makers are always extremely wary of social and economic problems and are always trying to spot any signs of potential crises and deal with them as early as possible. This is reflected in the language the central government has most frequently used regarding economic policy: "We are entering the most difficult times for the economy; the economy is non-sustainable unless we make fundamental changes; the eco-nomic transformation is now entering a moment of life-or-death and we must make relentless efforts to make the transformation a success." There is a Chinese saying that the paranoid survive. Chi-nese policy makers seem to be paranoid, and this is an important reason why so far they have successfully prevented major financial or economic crises from happening.

While the key decision makers are extremely cautious or even paranoid, they are also well informed about the external world, especially the West. Vice premier Liu He (in office 2018–2023) holds a master's degree in public policy from the Harvard Ken-nedy School. In April 2018, during the intense moments of the China-US trade dispute, I helped invite five Western and Singa-porean opinion makers, including Thomas Friedman of the *New York Times* and Martin Wolf of the *Financial Times*, to visit China in order to understand the Chinese perspectives. They met Vice Premier Liu and to my surprise, the meeting was like an aca-demic seminar totally in English, rather than a formal meeting with interpreters. On the walls of the meeting room were pictures of the vice premier meeting with Dr. Henry Kissinger and other Western statesmen and scholars. The meeting delved deeply into the various issues surrounding the trade dispute, mostly involving US domestic politics. After the foreign guests spoke, the vice pre-mier responded in fluent English. Indeed, the event could have passed for a policy seminar at a US university. Most interestingly, before the meeting, I was invited to his office and surprised to see it littered with the latest issues of the *Financial Times*, the *Econ-omist* (the UK weekly), and the *New York Times*. Apparently, he read them by himself and was highly knowledgeable about how the West perceives China. He is the very person negotiating with President Trump's trade representatives. Evidently, he had a knowledge advantage over his counterparts. Liu is not the only member of the cabinet with extensive knowledge of the West. Yi Gang, the governor of the central bank, obtained his PhD in economics from the University of Illinois at Urbana Champaign and worked as a professor at the University of Indiana for many years before returning to China. I cannot think of any other large countries except South Korea that are similar to China in this regard. Japan, for example, as of 2019, had only one American- or Western-trained top decision maker in the central government: the governor of the Bank of Japan.

The second reason that China is not a bubble is that it enjoys general although not 100 percent support from its population. Will China's political regime collapse and therefore bring down the China miracle? The ultimate answer will be given by the relatively young Chinese generation born after the late 1970s and raised in the era of reform and opening up. The popular wisdom is that when a population becomes wealthy enough, their demand for democracy will either foment revolution or a peaceful transition to democracy, and that China will go through this process, in which young people will be the most active agents advancing these changes. People who hold this view refer to the examples of Eastern Europe, as well as South Korea and Taiwan.

It may come as a surprise that China's younger generation born in the reform and opening up era (after 1980) may well be willing to support the current political regime for continued economic growth and social stability rather than support an "interruption revolution" like the Arab Spring.

Eric Li is an example of those in the young generation who are savvy, well educated, and pro-government in general. He was educated at UC Berkeley as an undergraduate and is an enormously successful venture capitalist and millionaire. He is now a popular political writer in China, authoring articles on *Foreign Affairs*, a major US journal, and giving TED talks. His basic point is that American and Western-style democracy is not the only model for the world, including China, and is not as exemplary as people believe. The Chinese political and social systems have their own virtues. Li is articulate, forceful, and convincing to many.

Eric Li represents a young generation of Chinese. They were born in the 1970s, are knowledgeable about the world outside China, and are also the beneficiaries of China's recent and rapid social/economic development. It is quite interesting to compare these young people with my generation, born in the 1960s. When these young people went abroad to study (and more of them did than those from my generation), they were much more critical of the Western system than we were. Interestingly, there have been studies showing that in recent years, some Chinese exchange students in the United States felt that they were discriminated against, and they turned more supportive of the Chinese government after returning from abroad.

My generation went to the United States and other Western countries as students at a time when China was "closed." Everything in the West seemed miraculous to us, and we thought China would never be able to catch up in its social and economic development. We believed that everything in the United States was much better than in China. The current younger generation is much more self-confident about China for the main reason that they grew up in a rising China, in which they witnessed a drastic improvement in living standards and social order. For example, when I was a child, there was no such thing as queuing in a line when waiting for a bus; people had to fight to get on, with the polite having no chance. Within a decade, this changed, and people are now much more relaxed and patiently queue for a bus. Fundamentally, this is because there are now more buses, and the attitude is, if you miss a bus, the next one is coming in a few minutes, so why fight? The other reason is that the West has had its own problems with issues like rising inequality. In fact, some of my Western academics deplore the degeneration of Western democracy and Western institutions. And it does not help matters that the West has become increasingly hostile toward China, examples including the chaotic interruptions of the torch relay for the Beijing Olympics in cities like Paris, due to anti-China demonstrations. People in the West may have long forgotten such incidents, but the younger generation of Chinese keep them deep in their memory, treating them as a sign of the West's hostility toward a rising China. I am not engaging in a debate about whether this is the case or not, but to be perfectly fair, Western democracy has not been doing a good PR job among the young and educated Chinese population.

A large proportion of young people I have talked to in China told me that the four years of President Donald Trump in the White House were one of the best illustrations of why China should not adopt the US sociopolitical system. They witnessed the chaotic situation created by the policies and tweets of President Trump. They were turned off by the president's policy of America First, often bullying less powerful countries and violating international rules. They concluded that if the US sociopolitical system is imported into China, China may become even more chaotic, and this will be disastrous.

A perhaps oversimplified but informative description of the political spectrum of the educated Chinese is as follows: Many of those born in the 1940s and 1950s harbor extremely positive feelings about the United States and Western politics, since they suffered the most during the Mao era before reform and tend to attribute China's success to its opening up to the West. Many of those who were born in the late 1970s and later and grew up in the reform era tend to be much more nationalistic and critical of the West and US democracy. My generation, born in the 1960s and early 1970s, stands in the middle.

Of course, the political views of young and educated Chinese may very well change if the Chinese economy stops growing steadily and potential social problems related to education, medical care, and housing are not mitigated. However, given the pragmatic and cautious nature of China's policy makers, the current trend of steady improvement in these areas is likely to continue. This gives me confidence that the political regime is unlikely to be undermined by a revolution waged by frustrated and anxious young people.

Given that the rise of China is unlikely to be a bubble and that China has been very different from a Western democracy, is China fashioning a new model of social, economic, and political governance, which will potentially be exported to other countries? This is the topic of the next chapter.

CHAPTER 15

Is There a "Chinese Model"?

B Y THIS POINT IN THE BOOK, YOU MIGHT NATU-
rally ask: Is China following its own model of sociopolitical
governance? That is, is there a Chinese model; is China different from the West; and is China's strength and influence likely to
continue rising? To answer this question, I may surprise you by
explaining that many Chinese scholars are not willing to discuss
such a question, since they feel that there are still many problems to
be worked out and thus it is too early for China to settle down with
a set of institutions. Also, even if there will be a Chinese model,
it would be highly unlikely for China to brand it and export it to
the rest of the world, since leaders in China know very well that
Chinese cultural and historical settings make such a job impossible. Given all these factors, I go through three pillars of what can
be called the Chinese approach to sociopolitical governance: all-
responsible government with a matching social mentality, internal discipline within the government, and respect-centered rather
than ideology-centered or interest-centered diplomacy.

IN WESTERN ACADEMIC AND policy circles, there is a great
deal of buzz around the concept of the "Chinese Model" or the
"Beijing Consensus," meaning China's approach toward sociopolitical governance, which could serve as a template for other
countries. Many people outside China may expect that Chinese

scholars and political insiders are extremely proud of the achievements of their country over the past four decades, and that they
must discuss the "Chinese Model" enthusiastically on a daily
basis. On the contrary, many if not most Chinese scholars and
many government officials are actually very reluctant to discuss
this topic, or you even might say are "allergic" to it. Furthermore,
the debate surrounding the "Chinese Model" is highly divisive
among Chinese elites today.

Why are many Chinese scholars, especially those in social sciences and humanities, so allergic to this topic? One obvious reason is that China is evolving rapidly, and all scholars, especially
those in the social sciences, have their own ideas about how the
country should change. Many are not pleased with China's current
situation and are hoping to see continued progress. I remember
a few years ago when I met one of my father's former colleagues
who was in his eighties and a well-read and thoughtful former
government official. When he asked what project I was working
on, I replied that I was writing a book on the economic development of China as a large country. He pleaded with me, "Please do
not talk about a Chinese model. We are still improving and it's
still too early to talk about a Chinese model." He didn't want the
younger generation to become complacent. He insisted on continuing to discuss the problems that existed, but he didn't believe
we had a "model."

Many of my close friends in academia and government echo
the concerns of this former official. Their advice is: "Don't talk
about a Chinese model. Talk about the Chinese experience, but if
you talk about a Chinese model then you are justifying a lot of bad
things that are in practice today."

While the Chinese people have a large and growing amount of
confidence and pride in their country, many higher expectations
still exist. The Chinese people want changes. One example of this
attitude can be seen with regard to education. Outside China, the
Chinese precollege education system is frequently praised for its

high levels of achievement in math, natural sciences, and even in English learning. In a survey conducted by the Organization of Economic Cooperation and Development (OECD) which compares the quality of academic achievements of high school students worldwide, Shanghai consistently ranks number one or two. China's precollege education is held in such high esteem that some Chinese teachers are even invited to teach in the UK. Yet if you ask a Chinese parent or a high school student, they all complain, and nobody says the education system is wonderful. They argue that there is too much competition and the study requirements are too demanding. But they do not offer any solutions. At the same time, there are numerous articles on the Chinese internet discussing how elite American high schools are so superior to their Chinese counterparts, citing the school Mark Zuckerberg attended (Phillips Exeter Academy). They argue that Zuckerberg was already well educated before attending Harvard (from which he famously dropped out to pursue the development of Facebook).

Another example about which many Chinese people feel there is a need for improvement is that China does not have any revolutionary entrepreneurs like Bill Gates, Steve Jobs, or Elon Musk. Although there are great Chinese companies and entrepreneurs like Jack Ma of Alibaba, people in China often argue that American entrepreneurs have changed the lives of people around the world. Chinese society must be more open and accommodating to allow such geniuses to emerge.

THERE ARE GENERALLY TWO opposing camps within China regarding whether there is a Chinese model. One believes the only meaningful model of political and social governance in the world is Western liberal democracy. This model espouses a certain set of universal values, including individual liberty and social equality. I have many respected and personal friends belonging to this camp. The proponents of this model believe these goals can only be achieved through Western democracy. They tend to be people born in the 1940s and 1950s who endured suffering during the Cultural Revolution as teenagers. So far, they seem to be the mainstream of the intellectual community if not of the whole society. When they argue for their views, they often focus on the problems of Chinese society and cite the United States as an example of social progress. You may think these scholars, many of whom are members of the Communist Party, would lose their jobs. In fact, most of them do not so long as they refrain from openly attacking top leaders. Again, this reflects how today's China is different from the former Soviet Union.

The second camp argues that China should evolve into a system featuring strictly Chinese characteristics. People in this camp maintain that China needs to improve, progress, and innovate, while at the same time taking into account Chinese history and Chinese culture. In the process, the argument goes, China may provide other countries with a solution in their efforts to modernize. Let's call this the camp of Chinese characteristics. So far, scholars in social sciences and liberal arts holding this view are relatively few in number but often are highly visible. In China, they are often labeled as leftist scholars.

I am not regarded as either an extreme rightist or leftist—I am usually perceived to be a moderate scholar. As a result, over the past one-and-a-half decades, I have been able to reach out to both camps and organize many closed-door sessions in my research center to discuss current policy issues, such as how to deal with China-US trade frictions. As the host and moderator at these events, I make special efforts to involve both camps. Discussions are usually very heated, with "leftist" scholars in the minority. On one or two occasions, some of them have even walked out of the room in protest. In such cases, I had to make special efforts to apologize to upset scholars and appease their anger. I have to say that I have learned more from the "leftist" scholars, since they have to work harder to convince the audience and present more evidence, while the "rightists" often just rely on what they call general common sense, such as the idea that democracy and rule of law are better than autocracy or authoritarian regimes.

THERE IS A VERY popular idea among Western scholars that when a country is economically better off, with a per capita income above $10,000, then Western-style democracy will emerge as the only model of sociopolitical governance. Favored examples of this in the East Asian region include Japan, South Korea, and Taiwan. Even in China, the renowned CNN anchor Fareed Zakaria once eloquently summarized this popular view. This was during a seminar in December of 2013, organized by a very senior advisor to a top Chinese political leader, who invited many influential Western scholars and opinion leaders to participate in dialogues with their Chinese counterparts. Unfortunately, the senior Chinese host was only reading his prepared notes, and the event was getting very boring. It was pushing lunchtime and as a world-class TV personality, Zakaria could not stand this extremely low efficiency of exchange. Thus, he broke out into a three-minute speech in which he argued that there is no historical exception to the rule that when people get rich, they will fight for democracy. Furthermore, he pointed out that mainland China is surrounded by such examples: Japan, Taiwan, and South Korea. Fareed politely suggested that the Chinese authorities should prepare to face this phenomenon as China becomes increasingly prosperous.

Despite the appealing logic of this argument, especially when relayed by someone as well-spoken as Fareed Zakaria, the conclusion that economic prosperity leads to Western-style democracy is far too simplistic. The argument misses two extremely crucial points. First, geopolitics. In all of the examples cited by Zakaria, the political influence of the West has been extremely important. In the case of Japan, after it lost World War II and was occupied by the United States, the Japanese constitution was drafted by two US military lawyers. In the cases of South Korea and Taiwan, the political elites sensed imminent threats from their respective military and political enemies and therefore felt compelled to conform to the US political system in order to strengthen military alliances. The former Taiwanese leader Chiang Ching-kuo famously asked his advisor in 1979: "Now that the US has abandoned us and established formal diplomatic relations with mainland China, how can we protect ourselves?" His advisor said, "Clearly, the only option is to become a democracy so that the US will protect us." Chiang started the process of democracy gradually by first opening up local elections and then the presidential election, much as in the US model.

The second set of variables refuting the view that economic development leads to Western-style democracy include culture and history. Culturally, many countries in Central and Eastern Europe that transitioned to democracy in the late twentieth century identify strongly with Western ideals due to their European identity. In Poland, for instance, which made the transition from communism to democracy in 1989, people perceive themselves as part of Europe. Historically, in such democracies as India and the Philippines, current political systems were strongly influenced by their former colonial rulers. In contrast with these examples, China is too large, too proud, and too independent to conform to the Western model. China was a unified, self-governing country for most of the past thousands of years. Unlike Japan, Korea, and Taiwan, mainland China has never been under US protection and there is no need to prove itself as a genuine friend of the United States by importing Western political and economic systems and institutions in wholesale fashion.

Furthermore, on the topic of culture and political thinking, one must recognize that Confucianism has been the dominant sociopolitical philosophy in China for over two thousand years. From an early age, Chinese students are taught to memorize classic stories conveying the values of Confucianism. They are educated to be obedient to their parents and told to respect social order and to follow the instructions of their teachers at school. As a result, Chinese people tend to rely on their parents first and then the government to solve their problems.

Perhaps the most important historical factor is the Chinese revolution and the emergence of the Chinese Communist Party. As explained previously, the party's original motivation was nation-building rather than promoting communism as an ideology. For the sake of improving public relations with the rest of the world, many scholars have suggested that the party should remove the word *communist* from its name. However, popular Chinese culture favors continuity, and due to domestic considerations, the title of "communist" has been kept. The party came to power through more than two decades of brutal warfare and has become extremely pragmatic and adaptive in battling many different enemies. In addition, the party made disastrous mistakes in the Great Leap Forward and the Cultural Revolution and is now extremely cautious and willing to adapt in order to stay in power. However, despite this flexibility, simply copying the model of multiparty political competition from Western liberal democracies is not on the menu. As previously explained, the party and the government are integrated in China, so having a new party running the government would create tremendous chaos.

China had an unsuccessful experiment with the system of village level democracy around the year 2000, when popular elections were introduced into Chinese villages—an event met with great enthusiasm from Americans, including representatives of the Jimmy Carter Foundation. However, democracy in Chinese villages quickly devolved into a brazen attempt by large families sharing the same last name to exploit minority families because Chinese villages had long been organized as kingships. As a result, that experiment today is widely perceived to have been unsuccessful, and the party has reinstated its involvement in the governance of villages. This establishes basic stability and fairness in the villages.

REGARDLESS OF WHETHER THERE will be a Chinese model, three important features stand out in the Chinese approach to sociopolitical governance.

The first feature is perhaps the most noteworthy, that is, an all-responsible government with matching expectations of the population. An all-responsible government is a government attempting to guard the welfare of its people. Such a government knows that if it does not perform up to the expectations of the population, it will be ousted from politics one way or another. As the Chinese top leaders starting with Mao have always said, "We are taking exams with the people giving the exam questions." This is why Chinese leaders are always worried and even paranoid about many socioeconomic issues.

I use the term *all-responsible government* as a neutral description of the Chinese system of sociopolitical governance. The Chinese government's motto is "serve the people," and it often takes many of the people's responsibilities onto its own shoulders. A similar term is *paternalistic government*, which was coined by my former Harvard professor, Janos Kornai, to criticize the behavior of the former Soviet Union and its Eastern European allies. He compared the behavior of those governments to the way that parents treat small children, leaving not enough room for freedom.

A good example of all-responsible government can be seen in its cautious attitude toward financial markets and the population's behavior. Whenever the financial markets become extremely active, whether in transaction volume or price, this causes the government to worry. The worry is that many small investors will lose money, and in turn will blame the government for the lack of proper market regulation. This is especially the case with companies in the peer-to-peer (P2P) business that issue high-interest-bearing bonds to investors and then lend out at even higher interest rates to individuals, usually for a short period of time. Oftentimes, when P2P companies default on their loans, hundreds or thousands of small investors gather outside government buildings demanding government action and compensation. Anticipating this, the Chinese government began issuing stern orders to strictly regulate the P2P business around 2019. In this example, the government behaves like a parent guarding the safety of a child learning how to drive a car, and the population is like a child needing support in case of an accident. In the United States, this type of structure is unimaginable—investors should bear their own risks and consequences of investment failures.

Perhaps the best example to illustrate the behavior of an all-responsible government is the COVID-19 pandemic. The Chinese government's response at the very beginning of the outbreak, around late November, was to prevent panic in society. To accomplish this, the Chinese Center for Disease Control performed its initial research while barring non-CDC doctors from releasing any news about the emerging virus. Dr. Li Wenliang, an eye doctor in Wuhan, propagated the news using his personal social media account in late December, and was later called to the local police station to plead guilty to his misdemeanor and publicly apologize on local TV. This doctor was later hailed by the general public as a whistleblower. Technically speaking, he violated a rule that all well-designed public health systems follow. That is, only qualified professionals in the disease control system are authorized to issue any news about a potential epidemic. However, in this case, he turned out to be right. Later on, by January 20, 2020, the Chinese government had determined that COVID-19 was a new and infectious virus, leading them to shut down Wuhan, a city of twenty million people. The entire nation was also put on a high level of crisis alert. Many scholars in China argue that the government was too slow early on, but too harsh later on. Here, a very simple explanation for the behavior of the Chinese government is that it tries to be all-responsible: The citizens are treated like children, while the government acts as a parent, trying to do everything to protect the children.

Almost the opposite occurred in the US case, where the federal government and many states issued orders asking people to practice social distancing and wear masks. Many people took to the streets to protest openly and emotionally about these rules. Their attitude was: We are responsible for our own lives, and we will never accept any order from the government on such issues.

My goal is not to evaluate whether the Chinese or US government performed better in dealing with the COVID-19 pandemic. Rather, the point here is that the two countries' pandemic strategies represent two drastically different models of government-citizen relations.

It is interesting to compare the mainstream libertarian belief with that of an all-responsible government. The libertarians of course find the idea of an all-responsible government repulsive. The libertarian belief is: "We the people are the bosses, and we delegate CERTAIN tasks to the government, in the process transferring SOME of our rights to the government. But if the government fails to deliver, we change the government." The belief of an all-responsible government is: "The people delegate MANY if not all rights to us in order for us to serve MANY if not all interests of the people." Matching this belief, in China, due to two thousand years of tradition, most of the population expects and counts on the government to take care of many issues and would be willing to delegate their rights. Furthermore, in the Chinese case, the ruling party is deeply worried that it will be driven out just like the last emperor in 1911 and the Nationalist Party under Chiang Kai-shek in 1949 if the party cannot live up to the high expectations of the population. For the time being, under President Xi Jinping, the political pendulum seems to have swung toward more government responsibility, as the government has become more ambitious in tackling many social problems, including inequality and environmental protection.

At the risk of oversimplifying, a typical government in the West is a quick carwash: The driver stays in the car, the washer only cleans the outside of the car. An all-responsible government is like a thorough detailing of the car: Give us the key, trust us, and we come back with a complete job of cleaning.

The second feature of the Chinese model concerns the internal discipline of the dominant party. China is not alone in having a dominant party that has been the ruling party. Singapore has one. So did Japan and Mexico. And one of the most popular and relevant criticisms of such political practices asks: How can a one-party system truly discipline itself? The argument is that in the United States and other democracies, parties compete against each other, and the party in power is watched carefully by the other parties. In addition, Western countries have legal systems that are intended to be independent of the government, allowing for further government discipline. In China, however, much emphasis is placed on internal discipline within the government and the ruling party.

In China, the State Supervisory Commission is in charge of internal discipline in the government and the Communist Party. The Commission conducts routine screenings of all government agencies. Also, when a government official or employee is suspected of work-related misconduct, they are first investigated by the Commission and then sent to the legal system for trial if found to have violated the law. That is, in addition to the legal system, the Commission is an extra layer of discipline overseeing the government and the party. It is like an amplified version of the compliance department of a large corporation.

The Supervisory Commission is an extension of the tradition of two thousand years of Chinese bureaucracy. In Chinese history, a local official was also the head of the local court implementing the laws of the emperor. Who could discipline the official?

The answer is an independent supervisory organization. Different dynasties had different names for this supervisory organization, but in each case, they functioned more or less the same way.

Wang Qishan was in charge of the party's anticorruption activities between 2012 and 2017, and was instrumental in strengthening the system of the Supervisory Commission. On one occasion, he invited American scholar Francis Fukuyama to visit China and discuss politics. During Fukuyama's visit, it was believed that Wang Qishan told him:

> I know all the theories and practices in the West regarding the rule of law and the necessity of the independence of the legal system, but in China, the independence of the legal system is not enough. Since we have a ruling party always in power, we need an additional system of internal discipline. We have such a tradition in Chinese history, while in the West, you do not.

The third feature of Chinese governance is respect-centered diplomacy. That is, the fundamental principle of China's diplomacy is to gain and maintain international respect for China, the people, the Party, and the government. Respect is even more important than real interests. This concept is a modern descendant of thousands of years of historical tradition, when the Imperial Chinese tributary system communicated to the countries of the region: We do not seek to obtain territory or economic interests and we do not seek to rule your country, but each year, send a delegate to us to show your respect for us as a large country and we will send our missions and gifts to reciprocate. This was a well-established practice in Chinese history, partly because Chinese emperors knew that their domestic affairs were already too burdensome for them to take on affairs in other lands.

I would argue that respect-centered diplomacy can explain most aspects of Chinese diplomacy. For example, the Belt and

Road Initiative—which is a program to build infrastructure projects and industrial parks in countries from China all the way to Africa—is not necessarily commercially profitable, but has great potential to garner respect from the leaders of relevant countries. Similarly, the two most contentious issues between China and Japan are the disputed sovereignty of the small rock-islands known as the Diaoyu Islands (or Senkaku Islands in Japanese) and the occasional visit of the Japanese prime minister to the Yasukuni Shrine, where some Japanese World War II generals who were convicted as war criminals are buried. Both issues are fundamentally tied to the issue of respect. In contrast, the Chinese government has long rejected Japanese offers for war compensation.

In another example, the actions of China in the South China Sea can also be understood this way. The Chinese government inherited claims of sovereignty on some of the islands in the South China Sea from the Nationalist government, and for many years, the Chinese approach has been to ask involved countries to recognize the disputed sovereignty claims while negotiating a way to share the benefits of economic development in the region, such as oil drilling. The key here is to earn respect from relevant countries in the region. Former president Duterte of the Philippines demonstrated a deep understanding of Chinese thinking in his policy decisions regarding the South China Sea. He was keen to show respect for China as a country and Chinese standing in the region without necessarily agreeing to Chinese sovereignty of the involved islands. In this way, he has been able to negotiate substantial economic deals between the Philippines and China.

Why is respect so important for Chinese diplomacy? First, it is a result of historical tradition. As Dr. Kissinger wrote in his book *On China*, China has thousands of years of tradition as a large, unified country, and for all this time it has been content with the idea of acting as the "middle kingdom" and requesting respect from other countries while not seeking to conquer them or interfere in their affairs. Accentuating this historical need for respect is the fact that over the past 160 years, China has suffered a gross lack of respect from Western powers. To make things even worse, today's China—despite being economically prosperous, technologically progressive, and militarily strong—is perceived in the eyes of many Western politicians as an alien and unfriendly power due to what they believe is its lack of institutions of liberal democracy and multiparty politics.

Looking through this lens, arguably the biggest mistake that President Trump made in dealing with China was not in his actual policy. Instead, it was his lack of respect for China as a country and for the Communist Party as the ruling party. Trump referred to China as an opportunist country taking advantage of the United States, and he dished out sudden and harsh policies against China without any warning or private exchanges with Chinese leaders. In an interview with CNBC, I said that it was not the actual demands placed on China by the Trump administration that irritated Chinese decision makers, but rather the barking dog approach toward China that caused the biggest rift between the two countries. When dealing with China, a polite negotiation style is just as important as what you ask for from the negotiation. In the United States, it may be more common to have tough and red-faced negotiations before reaching a deal and going out for a drink. In China, however, overly aggressive negotiation tactics can cause deals to collapse and leave both parties feeling bad.

Fortunately, perhaps the only thing President Trump got right in dealing with China was that he had always been polite with Chinese president Xi Jinping. Thus, China reciprocated by being polite with President Trump. Whenever I published an article about the United States in official Chinese media, I was always reminded to save face with President Trump and never mention his name when criticizing the US government. Personal attacks on President Trump are not allowed in Chinese official media.

THE BELT AND ROAD INITIATIVE (BRI) is a program for
Chinese private and state enterprises to help build infrastructure
and industrial parks in the silk road countries and the marine
silk road countries. These countries stretch from China all the
way to Europe and Africa. Many Western observers worry that
this is a form of Chinese neocolonialism, but this is not true.
First, colonialism of any form requires political control or influence and China does not intend to have them. In fact, inside
China, each year, there are reports that a Chinese BRI project
has suffered from a major loss because the host country has had
a change of government and the new government has turned
unfriendly to China. And there are many studies in China about
how to evaluate such political risks. That is, China does not have
any prowess to influence let alone control these countries. The
best examples are Kazakhstan and Ethiopia. Both countries
went through regime changes around 2021 with China watching
from far away.

The key motivation of the BRI is for China to gain international
respect through its economic capacity. In many internal discussions, Xi Jinping emphasized that mutual respect and friendship
are the top priorities rather than pure economic interest. Given
this principle, China will work out the issue of excessive debt
with relevant countries. Unlike debt taken on by poor countries
for everyday consumption, the BRI debt has been incurred in
order to build infrastructure. Arguably, the host countries are in
a good position: They got the hardware in use while the debt was
being postponed.

In contrast with the perceptions and worries of many Western
observers, China is not in a position to export its approach to
modern governance to other countries. In this regard, China does
not aim to spread any ideology and is not like the former Soviet
Union, which wove a network of Communist regimes. China is
also vastly different from the United States and its Western allies,

which have historically had an agenda to promote liberal democracy and the policy framework that comes along with it.

A few examples help illustrate how China is not interested in spreading any ideology or model of sociopolitical governance. First, the case of South Africa. The late Nelson Mandela used to claim to be a follower of Mao, and his African National Congress was very close to the Chinese Communist Party. The ANC even sent some of its senior cadres to the Chinese Communist Party's Central Party Schools to study. However, China never held any conferences or sent any delegates or advisors to South Africa to instruct the ANC on how to conduct its policies. Second, the case of North Korea. One may think that because China is a strong supporter of North Korea, it must have advisors residing in North Korea, or the North Korean government and ruling party must constantly send delegates to report to or seek guidance from China. In reality, almost the opposite is true. North Korea often makes decisions before informing China, if at all. China has constantly suggested that North Korea should be more flexible in its policies and implement reforms. Such polite suggestions have often been met with criticisms that China has betrayed the principles of communism. Third, the case of Russia, which is an even more interesting example. Obviously, China and Russia have become close allies in recent years, and they cooperate on many international issues, often going against the viewpoints of the West. However, China has little interest in persuading Russia to follow any specific policies or ideas of political governance. Ideologically, China and Russia are far apart. In November 2017, China celebrated the centennial of the Russian Revolution, which has been credited as having brought Marxism to China. However, Putin's Russia has been trying to distance itself from the Russian Revolution as much as possible. I happened to be a tourist in the summer of 2017 in St. Petersburg and visited the battleship *Aurora*, from which the first gunshot of the Russian Revolution was fired. To my surprise, there were more Chinese tourists than Russians there! In fact, President Putin requested that the history books be rewritten to denounce the Russian Revolution. In this anecdote, you can see that ideologically, China and Russia are completely different, and China has no intention of challenging the Russian authorities on this matter.

Since the outbreak of the Ukraine crisis in February 2022, China has been put under an uncomfortable spotlight. Days before the crisis, China's top leader promised to his Russian counterpart a good and unconditional relationship. It was clear that the Chinese leader did not have proper intelligence on what would happen. After the initial invasion, China switched to a neutral position: not supporting Russia in the United Nations, not joining the West in sanctioning Russia, not providing military support for either side, but maintaining economic transactions with Russia and Ukraine. More important, China has tried to push both sides to peace talks.

Why doesn't China export its approach to modern governance? The most important reason is that senior Chinese government officials know too well that the Chinese political system is extremely difficult to duplicate outside of China. Why? Because today's Chinese approach to sociopolitical governance is embedded in a tradition over one thousand years old, involving an extremely elaborate civil service system, and this system is almost impossible to transfer to other countries. The civil service system started with highly competitive nationwide exams to select government officials. The winners of the exams would be placed as government officials away from their hometowns to avoid nepotism and would be given the opportunity to gradually climb the ladder of the government hierarchy, gaining valuable experience along the way. In this way, any studious, determined, and lucky individual, no matter how humble their origins, could climb the ranks as high as the position of prime minister. As you can see, China historically has had a centralized and hierarchical civil service system. In the minds of many educated elites in China, the idea of maintaining social order with a well-educated and merit-based civil servant system is the social ideal. The kind of democracy practiced in India and the Philippines is not widely appreciated among Chinese elites. Despite India's claims that it enjoys noisy harmony in a diversified society, many Chinese elites perceive the Indian case as chaotic, dangerous, and lacking basic law and order.

In numerous surveys about the future career aspirations of Chinese primary school students, "government official" is one of the top choices. The tremendous investment by the government and families in education and the widespread desire to enter public service separates China from other developing countries. Outside of Japan, Korea, and Singapore, very few countries feature this tradition and culture. This is why it is extremely difficult for low-income countries without a preexisting strong foundation in civil service to duplicate the Chinese model. Professor Dwight Perkins of Harvard University started his career studying Chinese economic history and development and later studied economic development in Southeast Asia and Africa. He often commented in his class that if the Chinese system were to be transplanted to a low-income country in Africa or even to Southeast Asia, it would be disastrous, because few places in the world have a civil service infrastructure that could support the Chinese system.

Another reason that China does not export its approach to modern governance is very practical. That is, Chinese leaders are too busy with domestic affairs. The Chinese approach to modern governance is a top-down approach with much power concentrated at the top. This means that top decision makers are extremely busy dealing with domestic issues and crises. Almost every week, there are urgent domestic problems, and China's top leaders have to issue orders. The first half of the thirty-minute, national 7:00 p.m. evening news is occupied by reports on the busy activities of national leaders in dealing with many issues, mostly domestic and often provincial issues. In contrast, the US president does not have to deal with as many domestic issues. Governors and mayors are locally elected, and thus have the authority and autonomy to act in regional and local affairs. In academic language, the Chinese approach to governance has decreasing returns to scale; the larger the scale, the lower the efficiency. When applied to a city-state like Singapore, this system works well. For a huge nation like China, though, this approach is exhausting for the top leaders.

Some analysts in the West may argue that even if China is not positioned to export its political philosophy and practice, China has set an example of non-Western governance for the other governments to adopt. This view has ignored a simple fact that it is fundamentally an issue of domestic politics that decides whether a foreign government emulates anything from China. In such countries, a divide of pro-China and anti-China may arise, and, as respect-centered diplomacy implies, it is very unlikely for the Chinese government to step in to interfere. China will most likely be very passive and noninterfering.

MANY WESTERNERS ARE VERY concerned that China will export its social surveillance technology to other countries. First, China does have highly sophisticated surveillance technologies and they have been effectively deployed for law enforcement. A high-profile and horrible case involved a super-intelligent student at Peking University who killed his mother with a hammer and treated and stored her body very carefully in her room. He used her phone to text with her relatives and borrowed money from them. He claimed to have left China. Two years later, he finally was caught because he went to a Chinese airport to say goodbye to his friend. A few seconds' walk outside the car did him in. Without the camera at the airport, he could have been at large for many years or even forever.

A much less dramatic example is that my son always leaves

his laptop, iPad, and headphone in a university's library desk and comes out running errands for hours. I often suggest that he take care of his belongings, but they have never been stolen. He replies that theft is not an issue in libraries or classrooms, since there are cameras around. In general, a lot of crimes are solved or prevented with the assistance of the surveillance cameras.

Second, how intrusive are these surveillance technologies to ordinary people? Most Chinese I talked with feel comfortable and perceive that the technologies are their safeguards. Meanwhile, exchange students from Western countries seem to be visibly concerned when finding the cameras. I think the answer is that in general, for more ordinary people in China, the worry that government abuses the technologies is limited. I as a motorcycle rider should be worried about the omnipresent traffic cameras since there are many roads in Beijing banning motorcycle traffic. We motorcyclists have argued for years to change the restrictions. I often violate these rules, thinking that they are bad rules, but I am willing to pay the fine once I am caught by the camera. I have indeed gotten only some tickets. The police seem to be moderate, not going after all violations. The cameras are mostly meant for investigating major crimes and accidents.

Finally and most important, will China export the surveillance technologies? Such technologies are socially neutral and can be used to solve crimes or to prevent abusive behavior by the police. Fundamentally, it is up to the integrity of the importing government. At the US Capitol Hill on January 6, 2021, had there been a better surveillance system, law enforcement would have better means to find the offenders. China is not in a position to judge the qualifications of the buying government and then decide, on that basis, whether to export surveillance systems to them. In contrast, the United States sells billions of weapons to many countries. Weapons are only for wars, not to solve domestic crimes. In comparison with exporting weapons, selling surveillance technologies is a neutral act.

EVEN THOUGH CHINA IS not positioned to export its
approach to sociopolitical governance, China and the West will
certainly continue to have a growing mutual influence on one
another in sociopolitical governance. So far, such influence has
mostly been one way, that is, from the West to China. Eventually,
it will be a two-way exchange. I am confident that the West—
including the United States, which has historically been very
confident and proud of its model of governance—will pick up
something meaningful from China.

It has long been the case that China is learning from the West.
At my university, the joke is that before the era of reform and
opening up, whenever we would try to convince our president to
agree to do something, we would say, "Karl Marx said this. . . ."
During the reform and opening up, we said, "Harvard or MIT
does this. . . ." China is learning and will continue to learn a key
ingredient of success from the United States: Decentralize and
delegate decision-making rights to individuals or private entities
as much as possible, because once given sufficient liberty, they can
accomplish amazingly creative feats. That is the lesson behind the
success of Wall Street and Silicon Valley.

Now the reverse learning has begun in subtle ways. One example of this is the Massachusetts Institute of Technology (MIT), a
leading university in science and technology in the United States.
MIT's business school, the Sloan School of Management, has
been partners with Tsinghua's School of Economics and Management, and for many years now has picked up many new ideas from
Tsinghua. Starting around 2008, professors at the Sloan School
began to push their deans for faster decision making, especially
with regard to building a new office building. Their best argument: "Tsinghua did this and that, why can't we do the same?"
The whole university has had the same urge. Around 2018, MIT's
university board held its board meeting outside the United States
for the first time. They came to a hotel near Tsinghua and as one

item on the agenda, they had lunch with Tsinghua presidents and professors. I was there. The board members were curious about many aspects of Tsinghua's operations.

What are the areas in which the West will most likely learn from China? There might be a few areas, but I would argue that the most important lesson by far is how to create a greater capacity for independent government agencies to carry out long-term socioeconomic programs. In the United States, for instance, every two and six years there are congressional elections, and every four or eight years there is a change in the presidency. Due to these features of the US government, it is very difficult to make and stick to a well-debated long-term economic program. One solution is to establish or strengthen agencies that are independent of partisan politics, such as the Centers for Disease Control and the Federal Communications Commission. China maintains continuity; the same party stays in power, and usually every ten years we see a major change in the national leadership. Meaningful socioeconomic programs are deliberated, decided on, and implemented, such as programs for environmental protection, high-speed railroads, and scientific research.

Perhaps the trickiest lesson that the West may eventually learn from China is to be more flexible and open-minded when it comes to sociopolitical governance. The West has long taken pride in its liberal political system. However, there are many answers to the question of how a country can be effectively governed under the general principle that human rights are respected. Each country is different, with its own culture and history, and as such, various forms of government can be suitable depending on the scenario. Eventually, the rise of China will in effect remind many people in the world to be more open-minded and more understanding of other countries' history, culture, politics, and institutions.

In summary, although it is too early to claim that China has established a Chinese model of sociopolitical governance, there are already prominent features of Chinese governance, namely, all-responsible government, internal discipline of a dominant party, and respect-centered diplomacy. What do these three features imply for China's world view? That is, what is the thinking behind China's domestic and international policies? The next chapter will explore China's world view.

CHAPTER 16

China's World View

I N THIS CHAPTER, I ILLUSTRATE A SET OF VIEWS
regarding China and the world on which many Chinese policy makers, business executives, and educated people concur,
which I call China's world view. Among the seven points of China's world view, three stand out. First, China must take care of its
domestic issues properly before working on international ones.
Second, when dealing with foreign affairs, winning respect is the
most important thing. Third, it is important to try to stay coop-
erative with the United States but stand firm on issues of core
interest to China, that is, the issue of Taiwan and the ability for
technological improvement.

By world view, I refer to a set of widely agreed upon general principles shared among the country's top decision makers
and the educated general public. In fact, no country has a single
world view, and a country the size of China has a wide spectrum of views, depending on income, education, and exposure
to other parts of the world. However, there are a short list of
views that a country's policy makers and educated population
mostly share. For example, in the United States, most people would agree that individual liberty should be respected so
long as it is not in conflict with social welfare, as in the case of
a pandemic. In a country like China with a long history and

strong culture, the list of world views is likely longer than in many countries, and most are like folk wisdom and are taken for granted.

1. Governing China Is Like Students Taking Exams

Before entering the city of Beijing and assuming national power, Mao Zedong said: "We are like students going to take the civil servant exams given by the emperor in the court in the old days and we better stay on our toes and not fail them." By this, he meant that if the Communist Party messes up in governing China and causes widespread discontent, the party will be ousted by other political forces just as the Nationalist Party was driven out by the Communists. More important, unlike what happens when a Republican or Democratic president is voted out, the whole political regime in China will be undermined, and there will be no chance to come back as in a national election. The exam mentality and ensuing anxiety have always been on the mind of the Communist Party. For example, Chinese top decision makers have always put the utmost priority on grain security and have always been very concerned about inflation, since food shortage and inflation are likely causes of widespread discontent or even open protest. The exam mentality explains the extreme caution or even paranoia of China's policy makers. Whenever and whatever decisions they deliberate, the first and most important question is: Will this cause social instability? This is not well understood by many observers or analysts outside China, who believe that the Chinese government, with a large army and police force and tight control of many functions of society, should be very confident or even complacent. It is just the opposite. In an important sense, the exam mentality has kept Chinese policy makers always on their toes and rarely reckless. I sometimes call this the Chinese style of discipline on the government, instead of the conventional electoral democracy and separation of powers.

2. Homework First

Given that governing China is like students taking exams, home-work is most important in preparation. And the most important homework is to manage Chinese domestic affairs well. I call this the finish-homework-before-going-to-parties principle. When presidential candidate Donald Trump uttered his campaign motto "America First," many people in China tended to relate this to the Chinese view of homework. By "homework" I mean working to solve domestic issues. By "going to parties" I mean working out matters related to the international arena. This is because most people in China feel that since China is a huge country with a large population, solving Chinese domestic problems inherently makes a tremendously positive contribution to the rest of the world. People in China often argue that if China were to fall into crisis—be that due to economic distress, social unrest, or civil war—this would place an enormous burden on the rest of the world. Any experienced political leader in the West recognizes this.

One example of this view was exhibited during the China-US trade dispute, when President Trump did what previously had been unthinkable, such as labeling a Chinese company as a national threat to the United States and threatening to cut off its supply of computer chips. In China, this widely reinforced the belief that domestic issues should take priority, as dealing with President Trump proved to be essentially useless. The only sure way to resolve this kind of pressure from abroad will be to build domestic strength in technological innovation. In this way, it will be possible to avoid being at the mercy of foreign nations.

What are the major pieces of "homework" China must complete? First, to make sure the domestic economy is maintaining its momentum. It is clearly and widely understood that without stable economic growth and prosperity, everything is built on sand. Second, social stability has a firm foundation. That is, widespread social protests and grievances should be resolved at their roots. Most protests are not politically motivated and are not demanding freedom of speech, freedom of the press, or the formation of a competing party. Rather, mass protests in mainland China are concerned with mundane issues that affect people's daily lives, such as water pollution, military veterans not getting proper pensions, and people getting cheated of their savings by fake investment schemes, etc. Third, there is continued improvement in education, science, and technology, as they concern the future of the country. And fourth, environmental protection is a major priority due to its increasing consequences for the sustainability and health of both China and the world.

3. Historical Conservatism

Chinese foreign policies and even some domestic ones often originate from a philosophy that can be summarized as historical conservatism: Respect history and do not deviate from historical claims. The issue is: How far back does history go? For most practical policy matters, history starts with 1949, when the founders of the People's Republic, Mao Zedong, Zhou Enlai, and their colleagues, set the principles. This explains the puzzle of why China is so persistent in regarding the claim that many small and seemingly insignificant islands in the South China Sea belong to China, while China was not going after Russia for the huge amount of land obtained by the tsars in the mid-nineteenth century (the size of France and Germany combined). This also explains why China is persistent on the Taiwan issue and why China is keen to receive a proper apology from the Japanese emperor over the Japanese invasion of 1937–1945 even though the United States has never received an official, unabashed apology from the Japanese, either. Meanwhile, the Chinese government rejected multiple offers from Japan in the 1970s and 1980s to provide economic compensation for the war damage, thinking that such compensation might be viewed as a substitute for official apologies. The simple answer is that Mao and Zhou set the tone in the first years of the founding of the People's Republic.

The principle of historical conservatism also explains why China is not going after issues that had been settled by 1949. In Chinese textbooks, the Opium War of 1840–1842 with the ensuing unequal treaties was an evil act of the imperial powers. However, today's Chinese government never asked the queen or king or the prime minister of the UK to apologize for this, unlike the case of the Japanese government. The answer is that the case of the Opium War and the ensuing unequal treaties were in general already settled by the Nationalist Government before 1949. Therefore, the Chinese government after 1949 has not gone after the UK on such issues. In contrast, the issue of whether a few islands near Taiwan belong to Taiwan had not been settled by 1949. Neither had the issue of whether Japan needs to apologize to or compensate China for the invasion.

Most of China's current foreign policies can be understood from this perspective: The current Chinese government is not willing to deviate from previous policies established by Mao and Zhou Enlai. One exception is that many foreign policies during the Cultural Revolution are not followed, such as supporting revolutions and revolts in foreign countries, since the whole episode of the Cultural Revolution has been denounced.

Historical conservatism explains China's foreign policy dilemma when dealing with North Korea. North Korea was a close ally under Mao and Zhou Enlai. In Chinese official language, the friendship with North Korea was "forged with blood" due to the Korean War. Today's Chinese government is extremely reluctant to withdraw its support for North Korea despite the fact that North Korea's policy of pursuing nuclear weapons clearly goes against China's best interests, since this has provoked South Korea to station more US military facilities near the Chinese border.

This "historical conservatism" is in effect explained by the huge

228 CHINA'S WORLD VIEW

contrast between China's Communist Party concerning the legacy of Mao and that of the former Soviet Union concerning the legacy of Stalin. China's Communist Party under Deng Xiaoping and now Xi Jinping readily recognized that Mao was a great hero, although he made mistakes in his later years in waging the Cultural Revolution; on the other hand, Stalin's successor Khrushchev suddenly and completely condemned Stalin, which angered Mao and triggered him to wage the Cultural Revolution in order to prevent any "Khrushchevs" from coming to power after his death.

4. "Respect First" Diplomacy

China harbors a great desire to gain respect from the rest of the world, especially the West, and this is an area in which Westerners, especially Americans, may not understand or at least underestimate China's convictions. Looking through this lens, people can more easily understand the actions of Chinese leaders. Take, for example, the Belt and Road initiative. In May 2017 and April 2019, President Xi Jinping hosted two huge international events called the Summit of the Belt and Road Collaboration. Thirty to forty heads of nations attended, a larger number than would attend a UN general assembly meeting. Every day for a week, the official Chinese TV news programs showed President Xi Jinping hosting red carpet receptions for these leaders, each of whom came to China to express their willingness to understand and work with China.

Some may view this as a display of vanity, but when I speak to ordinary citizens they feel a sense of pride that China has now become a nation that warrants this kind of respect. The Belt and Road Initiative is not only designed to gain economic benefits from working with these countries, but also to gain international respect. President Xi has often expressed a new theory of international collaboration, which is based on a balance between moral leadership and economic interests, therefore allowing China to gain more respect on the international stage.

How to deal with China is perhaps more important than what

to ask from China. Again, the Belt and Road Initiative is a case in contrast. It is not totally clear whether China benefited economically in net from the BRI; however, China has obtained proper respect from the participants of the BRI. When provoked or insulted, the Chinese tend to become very nationalistic, and when treated with respect, they tend to be open to working together. Think of respect for China as a nation the same as economic and other interests to a Western country.

5. Do Not Export the Chinese Model

A majority or even overwhelming view in China among political leaders and scholars alike is that China should not export its political thinking or political system abroad, not only because it is unnecessary, but because it is also impossible. This has been a view that has been shared by Chinese leaders and most average Chinese people for the last decades. In 2012, when he was still the vice president of China, Xi Jinping complained to a group of reporters while visiting Mexico: "It is unfair for the West to criticize China. Over the past decades, China has not exported its ideology and political system to any other countries, China has not sought to overturn any foreign regime, and China has taken care of the welfare of its large population and has not exported poverty or refugees to the world. Why have we always been blamed and criticized? It is utterly unfair."

Pakistan is another example in which China has no intention of exporting its ideology and political system. Pakistan is arguably China's most stable friend as a neighbor, not just because of its common foe in India. In Chinese, there is an expression that Pakistan is as solid as steel as a friend and the friendship is weatherproof. No matter who becomes the leader on each side, the relationship is always well maintained. It is almost the same as the United States and Israel. Nevertheless, China has never asked Pakistan to follow a socialist ideology and implement China-like policies. In fact, as a Muslim country with national and local elections and parliamentary politics, ideologically and politically,

Pakistan is as far away as one can think from China. The Chinese side is not at all concerned by this.

There are many sources of suspicion regarding China's claims that it does not wish to export its ideology or political system. One comes from the observation of the Chinese government setting up many branches of the so-called Confucius Institutes next to many universities outside China. But these schools are all devoted to teaching Chinese languages and cultures. None of them teaches how great the Chinese Communist Party is, how wonderful the Chinese political system is, and how other countries should follow China.

6. Home Sweet Home

This is a commonly shared view by many Chinese going abroad: The goal of going abroad is to return home with fortune and glory instead of occupying foreign land and making it our home. This is what I call the Chinese mentality of "home, sweet home." And this explains well why overseas Chinese oftentimes are not as integrated into local politics as their economic success would imply. In history and throughout modern times, many Chinese have gone abroad either to study or more likely to escape war and famine. For them, the immediate goal is of course to make a better living, but their ultimate goal is to achieve fortune or fame in a foreign land in order to receive a hero's welcome when they return home. In Chinese, there is a popular saying describing this: "to do well in the outside world and then dress up well, return home, and be received with honor and glory." For those who are not fortunate enough to achieve success abroad, they will still need to return home once they reach old age. The popular saying is that "one needs to land in the homeland like a falling leaf on the root of the tree." Chinese people travel to other countries as visitors and sometimes immigrants, but rarely or ever colonists.

The story of Mr. Wu Shunde is a good illustration. His father had already been a successful businessman in Malaysia for many decades when Shunde was born in 1912 in Malaysia. Many Chinese were forced to go abroad because of war or famine. When he was two years old, his parents sent him back to China's Guangdong to receive formal education with the goal of making sure the family had good connections with their homeland. Wu attended Lingnan College, a Catholic school in Guangzhou. He later conducted business in Hong Kong. He eventually came to own the second-largest company in Hong Kong in terms of employment, the Maxim Group, which manages chains of restaurants ranging from formal and expensive Cantonese restaurants to cafeteria-style fast food. His extended family now owns the whole Starbucks franchise in greater China. When he became successful in business, Wu donated money mostly in mainland China, including five buildings at Tsinghua University, such as that of the School of Economics and Management and the School of Public Policy. My small complaint is that the buildings are all similarly named after him, so my ordered lunch boxes are often misdelivered.

John Cecil Rhodes was just the opposite of many Chinese like Wu Shunde. Rhodes was one of the most famous British colonial entrepreneurs in the late nineteenth century. He made his fortune in the countries now known as South Africa, Mozambique, and the countries then known as Northern and Southern Rhodesia (Zambia and Zimbabwe today). He was once one of the world's richest people, monopolizing the supply of diamonds from South Africa. His company, De Beers, now belongs to the Anglo American Group, which is listed on the London Stock Exchange.

Rhodes's dream was not to return home with fancy clothing and glory, but to expand the British empire. He even deeply regretted that America had gained independence. As a bachelor with no heirs, he faced the issue of how to allocate his huge amount of wealth after his death. He decided to donate his money to the cause of expanding and reviving the glorious days of Great Britain. For this, he initially wanted to work with Nathan Rothschild, another tycoon of the time; Rothschild politely refused.

Ultimately, Rhodes donated most of his wealth to Oxford University, establishing the Rhodes Scholarship. The original purpose of the Rhodes Scholarship was to train the brightest future leaders of the English-speaking world, including Australia and the United States, in order to create loyalty toward Britain among the elites and eventually lead to a return of British rule in those countries.

No matter how successful Mr. Wu was in the pursuit of his personal goal, his ultimate dream was to return home to China to be respected by the Chinese people. "Home sweet home" was always in Wu Shunde's mind, whereas the dream of John Cecil Rhodes was to expand the influence of his home country.

This difference in behavior and mentality still persists among today's young Chinese students. When my generation went abroad to study in Western countries, many of us had the dream of returning to China to excel in career development. Today that mentality has grown even stronger. Many young Chinese are not willing to study overseas, and those who do intend to return home as early as possible after earning their degrees. According to a report by Huaqiao University based in Fujian, China, 80 percent of Chinese students who studied abroad from 2010 to 2020 have returned to China, rather than staying in foreign countries. This is consistent with my casual observations.

The Chinese word for China literally translates to "Middle Kingdom." I would argue that this does not necessarily refer to a political concept, but rather expresses the idea of home—central to the mindset of many Chinese. This is why most of the Chinese dynasties of the past two thousand years were not expansionary. In fact, the most expansionary dynasties were led by the Mongolians or the Manchurians, who were invaders from the North and then came to rule the whole country.

7. The Business of Diplomacy Is Business

While President Trump made a splash by combining business with diplomacy and geopolitics in his first foreign visit after taking office, Chinese leaders have long made it routine to witness the signing of a large number of business agreements during visits by foreign businesspeople. For example, I have been the only academic member of the Sino-German Economic Advisory Council, consisting of one academic and twelve business executives on each side. One benefit for business executives in joining the committee is to be able to push for business deals with the Chinese Ministry of Commerce, which is often responsible for giving the green light to Chinese foreign projects before a state visit of a Chinese leader to Germany or a German leader to China. Such state visits accelerate many business deals.

When a Chinese leader plans to visit African or other developing countries, Chinese businesses would always line up business deals. The special state-chartered flights would be full of business executives accompanying Chinese leaders, and they would later sign business deals in the presence of the leaders.

Behind this pattern of Chinese behavior is the philosophy that economic development should be promoted across countries. Chinese leaders often argue that the right of economic development should be a part of human rights and one of the most important ones for people in a poor country; that is, to benefit from economic development and to have opportunities to participate in economic development is as important as political freedom and freedom of speech. In the language of Chinese leaders, the foundation of political freedom is economic development, and economic development emanates from international collaboration and investment. It is wrong, the rationale goes, to first demand that a foreign country obey certain political rules, develop rule of law, and adopt democracy before agreeing to do business.

In Chinese philosophy, one has to push for economic growth first; political development will come later as a consequence of a higher quality of life. This often ignites a dispute between China and Western countries. Western countries tend to precondition their business deals and economic aid on political freedom and human rights.

8. *China Should Work with the United States . . . with Principles*

China should work with the United States while standing firm for China's own long-term interests. Yes. You read that right. This is still the dominant view inside China, despite the surging hawkish US attitudes toward China starting with the Trump presidency.

The Chinese nickname for the United States reveals the true image of the United States in the minds of most Chinese. Americans and their country are called: the "Old Americans" (alternatively translated as the Big Americans). In Chinese, "old" is not necessarily a reference to age. It is a prefix added to someone's last name in order to describe a person who is the most senior in rank, or physically strong and big, bossy, confident, stubborn, self-centered, and often times, grumpy. In contrast, the Chinese would never use the phrase "Old Japanese." Instead, they say "Little Japanese," which refers to Japanese who often appear to be very modest, polite, and clever. These nicknames are of course stereotyping and I disagree with them, but they are reflective of the Chinese perception. In the minds of most Chinese, America remains the "big boss," and the "big boss" might not always be reasonable—it can be grumpy like an old grandfather.

The majority of Chinese believe that dealing appropriately with the United States is China's top priority in international affairs. Some people go as far as to argue that without the United States, China's forty years of economic reform and opening up would not have been as successful. Furthermore, most educated people in China agree that the current world order, essentially established by the United States at the end of World War II, has been more or less beneficial to China for the past four decades. This view is consistent with the fact that China is one of the five permanent members of the UN Security Council.

Facing the increasingly hawkish stance of the United States toward China, is there a consensus view among most people in China? This is a difficult question since the China-US relationship is a hot and divisive topic in China. Aside from the ultra-nationalistic or the highly pro-Western views, the middle or consensus view seems to be rather clear. The consensus view is that facing pressure from the United States, China needs to respect and negotiate with the United States as the "Old American" but stand firm and not give in on issues of long-term interest to China. Such issues generally include that of Taiwan and policy options to promote continued economic and technological progress.

The Russia–Ukraine war is a good illustration of China's cautious, restrained, and principled dealings with the United States. China had been friendly with both Russia and Ukraine for decades before the war. In fact, Chinese business had invested heavily in Ukraine, including a few large grain warehouses that were destroyed in the war. Therefore, the top priority is for China to broker a peace agreement between the two countries, and this would also enhance China's leadership profile in the world. Meanwhile, China does want to maintain its good relations with Russia, with which China has one of the world's longest borders. A highly sensitive issue is whether China should placate Moscow's appetite for military equipment, as this will irritate the United States and its allies. Taking all these considerations into account, China has played a nuanced role in the conflict, trying to broker peace, maintaining good relations with Russia, but stopping short of selling military equipment to Russia.

An example of standing firm against US pressure by promoting China's own technological innovation is Huawei. Long before President Trump's policy of cutting off Chinese high-tech companies from American suppliers, some high-tech companies such as Huawei began working on a contingency plan that they internally referred to as the "spare tire," intending to establish their own operating systems and computer chips just in case the United

States were to cut them out of the computer technology ecosystem. This was only meant to serve as a backup plan that would never have to be implemented. But by 2019, many companies realized that the possibility of having to use their "spare tires" was increasing substantially. In September 2020, Huawei officially launched the Harmony OS, which is an operating system not only used by mobile phones and laptops, but also by all devices hooked up to the 5G network. The Harmony system would not have been developed had the US administration not treated Huawei as an unreliable entity.

Now that I have illustrated and argued that the rise of China most likely will continue and China has its unique approach to managing the country's affairs and its own set of world views, a natural question is: Will the rise of China be good or bad for the rest of the world, including the West? In the next and final chapter of the book, I argue that the rise of China will be good for common people in the rest of the world.

CHAPTER 17

Why Is the Rise of China Good for the World?

I N THE LAST CHAPTER OF THE BOOK, BUILDING ON the analysis of previous chapters, I argue that the rise of China is good for the world and more specifically, the rise of China is good for the common people of the world. I first explain that the rise of China will not cause a war, cold nor hot, between China and the United States, despite the fact that many scholars have predicted or even argued for such a war. My main argument is that China has not been following the path of the rise of a Western power and therefore such predictions for a China-US war based on Western history are not applicable. I then explain that the rise of China will provide new economic opportunities for most people in the world. Also, the rise of China will bring more global public goods such as faster progress in science and technology, space exploration, peacekeeping in war-torn regions, and a more effective fight against climate change. In addition, the rise of China will raise the pressure of competition and therefore push many countries, including the United States, to spend more on science, technology, and education, which is beneficial for these countries.

M ANY POLITICIANS AND POLICY analysts in the West, especially those in the United States, have identified China as the biggest strategic enemy. Former US president Trump certainly made a critical contribution in this regard. Even before COVID-19 and during his campaign for election, he labeled China as the biggest and most present danger to the United States, just like the former Soviet Union. While in office, copying a Cold War tactic, he shut down the Chinese consulate in Houston with only seventy-two hours' notice in July 2020. This was a particularly symbolic decision: The Houston consulate was the very first one opened as a result of Deng Xiaoping's historic visit to the United States in 1979, during which Deng stopped by Houston and snapped a charming photo wearing a cowboy hat. Besides the incident of the Houston consulate, four Chinese scholars were arrested by the FBI for allegedly hiding their history of employment with the Chinese military. Chinese hi-tech company Huawei, despite being a privately held company, was also blocked from buying computer chips from all companies under US influence. On top of these events, President Trump's secretary of state, Mike Pompeo, made a shocking speech proclaiming that the past fifty years of US engagement with China had been a failure, and that China was an evil force to be met with resistance and containment. He chose to make the speech at the Richard Nixon Presidential Library and Museum on July 23, 2020, implicating the strategic mistake that President Nixon (of his own party) had made in normalizing relations with China half a century earlier.

Meanwhile, the US Congress has become increasingly hawkish toward China, even after the Trump presidency. The normally disagreeable and argumentative US Congress has shown a rare solidarity when it comes to proposing legislations condemning China for various problems. In particular, the US Congress passed legislation urging the White House to provide more military and political support for Taiwan with the clear purpose of showing defiance against the Chinese government, while for the past four decades, the US White House has reassured the Chinese government that Taiwan is part of China and military sales to Taiwan should taper off from the levels of the late 1970s.

THERE IS ONE GENERAL theory and two practical arguments behind the view that the United States and the West should treat China as a strategic enemy. The general theory is often called the Thucydides Trap, which is based on the history of Ancient Greece that when a new power rose, the incumbent power felt challenged and as a consequence, wars between the new and the incumbent powers broke out. Professor Graham Allison of Harvard University, an expert on the Cold War between the West and the Soviet bloc, is responsible for proposing and publicizing this theory. He published a book in 2017 titled *Destined for War: Can America and China Escape Thucydides's Trap?* He argues that when China grows bigger and stronger, China will face pushback from the world's incumbent hegemon, the United States, much as in the wars fought between the number one powers and their challengers in ancient Greek times. He argues that World War I was fought between Germany, a rising power, and the UK, the incumbent, and World War II was a sequel to it. In China, quite a number of analysts seem to echo the view of Professor Allison. As early as 2010, a leading media analyst, Peng Xiaoguang, wrote a long article predicting that the United States would turn against China much as the United States waged the Cold War against the Soviet Union after World War II.

Besides the theory of the Thucydides Trap, there are two specific arguments for why the United States and the West in general should treat China as their biggest strategic enemy. The first concerns ideology and world order. The former secretary of state, Pompeo, and the ex-vice president, Pence, have made it very clear in their speeches: China is under a non-Christian and nondemocratic political regime, which has remained unchanged since China and the United States normalized relations in 1979; to make things worse, the stronger economy that China built with its close economic ties with the United States strengthened rather than weakened its political regime. An extension of this point is that when China keeps on rising, it will challenge and eventually change the world order that the United States and the West have built after World War II. One of the examples of China changing the world order is that China has not been siding with the United States on issues such as sanctioning Iran, Russia, North Korea, and Syria.

The other specific argument for why China is a strategic enemy is economics. This has often been claimed by former president Trump: The rise of China has been at the expense of the US economy. Many US workers have lost jobs due to companies relocating factories away from the United States to China, and Chinese products are sold at low prices in the US market, outcompeting the remaining US manufacturing firms. Thus it is time for the United States to fight back. Tariffs are a great weapon against China in this regard according to former president Trump.

THERE ARE SEVERAL REASONS the Thucydides Trap is not applicable to China and the United States. First of all, the Thucydides Trap theory is based on internal competition within Western civilization. As a simple historical fact, intra-civilization and civil conflicts are often much more fatal and brutal than inter-civilization conflicts and international wars. For example, for the past five hundred years, most wars were fought among Western nations, one per year, with the two world wars mostly involving Western nations. Also, American casualties were higher in the US Civil War than they have been in all US foreign wars combined. In China, civil wars, including peasant revolts, have often caused more deaths than wars against other nations.

Second, and much more important, historically, most Chinese dynasties of the past two thousand years, with the exceptions of the Yuan Dynasty ruled by the Mongolians (1271–1368) and Qing Dynasty ruled by the Manchurians (1636–1911), were not expansionist and instead practiced a tributary system. In a tributary system, each year foreign ambassadors would pay homage to the emperor to demonstrate respect for him, and the emperor reciprocated with his gifts and might even send one of his daughters to marry the head of a foreign land. The foreign countries were in effect independent and self-governed. This is totally different from the history of Western colonialism.

Why have a tributary system rather than territorial expansion? A simple reason is the Confucian doctrine of peaceful coexistence. That is, avoid fighting with neighbors. If fighting is necessary, try to win the war and then retreat in order to win the heart of the new local ruler, and then each year ask the neighbor to pay homage to the Chinese emperor. The idea is that winning the heart brings eternal peace while winning a war brings only temporary peace. And, winning a war is only a means to winning the heart.

All signs indicate that today's China follows that cultural tradition of Confucianism and is leaning toward the tributary system rather than the expansionist approach of the exceptional dynasties and emperors.

In short, it takes two to tango. Given Chinese historical and cultural tradition, the Thucydides Trap theory does not hold.

I WOULD ARGUE THAT a China-US war, cold or hot, is avoidable and unlikely to happen. To begin with, the so-called Thucydides Trap theory is not applicable to today's China, despite the attractive simplicity and beauty of the theory with a fancy Greek name. The Thucydidean analysis is based on Western history. Its key assumption is that China is like Germany in the 1910s and the former Soviet Union in the 1930s, or earlier rising powers in Western and Greek histories. In this book, I have gone into details arguing that China is different from all such previous rising powers. In fact, in the last chapter, I have illustrated China's unique world view, which is nonexpansionist.

How about the concern that China will seek to change the world order that the United States and the West have built? Let us not forget that China is in fact a beneficiary of the modern world order with the United Nations, World Trade Organization (WTO), World Bank, and International Monetary Fund (IMF) being the pillar institutions. Whenever there are international crises, whether with Iraq, Iran, North Korea, or Syria, China has always called for the UN to play the most prominent role in resolving these issues rather than through unilateral actions by the United States and its allies. The Chinese economy thrived by greatly expanding international trade after joining the WTO, and Chinese policy makers have benefited significantly from the policy advice of the World Bank and the IMF. China has maintained very good working relations with all these international institutions. There is no reason for China to seek to undermine the world order. As a matter of fact, it is the United States that failed to pay its dues to the United Nations and often complained about the World Bank and the IMF, and even withdrew its membership from the WTO.

Will China seek to form alliances to challenge the United States and the West? The answer is clearly no. Unlike the former Soviet Union, China is not built upon an ideology that it seeks to export. In addition, as has been argued previously, unlike Germany of the 1910s and the 1930s, China's foreign relations are centered around the idea of obtaining respect rather than real interests. One example I discussed in other chapters in the book is that China does not try and has not tried to cultivate its own satellite countries. Another example is that despite having already become the world's largest trader relying on ocean freight, China does not have and has not attempted to build any military base overseas, while the United States had maintained 374 overseas military bases by the end of 2022. China has shown no intention of challenging the United States in this regard. In short, I have illustrated several times in the book that China's world view takes "doing our homework" as task number one. China is not a global expansionary force. It is not seeking to expand its territory, nor is it seeking to export its ideology.

Will China fight a war with the United States over Taiwan? The answer again is no. To begin with, unlike Crimea, which had not been recognized by most countries as part of Russia before Russia annexed it by force in 2014, Taiwan has been recognized as part of China by almost all countries except for a dozen small ones. Most importantly, mainland China and Taiwan still have a good chance to negotiate some kind of peaceful union in which Taiwan has the utmost autonomy, including keeping its military force, and is much more independent than Hong Kong and Macao. This would allow mainland China to claim that it has accomplished the mission of reunification, therefore ending the so-called Century of Humiliation. In the unlikely and unfortunate scenario of the Taiwanese authorities declaring independence and the mainland being cornered into waging a military campaign, it is very unlikely for the United States to be involved militarily, since there is no US legislation committing the White House to make such a decision. More importantly, one hundred miles off the coast of mainland China, Taiwan would be a highly asymmetrical theater of war between mainland China and the United States. The Chinese military has played out this scenario time and again. The US White House and Pentagon will be extremely reluctant to engage in a military conflict with China in this region, knowing that China has much more political will and stronger military capacity in such a war than in the case of the Korean War, 1950–1953, in which the United States and its allies did not prevail.

Will China and the United States fight a war in the South China Sea, where China also has sovereign claims over many islands? Again, it is unlikely. The issue of the South China Sea is not as severe as it is interpreted to be by many people in the West. China has not claimed sovereignty over the entire area of the South China Sea. Rather, it only claims many islands within the South China Sea. Additionally, China has repeatedly shown a willingness to work with many countries on economic development in the region, such as by sharing the economic benefits of oil drilling, while putting aside the sovereignty issue of the islands. For the United States, there is a vague notion that as a superpower, it needs to continue projecting its influence and authority in the South China Sea region. However, waging a military campaign in the region just for the vanity of supremacy would be excessively costly for both China and the United States.

MOST PEOPLE IN THE United States and the West do not understand or even care about the issues of ideology or the world order, and may not be able to point out on a map where Taiwan and the South China Sea are, but they care about a simple question: Is the rise of China good for me and for my children? This is a simple and fundamentally important question, since in a democracy like the United States, the answer to this question strongly influences whether China and the United States will be headed toward a significant conflict.

Based on the analyses in this book, I argue that the rise of China is good for common people around the world, including people in the United States, and that people like former president Trump are wrong in claiming that the rise of China has caused economic damage to people in the United States.

There are three important factors making the rise of China beneficial to people in the United States and the rest of the world. The first and most obvious factor is the enlarged size of the world's market economy due to the rise of China, which implies more economic opportunities and benefits for the rest of the world. China is home to about 18 percent of the world's population. A half-century ago, China was not connected to the world economy.

Now, China is very much a critical part of the world economy. China is currently home to 18 percent of the world's economic activities, and this share is still rapidly increasing. In the following, I lay out specifically how the huge and still increasing Chinese market benefits people outside China.

LOWER PRODUCT PRICES

A highly visible benefit of the rise of the Chinese economy is that the prices of many goods sold in superstores have been kept very low, and this has helped low-income families everywhere. For the past four decades until 2021, most countries in the world have mostly avoided the problem of high inflation. Besides prudent monetary policy in most developed countries, the rise of China also has been an important factor.

Consider the Dollar Store franchises in the United States, where every good used to be sold for $1 and only in recent years moved up to $1.25. Such stores have been in operation for over twenty years without significantly changing their prices. How is such a business model possible? The answer is China. Almost all goods sold in these stores are produced entirely or partially in China.

A specific example of the benefits of low-cost Chinese production in the rest of the world can be seen in the community of audiophiles, who treasure specialized equipment such as amplifiers with vacuum tubes. Such equipment was previously very expensive because it requires skilled labor to weld together the electronic components. As China has risen, the price of amplifiers with vacuum tubes has fallen into a much more affordable range—a few hundred US dollars rather than a few thousand US dollars. There are many more products than just vacuum tube amplifiers that are now made in China for the rest of the world.

In the economy overall, how large is the contribution of goods made in China to lower inflation and a lower cost of living for people in the United States? A study by economists of the Federal

Reserve Bank of San Francisco in 2011 showed that about 2.7 percent of US household consumption comes from China. Another study, published by the *Journal of International Economics* in 2020, estimated that Chinese exports to the United States helped reduce inflation by 0.49 percent per year between 2000 and 2006. Meanwhile, the inflation target of most central banks is 2 percent, and the US inflation rate was mostly below 2 percent between 2000 and 2019 before President Trump's tariff. In short, the Chinese contribution to helping control US inflation was significant.

More Jobs

The rise of China also means more job and career opportunities for people outside China. One high-profile example of this is the story of Stephon Marbury, a former NBA star. He was drafted as the fourth pick by the NBA in 1996 as a future superstar. Unfortunately, instead of flying high in his NBA career, he ran into troubles on and off the court. Half persuaded by a Chinese sports agent, he decided to sign a contract with the Beijing Ducks and try his chances in the budding Chinese Basketball Association (CBA). To everybody's surprise, including himself, he excelled in China, helping his club win three CBA championships. He was nicknamed the political commissar, meaning that he is a leader and motivator for his teammates. He was deeply loved by his fans. After retiring from the Beijing Ducks, he competed successfully to become the head coach of another club in the city of Beijing in 2020 and helped turn around the performance of his new club. The moral of the story is simple: Those who have not done well in their home country may achieve success in China! Marbury is not alone. Each CBA club has a few foreign stars, mostly from the United States. They bring with them coaches, trainers, and assistants. Altogether, in China's CBA, there is a contingent of over one hundred basketball professionals from the United States, Europe, and Australia working in China. Other professional sports are the same, thanks to the expanding Chinese sports markets.

How many jobs has the growing Chinese economy created outside China? After all, not everyone can be a sports star like Stephon Marbury. There are no official statistics, but we can do a quick estimation. Each year, China imports about one trillion US dollars of goods from OECD countries (about 48 percent of all Chinese imports), which are mostly the Western countries plus Japan and Korea, and those imports have been growing at a pace of roughly 8–10 percent. Most of the imported goods from OECD countries are manufactured products rather than crude oil or minerals. How many jobs does one trillion USD of products create? The average product an OECD worker produces in a year is 83,000 USD (47 USD per hour multiplied by 1,769 hours of work per year). This results in 12 million jobs, which is about 2.2 percent of the OECD's total employment of 557 million. This is about 11 percent of the OECD's total employment in agriculture and manufacturing, since most of China's imported goods are agricultural and manufactured products and the OECD's average ratio of manufacturing and agriculture to total jobs is around 20 percent. This means that in the West plus Japan and Korea, one out of fifty jobs in the whole economy and one out of nine jobs in the manufacturing and agricultural sectors are serving the Chinese market.

Who are the laborers producing for the Chinese market? They are the farmers in the US Midwest, who rely heavily on China for their corn and soybean sales. They are the fertilizer producers in the United States. They are the car manufacturers in Detroit and Munich, whose high-end models are strategically produced in corporate headquarters for the sake of maintaining brand authenticity, but whose biggest sales are in China. They are also the small family workshops making niche products for audiophiles and sportscar parts, who get their biggest orders from China.

Besides agriculture and manufacturing, let us not forget the service sector jobs associated with, if not created by, the rise of the Chinese economy. Outstanding among them are education and tourism. Before COVID-19, each year, there had been as many as 155 million Chinese visits to the rest of the world, at least 50 percent going to OECD countries (the other popular destinations are the Southeast Asian countries). Each tourist spent on average 1,600 USD. This means 124 billion USD of services in total for the OECD countries, which have 27 million employees in the tourism sector, each job creating 68,000 USD in monetary value a year. This means that Chinese tourists helped create 1.84 million jobs, or about 6.8 percent of the total employment in tourism. In other words, one out of fifteen tourism professionals in OECD countries serves Chinese tourists.

Education is another sector in which the rise of China has created new demand for foreign countries, especially the United States. As of 2019, each year, about 660 thousand Chinese students go abroad, mostly studying in colleges, with 42 percent going to the United States. Tuition and room and board for the majority of them is paid by their parents who, as I explained in the chapter on education, are often more than willing to spend on their children's education. In the United States, each student easily spends as much as 80,000 USD per year on tuition plus room and board. The total number of Chinese students studying in the United States is about 400,000, spending a total amount of 32 billion USD. This amount is roughly equivalent to the United States exporting 10 percent of its total automobile output to China.

Of course, the increase of Chinese exports to the rest of the world has meant that many factories, companies, and workers in the United States and the West have been replaced. As many people have argued, this should not be taken as evidence that the rise of China is damaging to Western society. A careful analysis shows that the proportion of manufacturing employment in the United States is already very low—less than 10 percent of the US population is directly involved in manufacturing. Therefore, even without the rise of China, manufacturing jobs would move toward Southeast Asia, India, or Africa. The West is thus left with the challenge of transitioning from manufacturing to other sectors, including the service sector.

The new jobs outside China created by the rise of China require necessary and proactive adjustments by enterprises and workers. Workers need to move to sectors that cater to the demand of a rising Chinese market, including education, tourism, and premium manufactured products. The process might be difficult, and it is the responsibility of the relevant government to smooth the adjustment. The Chinese government also had to do this for its own economy because many previously profitable factories went bankrupt due to the competition from imports.

MITIGATING THE DAMAGE OF FINANCIAL CRISIS

China, due to its high savings rate and cautious management of its economy, as discussed above, has been holding trillions of dollars of foreign assets and has become increasingly important as a force that can help mitigate the impact of financial crises in the rest of the world. For many reasons, the US and European economies have had financial crises or panics every ten to fifteen years, or even more frequently. Most recently, in early 2023, Silicon Valley Bank (SVB) and Credit Suisse (CS) caused widespread panics. Although the SVB and CS panics occurred on the heels of the balloon incident, preventing US Treasury Secretary Janet Yellen from visiting China, it is widely believed that her team coordinated closely with their Chinese counterparts in order to stabilize the global financial markets. In the case of the European debt crisis between 2010 and 2015, the EU leaders worked hard to woo China to invest in their bailout funds. Although it was unclear in the end how much China invested in such funds, China made a large number of real investments on the ground in European ports and road building. Such investments helped maintain European jobs and sped up economic recovery.

MORE GLOBAL PUBLIC GOODS WITH CONTRIBUTIONS FROM CHINA

The rise of China benefits ordinary people in the world by providing public goods from China. Public goods are goods that each of us need and all of us can share. One example is scientific knowledge. Such knowledge leads us to better treatment of disease or cleaner energy for the whole world. Every year, more than four million Chinese college students graduate with degrees in science and engineering. The cream of the crop in academic performance among these graduates go on to conduct scientific research. As modern science is now mostly experimental and is extremely dependent on millions of hours of input by junior scientists, it is therefore very costly in labor. The rapid increase of Chinese college graduates has provided the US and other Western universities and research institutions with a huge supply of scientific labor. Check out the website of any department of natural science of a university in the United States or other Western countries, and 50 percent of the graduate students or junior scientists are easily from China. The average pay for them is much lower than that of a manufacturing worker in the United States, and therefore, there has been a shortage of supply of US students for this kind of work. The influx of Chinese students has become a lifeline of scientific research in the United States and the West. No wonder that whenever the US government considers cutting down on student visas from China, US universities are united in fighting against it.

Another example of a public good is space exploration, and here China has also made meaningful contributions. The need to build space stations explains itself: It is not done just to whet the curiosity of a few scientists or the vanity of involved nations; it is also important because we human beings must prepare for the days when we have to migrate to outer space or to another planet. Furthermore, scientific experiments are also done in space stations, often with immediate benefits. One example is that new and better seeds of grains, vegetables, and fruits can be bred in outer space much faster than on earth. The United States, together with Russia and the European Union, agreed to build an international space station in 1998. The United States has spent roughly 100 billion USD, about 650 USD per taxpayer, on this project. Unfortunately, the space station will stop functioning by 2030 due to a lack of continued funding. China wanted to collaborate with the United States and build a joint space program, but the United States said no to China due to a lack of trust. China went ahead on its own. With a much lower cost in engineers' salaries, China had already built a space station by 2022 and keeps expanding it. Meanwhile, the US, Russian, and European program faces significant challenges due to the Ukraine crisis and a lack of funding. Decades or even centuries from now, the whole human race will benefit from the efforts today in building and maintaining space stations. China is making a contribution to the whole world. It is ideal and also probable that China, the United States, and other countries will collaborate on this. Besides the many benefits such collaboration could bring to the world, the United States would be able to avoid spending its valuable tax revenue on such programs. The rise of Chinese economic capacity makes this possible.[1]

International peacekeeping is another example of a public good. There are many regions in the world suffering from the lack of basic law and order. The ensuing fights often spiral into regional military conflicts and cause a huge exodus of refugees to the rest

---

1 Will Elon Musk and other private entrepreneurs change the picture? In recent years, they have entered the business of space travel and greatly lowered the cost of launching rockets. However, it is unlikely that they will be able to replace the role of publicly funded programs, which are for pure science exploration and mostly will not be profitable.

of the world, which has been a headache for the West. Maintaining law and order in such regions is a public good for everyone in the world. International peacekeeping is a United Nations program to deploy military forces in war-torn regions in order to maintain law and order. It is not a controversial program of the UN, since the military forces are only deployed to regions where fighting parties have already agreed to a truce. The peacekeeping program of the UN has made important contributions to many otherwise unstable regions. By now, China has become the largest contributor to the peacekeeping troops in terms of military personnel and funds. China has stated that it is willing to contribute more to the peacekeeping program. With more collaborations between China, the United States, and other countries, it is imaginable that the UN peacekeeping program can grow much bigger.

Artificial Intelligence (AI) is a leading issue on which China and the United States are likely to coordinate closely, since both sides, as large nations, have a common stake in its safe development, just as the Soviet Union and the United States worked effectively to prevent a nuclear war. AI, if not properly developed, poses potentially fatal danger for humankind, just like nuclear technology. China and the United States, as leading countries in AI, will have to cooperate to come up with something like a constitution of AI, prohibiting certain kinds of AI development.

A More Effective Fight against Climate Change

China will arguably be the most important country in helping to lower the cost of the fight against climate change and speeding up this fight. This can be demonstrated in monetary terms. In the United States and the West, as of 2022, the cost to reduce carbon levels can be as high as 70 USD per metric ton. If you bring China into the picture, the cost may come down to as low as 10 USD. Why? First, China, as a center of manufacturing for the world, has become the world's largest source of emissions of carbon dioxide since around 2005. Meanwhile, China has also been rapidly investing in green technology. Therefore, reducing a unit of carbon in China is much cheaper than in Europe, where old technologies are slower to be phased out than in China. More importantly, China is home to 70 percent of the production capacity for the world's solar panels and 50 percent for wind turbines, at only a fraction of the cost that it would be in other parts of the world. The huge and low-cost supply of solar panels and wind turbines helps speed up the process of fighting against climate change. On climate change, China has already garnered cost-effective carbon neutral technologies. For example, China has used its super low-cost solar and wind energy to produce methanol to replace coal, gasoline, and diesel and use it in redesigned internal combustion engines. The United States, intending to continue being a global leader, will push for effective technologies to reach carbon neutral for the world and therefore will work closely with China in this regard.

CHINA PROVIDES COMPETITION THAT THE UNITED STATES AND THE WEST NEED

The third and perhaps the most interesting avenue in which the rise of China helps the West, especially the United States, is through competition and rivalry. No doubt, the rise of China has caused a widespread sense of urgency in the United States and other Western countries in general to make sure that they don't fall behind. In many ways, this is an impetus for the United States and the West to speed up necessary social reforms.

Take the example of US federal expenditures in science and technology. For many years, despite repeated and extensive calls from the US communities of higher education and science and technology, the United States has been steadily cutting its budgetary allocation to these areas. This has been mainly due to budgetary pressure facing the US federal government. There is mounting evidence that cutting funding for scientific research will hurt the long-term competitiveness of the US economy, even though the private sector may fill some of the gaps left by the funding cuts. By early 2020, the trend of a declining federal budget for science and technology was suddenly reversed, and it took the so-called China threat to get it done. Senator Chuck Schumer from the state of New York, one of the most outspoken China bashers on Capitol Hill in the United States, whom I met and found to be an eloquent and passionate politician in a Tsinghua classroom during his very first trip to China, proposed a piece of legislation called the Endless Frontier Act in 2020. The Act calls for a massive increase in the amount the US federal budget allocates for science and technology, increasing from 10 billion USD a year for the National Science Foundation to 100 billion USD in total for five years to come. The Act was instantly welcomed by presidents of leading US universities. The direct motivation: China. Senator Schumer's argument was straightforward: Without such a program, the United States will fall behind China in areas like AI, quantum computing, biotechnology, etc. His list covers as many as fifteen key areas. The US economy and society will benefit from such an act, based on historical experience. After many modifications, the Endless Frontier Act eventually became a law by August 2022. Even though the Act has many anti-China provisions, it will have a major impact on US scientific research.

Education is another example in which the perceived threat and competition from China motivates US and Western policy makers to make progressive changes and to try to explore reforms. There is a general sense that the US education system at the precollege level overall has been lacking intensity in general and has been very weak in particular in the STEM (sciences, technology, engineering, and mathematics) area. This is obviously an extremely complicated topic. But in policy debates, the word "China," or more specifically, "Shanghai," is motivational, since many cross-country studies rank China (oftentimes choosing Shanghai as the representative city, a biased choice) to be on top, way above the United States. Without getting into the details of the debate, I believe that there is a consensus among US policy makers and education experts that something has to be done to put more resources into the US education system. Vice versa, in China, the United States is a perennial motivation for educational reforms. Interestingly, education experts in China often cite universities like Harvard, Yale, and Stanford, and high schools like the Phillips Academy, as examples of how creative the US education system is in cultivating talents and by contrast, how bad the Chinese system has been. Competition works! Both China and the United States are attempting to improve their own education systems, using each other as motivation.

I HAVE ARGUED REPEATEDLY that the rise of China is good for the United States and the West, but how do individuals in the West benefit from the rise of China? I have two specific suggestions, mostly for young people. But before going into the specifics, I cannot emphasize enough that one needs to avoid the mistake of stereotyping people according to culture and nationality. All Chinese people are different, just as all Americans, Europeans, and Indians are different. One must be open-minded and patient in understanding a country or a culture.

Given this premise, my first suggestion is to study basic Chinese in order to understand the culture. Language is a conveyor of culture, and culture is essentially a set of norms about how people behave. This especially applies to young people. The Chinese language is a particularly easy language to start learning because the grammar not only uses the same system as English (the most used international language) but also is simpler than English. It is perhaps the easiest and simplest grammar of all languages, and therefore the payoff-to-effort ratio is extremely high in learning beginning Chinese. Of course, the best way to learn a foreign language for a young person is to make friends with people from the other country and never be shy in asking questions about the language. The Chinese language provides an invaluable window into understanding the country as a whole. For example, when two Chinese first meet, they may say to each other *Xing Hui*, meaning that it is a good fortune to meet you. The implied meaning is that of all the countless people in the world, you and I meet, this is a serendipity, and we should treasure it and let us hope good things will happen.

My second suggestion is to visit China if you have not done so, or at least get a copy of a Chinese map. No matter how much you read or watch reports on the internet, you can never really understand a country without carefully reading the map and actually visiting it. Nowadays, with the world's largest network of rapid rail and almost the largest volume of air traffic, tourist facilities are highly developed and many tour options are available. Even more importantly, generally speaking, China is a very safe country for tourists. And when you visit, you will almost certainly develop an entirely new perspective on the country and the culture. You may even discover opportunities for professional development or business collaboration.

I am very confident that by acquiring a basic knowledge of Chinese and visiting China, a person will open up a window of new opportunities. It will be as exciting as some of my generation of Chinese who have had the good fortune to study English or other Western languages during the past decades and then to study in countries like the United States. Our lives were transformed and, in turn, we helped many fellow Chinese change their lives. The same surely can be said of young generations in the rest of the world.

Acknowledgments

WRITING THE BOOK HAS BECOME AN INCREAS-
ingly challenging task for me. When I had the idea to
write it in 2011, China was perceived to be a rising force that the
West could work with. However, when I was almost done with the
draft, China had become, for many, the imagined opponent in a
new cold war. Such a drastic change makes my initial purpose of
demystifying China to prevent global conflict even more important and urgent. Meanwhile, the thesis of the book that the rise of
China is good for the world has become increasingly difficult to
present and to argue for. Moreover, I anticipated mounting pressures from ever more nationalistic Chinese readers who believe
that I am misinterpreting China to please the Western audience.
Facing the rising pressures, I seriously considered abandoning
this project at various stages of the writing.

It is an unusually large number of friends in China and in the
West who motivated me and propelled me to finish the long and
challenging job. First and foremost is Neil Schwartz, who was my
former student and later my colleague at Tsinghua University. He
not only provided excellent research and editorial support but also
was so persistent in reminding me to work and finish writing the
book that I subconsciously avoided bumping into him to hide the
embarrassment of my slow progress. However, my mindset was
completely changed by his passing away due to COVID, which

prevented him from coming back to work and live happily in China, and his parents' decision to donate his pension to establish a scholarship for foreign students at Tsinghua. This convinced me that I definitely had to finish the book, since the young generation deserves a better world of peaceful mutual understanding between China and the world so that they have the freedom to choose to live in a country of their choice. Therefore, the book is dedicated to Neil and to future generations in China and the United States. Many friends not only helped but more importantly inspired me during the long writing process. I owe the title of the book to Niall Ferguson, with whom I used to participate in many international forums. He consistently encouraged me to write a book for the general reader, as he has done so successfully. In a bar at Central Square in Cambridge, Massachusetts, he came up with the title of the book, *China's World View*. I would not be surprised if he does not agree with many of its arguments and even the thesis of the book. However, I am very grateful to his ingenious suggestions and his help in navigating the process of working on the book. Thanks to an introduction by Niall, Andrew Wylie efficiently managed the process of the project. I still recall a sunny morning in New York City when he sat on his couch in his office and went through with me my sample chapters, offering me many critiques that were initially shocking but proved to be critically valuable.

I am grateful to the editor and highly capable production team of W. W. Norton. They had to go out of their way to help me as a non-native writer. Tom Mayer was much more than an editor for the book. He actually functioned like a director of a movie, reading an early draft of the book and suggesting many critical changes and additions at various stages. Even more important, I am grateful to him and his colleagues for not giving up on me as I have embarrassingly missed all possible deadlines.

I am indebted to many journalists and Western opinion leaders including Keith Bradsher, Mike Cronin, Thomas Friedman, and

Martin Wolf. They not only provided many good suggestions on my writing, but more importantly, when they interviewed me, I sensed the most urgent concerns of Western readers about China. Moreover, Tom told me a twist of an old saying: The only thing worse than attack is no attack. And this raised my writing spirit whenever I worried about future criticisms or attacks.

I am blessed by the help from a huge number of friends based in China during the book project. Emily Finkelstine and Luke Witzaney did a wonderful job in research assistant and editorial work. Joan Xu read the draft and made important suggestions as a young professional versed in both the Chinese and American cultures. A few Chinese colleagues provided very useful comments and suggestions after reading a machine-translated Chinese version of the draft. I would not list all the names in order to avoid any speculation about their responsibilities for the views in the book. The same applies to all the people I thanked above. That is, I myself stand to be responsible for any criticisms and liabilities of the book.

As a first-time writer for non-academic readers outside of China, I face the particular challenge of making the book as popular as it deserves. I am more than fortunate to have been helped by generous reviews of the book draft from many world-leading thinkers and opinion-makers. They are Niall Ferguson, Mark Leonard, Kishore Mahbubani, Eswar Prasad, Lawrence Summers, and Jeffrey Sachs. It is not that they all agree with the views in the book that I appreciate most. Rather, it is that they all highlight the need for the West to understand how China works and the Chinese perspectives on critical world issues.

The long process of writing has been particularly taxing for my family, who have been used to my missing many holiday gatherings and have been convinced that the tax was paid not to me but to contribute to a public good. I am grateful to them and wish the public good will prove to be valuable for years to come.

Index

Great Leap Forward, 42–43, 45, 115–16, 206
Gree Electric, 118
green technologies, 162, 166–69, 253
grievance cases, 79, 93, 100, 186–87, 226–27
gross domestic product (GDP)
  of China, 13, 18, 27–28, 32
  consumption ratio as share of, 188
  debt-to-GDP ratio, 29
  intense focus on GDP growth, 82, 95,
    133, 185
  percentage of annual national savings, 188
  percentage spent on elderly, 179
Guan Hanhui, 32
Gu, Eileen, 149–50
Guangdong province, 67, 167
  Guangzhou, 81, 111
  Shenzhen special economic zone, 111
guerilla warfare, 40
"Guerrilla of Kids, The" (TV show), 175
Guizhou province, 80–81
Gu Junshan, 90
Guo Boxiong, 89–90
Guomei home appliance seller, 136

Haier home appliances, 110–11
Harmony OS, 236
Harvard University, 14, 131, 183–84, 195,
  202, 207, 217, 220, 239, 255
Hebei province, 144, 165–66, 168
Hefei, Anhui, 114–15
Hengshui High School, 144
history, 24–35
  avoiding the "Thucydides Trap," 239–42
  "century of humiliation," 24, 31–33, 34,
    227, 243
  civil wars in Chinese history, 31, 225, 240
  Cultural Revolution, 42–44, 45, 47–48, 53,
    68, 203, 206, 227–28
  cyclical view of, 31
  founding of the People's Republic of
    China, 41, 115, 207, 226–27
  Great Leap Forward, 42–43, 45, 115–16,
    206
  historical conservatism of China, 226–28
  1911 Revolution, 31, 209
  "reform and opening up" period, 19–20, 27,
    38, 45, 64, 115–16, 171, 196, 220, 234

when China was "closed," 197
  See also China, rise of; warfare
Hollywood, 16–17
Hong Kong, 24, 32–35, 96, 108, 173, 231,
  243
HSBC, 115
Huang Guangyu, 136
Huaqiao University, Fujian, 232
Huawei, 186, 235–36, 238
Hu Jintao, 45

ideology, 8–9, 13, 19–20, 22, 46
  avoidance of debate, 27, 81
  China's inability/disinterest in exporting
    its, 8, 11, 18, 200, 214–18, 220, 229–30,
    242–43, 244
  European social democracy, 46
  libertarianism, 158, 209
  Marxism, 38–39, 46, 157, 215, 220
  shift in Chinese Communist Party
    ideology, 46, 206
  socialism, 38, 42, 48, 115, 117, 229
  Stalinism, 42–43, 124, 228
  state-owned enterprises (SOEs) and, 117
  and US-China relations, 239
"imperialist companies," 115
Independent Commission Against Corruption
  (ICAC), 96
India
  Chinese businesses in, 186
  corruption in, 90–91
  democracy in, 205, 217
  education in, 150–51
  environmental issues in, 164
  jobs in, 249
  Pakistan and, 229
  population of, 171, 180
indirect elections, 59–61
Industrial and Commercial Bank of China
  (ICBC), 113, 119
inequality, 31, 191–92, 197, 209–10
  in Chinese communism, 38
  Gini coefficient, 191
  regional disparities, 192–93
  taxes and, 191–92
  urban/rural disparity, 191
  See also cities; rural populations